CORRESPONDENCES *of the* BIBLE

CORRESPONDENCES *of the* BIBLE

The Human Body

John Worcester

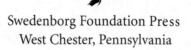

Swedenborg Foundation Press
West Chester, Pennsylvania

First edition published as
Physiological Correspondences in 1889
by the Massachusetts New-Church Union, Boston
Reprinted in 1987 by the Swedenborg Scientific Association
Reprinted in 2009 by the Swedenborg Foundation,
West Chester, Pennsylvania

Correspondences of the Bible by John Worcester
The Animals ISBN 978-0-87785-112-7
The Plants ISBN 978-0-87785-113-4
The Human Body ISBN 978-0-87785-114-1
Three-volume set ISBN 978-0-87785-111-0

Editing and index by Morgan Beard
Designed and typeset by Karen Connor

Printed in the United States of America

For more information:
Swedenborg Foundation
320 North Church Street • West Chester, PA 19380
www.swedenborg.com

CONTENTS

About This Book   vii
Introduction   ix

THE LIPS, TONGUE, AND TEETH   3
THE SALIVA   18
THE ESOPHAGUS   25
THE STOMACH   28
THE INTESTINES   38
THE MESENTERY   51
THE LIVER   58
THE SPLEEN AND THE PANCREAS   72
THE OMENTUM   80
THE SUPRARENAL CAPSULES   86
THE KIDNEYS   90
THE PERITONEUM   96
THE HEART AND THE LUNGS   101
THE NOSE   116
THE ORGANS OF SPEECH   128
THE PLEURA   137
THE DIAPHRAGM   141
THE MUSCLES IN GENERAL   145
THE BONES   147
THE CARTILAGES   150

Contents

The Skin   152

The Hair   164

The Hands   168

The Feet   178

The Ear   183

The Eye   195

Generation and Regeneration   211

The Brain   246

About This Book

"CORRESPONDENCES" REFER TO THE SPIRITUAL MEANING behind everyday objects or ideas. For example, the heat and light of the sun correspond to God's love and wisdom, so heat and love and light and wisdom are correspondences. Throughout this book, Worcester gives examples of how specific aspects of human anatomy represent certain spiritual principles, and you can read more about how this applies to the natural world in the companion volumes *The Animals* and *The Plants*. These correspondences reflect the inner meaning of the Bible.

John Worcester originally released this book under the title *Physiological Correspondences* in 1889 as an aid to studying correspondences as described in the writings of Emanuel Swedenborg (1688–1772).

Emanuel Swedenborg was a Swedish scientist, inventor, and mystic who spent his life investigating the mysteries of the soul. Born in Stockholm to a staunchly Lutheran family, he graduated from the University of Uppsala and then traveled to England, Holland, France, and Germany to study the leading scientists of the time. He gained favor with Sweden's King Charles XII, who gave him a position overseeing the Swedish mining industry. Later, he was granted a seat on the Swedish House of Nobles by Charles XII's successor, Queen Ulrika Eleonora.

Between 1743 and 1745, a lifetime of religious study culminated in personal contact with the spiritual realms. He wrote a steady stream of books describing his experiences traveling in spirit form through heaven and hell, his conversations with angels and demons, and the inner meaning of the Bible as revealed to him through the Lord.

Because this volume was written for Swedenborgians, Swedenborg's books are cited without bibliographic information. A full list of Emanuel Swedenborg's spiritual works is included in the back of this volume to aid those who would like to do more research.

INTRODUCTION

"The states of spirits and angels, with all their varieties, can in no wise be understood without a knowledge of the human body; for the Lord's kingdom is like a man" (*Spiritual Diary* §1145 ½).

"That heaven as a whole is like one man is an arcanum not yet known in the world; but in heaven it is most certainly known. To know that, and the specific and particular things concerning it, is the chief of the intelligence of the angels there; very many things also depend upon it, which without that as their general principle do not enter distinctly and clearly into their minds" (*Heaven and Hell* §59).

"The chief of the intelligence which angels have is to know and perceive that all of life is from the Lord, and that the whole heaven corresponds to His Divine Human, and consequently that all angels, spirits, and men correspond to heaven; also to know and perceive how they correspond. These are the chief things of the intelligence in which angels are above men; from these they know and perceive innumerable things which are in the heavens, and hence also those which are in the world" (*Arcana Coelestia* §4318).

The correspondence of the whole heaven with the Divine Human, and of individual men with the heavens, is the subject of these studies.

CORRESPONDENCES *of the* BIBLE

The Lips, Tongue, and Teeth

To the lips is assigned the threefold duty of expressing the thoughts and feelings to the sight by means of their motions and changes of form; or modifying and articulating the voice, and thus communicating the activities of the mind to the ear; and of receiving and drawing in the food by which the body is nourished. To the last use we will attend first, leaving the others till we have studied the correspondence of the lungs and of the face.

The use of the lips in receiving food is most evident in infancy, during the period in which nourishment is obtained by sucking. Afterwards, in drinking, they have a similar duty through the whole of life. In these operations the lips apply themselves to the mother's breast, or to the cup, and in conjunction with the cheeks, tongue, and fauces, by alternate expansions and contractions, draw out the pliant food, and introduce it into the mouth.

Such food needs no mastication; the function of the lips is merely to draw it in and introduce it, and then it is received by the soft parts of the mouth, and is quickly conducted to its destination. The lips have a similar use in laying hold of and drawing into the mouth solid food that is presented to them, and in caring for this they have the further duty, in cooperation with cheeks and tongue, of pressing it between the teeth, and compelling it to submit to the grinding process by which its interior parts are opened and separated.

It is, perhaps, worthy of mention also that on the inner surfaces of the lips are little glands, which begin the process of moistening and lubricating the food, to aid in digestion and in its passage to the stomach. Undoubtedly there are also absorbents, by which a small amount of the purest part of the food is taken at once into the circulation of the body, and introduced into its life and uses.

To see the correspondence of these uses of the lips, on a grand scale and in perfection, we must think of the great community from which men derive their humanity, and which, because it receives the Divine Influence immediately and the greatest measure, Swedenborg calls the "Greatest Man" (*Arcana Coelestia* §3741).

This Greatest Man is the heavens. It includes all good men, recipients of good life from the Lord, who have lived upon any of the earths in the starry universe from the beginning of time. Of these, "the inhabitants of this world are very few comparatively, and almost as a drop of water in comparison with the ocean" (*Arcana Coelestia* §3631).

Of this Greatest Man the Lord is the Life. It is formed to receive His life, and to live from Him; and it is Man because He is Man. All its parts are human, and do human uses corresponding to the uses of the organs and members of the human body.

The nourishment of the heavens is of two kinds: they receive an influence of love and wisdom, or of warmth and light, immediately from the Lord; and they receive additions of new members from the earths.

These two kinds of nourishment are comparatively like the inflow of life from the soul into the human body, from which every particle of the body draws its gift of human life, and the additions of new particles from the food. Both kinds of nourishment are necessary to useful activity. Continual inflow of spiritual life of course is necessary to those who in themselves are dead; and frequent supplies of new experiences, new subjects of thought, new applications of truth, and new opportunities of use are also necessary, to those whose happiness is by their very constitution made to depend upon eternal progress.

New things, necessary to the growth and happiness of the heavens, are as food supplied from the earths. Like food the comers from the earth must be received by the heavens, examined, sorted, instructed, and trained to heavenly states, as by a kind of digestion, before they can be assimilated; and this is the function of the world of spirits. Swedenborg says:

> The life of man when he dies and enters into the other life is like food, which is received softly by the lips, and afterwards is passed through the mouth, fauces, and esophagus into the stomach; and this according to the nature derived from his works during the life of the body. Most are treated gently at first, for they are kept in the company of angels and good spirits; which is represented in food that it is first softly touched by the lips, and afterwards tasted as to its quality by the tongue.
>
> The food which is soft, in which is sweetness, [essential] oil, and spirit, is immediately received by the veins, and borne into the circulation; but food which is hard, in which is bitterness and foulness, and little nutritiveness, is more hardly treated, and is cast down through the esophagus into the stomach, where it is corrected by various methods and tortures. What is still harder, more foul, and worthless, is thrust into the intestines,

and at length into the rectum, where first is hell, and is cast out, and becomes excrement.

Resembling this is the life of man after death. First man is kept in externals; and because he had lived a moral and civil life in externals, he is with angels and good spirits. But afterwards externals are taken away from him, and then it appears what he was within as to thoughts and affections, and at length as to ends; according to these his life remains.

As long as they are in this state, in which they are like food in the stomach, they are not in the Greatest Man, but are being introduced; but when they are representatively in the blood, then they are in the Greatest Man. (*Arcana Coelestia* §5175–5176)

The angels, then, who softly receive man at his entrance into the spiritual world, who cooperate with the Lord in drawing him out of the world and introducing him into the spiritual world, are in the province of the lips. Perhaps we see some effect of their presence even before the moment of death, in those whose feelings and thoughts are strongly drawn towards the other world as the time of death comes near; and especially in those for whom open vision of spiritual things, more or less distinct, produces an anticipation of the peaceful gladness which we commonly see represented in the face after the natural life ceases.

Swedenborg says that celestial angels, who belong to the kingdom of the heart, come to a person at the time of death, and take charge of his affections and thoughts; and that at their approach an aromatic odor is perceived, and then all *spirits* leave the person exclusively to their care (*Heaven and Hell* §449).

The office of the lips and tongue, and of those in the corresponding provinces of the heavens, is twofold: they are organs of speech and organs for receiving food. As organs of speech their use is spiritual, and as organs for receiving food it is celestial. As Swedenborg writes:

> The tongue affords entrance to the lungs and also to the stomach; thus it presents a sort of courtyard to spiritual things and to celestial things; to spiritual things because it ministers to the lungs and thence to speech, and to celestial things because it ministers to the stomach, which supplies aliment to the blood and the heart. (*Arcana Coelestia* §4791)

It is noteworthy that the angels who first receive man at death do not speak; but sit silently looking into his face, communicating their own affection. They apply themselves to him from love of introducing him into the joys of heaven, and of adding new members to heavenly societies. From this love they hold his thought fixed upon the future life, and lead it by various happy things into as full sympathy with their own thought as is possible. Then the Lord separates him from the body and he awakes in the world of spirits. Swedenborg writes in his *Diary*:

> Two or three times I have been sent into the place where is the resurrection of the dead. It is known from this: that something balsamic is perceived from the dead when the Lord is present, and celestial angels. And it was said that the Lord is especially present there, and therefore also celestial angels are there; because without such presence of the Lord, there would be no resurrection of the dead" (*Spiritual Diary Minor* §4702).

7

After he is raised up, if the new spirit belongs to the very few who by instruction in heavenly truth and by training in heavenly love and usefulness are already prepared to enjoy the life of heaven, these angels receive him among themselves, and by ways in their own societies, like the absorbing vessels of the lips, and especially of the tongue, they introduce him at once into heaven, and lead him on the way to his permanent home.

In this work the angels of the tongue and the cheeks cooperate with those of the lips. If the new spirits be interiorly open, gentle, and good, they are most kindly treated by the angels of these provinces. Those of the tongue, especially, delight to perceive the new varieties of goodness and truth which are introduced from the world, and are eager to convey the pleasing intelligence of their arrival, and if possible the spirits themselves, to the societies which will be enriched by them; for the tongue abounds in porous papillae, which erect themselves on the approach of food, to touch it, and to feel its quality; and if there be in it that which is spirituous and aromatic, to absorb it for the immediate benefit of the brain and the whole system.[1] "The angels love everyone, and desire nothing more than to perform kind offices to all, to give them instruction, and to take them into heaven, in which consists their supreme delight" (*Heaven and Hell* §450).

The angels of all the societies desire to receive new members; and being informed by the tongue of the advent

---

1. The tongue "as an organ of taste signifies the natural perception of good and truth; whereas the smell corresponds to spiritual perception; for the tongue tastes and relishes meats and drinks, and by meats and drinks are signified good and truth which nourish the natural mind" (*Apocalypse Explained* §990).

of those who are suitable for their respective societies they prepare to welcome them. Their eagerness and desire excite appetite in all the intermediate receiving societies, and all combine to invite and guide the new spirits to their destination.[2]

With such soft welcomes are good, open-minded spirits received, and especially is such kindly embrace extended by angels to those who leave this world in infancy and childhood. No harsher treatment do they need than to be separated from evil spirits, and taken up at once into heavenly societies, to be made wise with the wisdom of angels.

The work of reception which we have been describing is done in the province of the mouth of the Greatest Man, in what Swedenborg calls "the first state of man after death" (*Heaven and Hell* §491). And spirits who are interiorly open, and whose thoughts and feelings appear frankly, undergo no treatment less gentle than this. But with the greater part even of good men, at the present day, the interiors have never been consciously opened. They have done good works, perhaps from good principles; but they have attended, as others have, only to the appearances of their lives before men; which, like the hulls and skins of various grains and fruits, must be broken up with some force, that their real life, their purposes and intentions as well as their outwards acts, may be disclosed. This

---

2. "Men, after death, as soon as they come into the world of spirits, are carefully distinguished by the Lord; the evil are immediately bound to the infernal society in which they were in the world as to their ruling love, and the good are bound immediately to the heavenly society in which they also were as to love, charity, and faith" (*Heaven and Hell* §427). "This is the case with all as to internals; but not yet as to externals" (*Heaven and Hell* §497).

disclosure is necessary both for a fair judgment of the characters of the new spirits, and as the first step towards the separation of good from evil, either in the same or in associated persons.

The love of introducing good spirits into heaven, and the love of perceiving the interior quality of new goodness and conveying a knowledge of it to the heavens, urge, therefore, the opening of the whole life of the newcomers. We see an image of their operation in the action of the tongue and lips upon the food, which they press gently, subdivide, and examine, and bring into contact with all the soft absorbing surfaces of the mouth. And if in this examination hard morsels are discovered which do not open to gentle pressure, these are quickly conducted between the teeth, by the pressure of which they are broken up, and all their contents disclosed for examination; or, if they cannot be broken, they are rejected as worthless. So the angels who are in the love of receiving good spirits, and conducting them to heaven, presently lead those spirits whose interiors are closely concealed by externals into the province of other angels whose function is to open the interior memory of life.

These angels whose use is in some respects similar to that of the gates of pearl, in conjunction with the angels of the tongue, guard the way to the greater part of the world of spirits, and of heaven and hell. They know that all newcomers are now to be judged—not according to their professions, but their lives. They say to them, therefore, "None are received here whose quality is not known; and the quality of everyone is known from his life; now, how have you lived? What good have you done? What evil have you resisted? And what evil have you done and what did you love to do and think?" Thus they open the whole memory of the life (*Heaven and Hell* §462).

No doubt many other simple truths or facts concerning the other life they hold and press home in the same way. They are not in themselves sensitive, except to the resistance of spirits to this opening. They deal simply with matters of fact. They do not judge of the quality of the things they discover; this is the duty of the tongue. Their work is, as warders, to compel those who approach to show their true colors, to warn the tongue and to assist in shutting out such, and any others whose quality is too repugnant to the life of the Greatest Man. We are told by the Scriptures that some who are admitted will be spewed out of the mouth. No doubt some will be ejected with disgust as soon as their quality is perceived. Perhaps these are the lukewarm, who can be received neither in heaven nor in hell, but are beneath the hells, in a state almost without life (*Apocalypse Revealed* §204; *Apocalypse Explained* §1158).

There are some other particulars in regard to the action of the teeth which should be considered before we leave them. The teeth hold the food, and bite it off; in which they correspond to the truth that all men must die, and that the purpose of their life is to be prepared for heaven, and to be added to the heavens. Compared to the gentle drawing of all the thoughts and affections towards heaven, inspired by the angels of the lips, this is stern teaching; but it is necessary for those who cling to the world, and are unwilling to die. It is such truth as we apply to men to separate them from their worldly pursuits and attachments, and to turn them towards heaven. The angels of the incisors must influence us to do this.

This is the duty of the twice four front teeth, which have no part in the grinding of food, but only in the breaking off. The next four teeth, called "canine," or "eyeteeth," are, in man, much like the incisors, and join in their work;

adding, perhaps, a special duty of *holding* the food and, in the carnivora, of penetrating and rending it.

Then come the bicuspids (2 x 4), whose use it is to break or cut up the food into small pieces, ready for grinding; and then the molars (2 x 4 + 4), which separate all the particles.

As the incisors correspond to the truth that all must die and enter the spiritual world, the grinding teeth, in their several degrees, represent the further truth that there, all are judged according to their works; and all therefore the lives of all must there be opened and explored, to show their real quality. Such truth, also, we apply in the world to bring out the fitness or unfitness of men for various uses and positions in society.

The teeth are in two sets, the upper and the lower. The upper are fixed in the head; the lower, exactly similar in number and character, are fitted into the moveable jaw, and press, each one against its correlative above. The upper teeth correspond to truth founded in the nature of the world they guard; the lower to similar truth applied to the individual cases presented. The upper say to those who approach, "All men are created for life in the spiritual world; there are none in heaven who have not once lived upon the earth, and there died." The lower add, "You also are born for the same end; you too must die." The upper say, "Here all are judged by their life, by what they have done and what they have loved to do and to think." The lower continue in turn, "You, too, are to be judged according to your lives; now, what have you done, and what have you loved to do and to think?" And thus they compel the opening of all the particulars of the life.

They also have a delicate tact for hypocrisies and concealments; just as the natural teeth have for even the smallest hard particles which come between them, and they feel just where the pressure is necessary.

Swedenborg speaks of the teeth as corresponding to the "sensuals of the understanding" (*Apocalypse Revealed* §435), or to truth held merely naturally and obediently, without interior understanding. And the work of those who are in the teeth of the Greatest Man is not the work of intelligence, or of interior perception; it consists in strong compulsion, and is performed by those who hold Divine Truth firmly and uncompromisingly, but not intelligently. They who are in tender states cannot do this work; but leave it to those whose life it is to insist upon submission to the rules. They are simple, honest doorkeepers, who admit all who present themselves for admission, on the one condition that there shall be no concealment of who they are, or what they have done; but their lives shall be open for judgment.

Swedenborg often speaks of the disputes of the evil as sounding like gnashing of teeth; because they hold literal truths or falsities in the memory, and clash them together in a kind of clamorous argumentation (*Heaven and Hell* §575). The teeth in the hells seem to be related especially to the cruel, tearing teeth of the carnivora; and their purpose is to injure others, and to claim all things that can minister to self-love and love of the world. The gnashing of the teeth is the angry clashing of assertions of fact, or of literal statements, by which they urge such claims against one another and against the Lord and the heavens.

Of some who cause pain in the teeth, he says, "Hypocrites who have spoken holily of Divine things, with affection of love concerning the public and the neighbor, and testified what is just and right, and still have despised these things in their heart, and also laughed at them, when it was allowed them to flow into the parts of the body to which they corresponded from the opposite, produced pains in the teeth, and on their near presence so severe that I could not bear it" (*Arcana Coelestia* §5720). Which appears to have been because the truths which they held in the memory and produced from the memory were like teeth, and their interior contempt for them was like death to the life and support of the teeth.

Again he says that "those who have been rich in the life of the body, and have dwelt in magnificent palaces, placing their heaven in such things, and have despoiled others of their goods under various pretences, without conscience or charity . . . exhaled a sphere of fetor of teeth" (*Arcana Coelestia* §1631). Which, apparently, was because with them a life of pleasures was substituted for a truly heavenly life, and the principles which insist upon interior exploration of those pleasures before they are received into the life were neglected and allowed to become foul and to decay.

A similar consequence follows from the habit of thinking over things that seem pleasant, in an indolent fashion, like food retained in the mouth, and rolled with the tongue, without regard to its rightness or usefulness; from which our principles decay, as the teeth do when not kept clean and bright.

The pains and dangers which children pass through in cutting their teeth correspond to the natural reluctance and difficulty in forming principles by which apparently pleasant things are thoroughly examined, and the evil resolutely rejected.

A child's first principles are scarcely more than his parent's words, held without thought. These are succeeded by natural principles better understood, as the first set of teeth, lightly rooted, are replaced by those that are larger and firmer.

When old people pass from the state of parents to that of grandparents, and leaving the disciplinary stage of life, pass again into a childlike state, they become indulgent, and lose their teeth spiritually as they do naturally.

In this view, soundness of the teeth would correspond with the love of having enjoyments of life thoroughly good; especially with the love of thoroughly good work, and not of what merely appears well. And unsoundness of the teeth would correspond to content with good appearances, and work that will pass.

The dentist's work, spiritually, is to point out the carelessness of such principles of judgment, and suggest what is necessary from principles of love to the Lord and the neighbor to make them sound. Such suggestions are like fillings of gold and silver.

Artificial teeth seem like the conventional standards which must replace the natural when they are gone.

There is an influx from the heavens into man, and from every province of the heavens into the correlative province of man's mind and the corresponding organ of his body. It is from this influx that his mind lives and loves and acts, and that the body also lives and performs its functions. The desire of the angels to receive new members, and introduce them into the uses and the happiness of the heavens, flows into our minds as a desire for the elements of which angelic spirits can be formed in us. It causes us to apply our minds to any source from which we can drink wisdom, and to drink it in for examination. It gives us an interest also in good works, from which we can get instruction and encouragement in regard to good life. It incites us to attend to these things, to receive them, taste them, be affected by the goodness of them, and to absorb this into our affections and lives. Therefore Swedenborg says that the use which the tongue performs in tasting, absorbing, and preparing nutriment for the body, "corresponds to the affection for knowing, understanding, and being wise in truths" (*Arcana Coelestia* §4795).[3]

That heavenly spirits are formed in us by thus receiving genuine wisdom and the goodness of wisdom is plain to everyone. And it is also evident that the influx of the angels' love of receiving new angelic spirits must produce in us individually a desire for the heavenly elements of which such spirits are formed.

In this influx all angels who belong to the provinces of the digestive organs combine; and, indeed, in a general way, the whole heaven, since all angels desire to receive new brothers; and this hunger of the whole heavens for new brothers flows into us, and is felt as a hunger for wisdom. Specifically, those in the province of the lips impart to us the power of application to new truths; those in the province of the tongue inspire the capacity for tasting and discerning the quality of new ideas, before we finally adopt them; and those in the province of the gums and teeth, who cooperate so effectively with the tongue in its explorations, inspire the desire to open the interior quality of whatever is presented, and to receive nothing that we do not thus know, and that does not agree with our life.

We may hear thoughts which do not especially concern us, and may *look* at them with much or little interest, perhaps merely because others value them; but not until we think of them as relating to us, and desire to receive them

---

3. "*Quapropter etiam sapientia, seu sapere, dicta est a sapore.*"

into our lives, and so apply our minds to grasp them and understand them—not till then do we do that which is represented by taking food with our lips, masticating it with the teeth, and tasting it with the tongue. And then, if we assent and resolve to adopt it, we spiritually swallow it. Sometimes, also, people swallow what they do not understand, or even what they do not like, with very little mastication.

Yet, as thorough mastication is essential to good digestion of food, so the thorough understanding of the knowledge of life which we receive is essential to its proper assimilation.

THE SALIVA

THE OFFICE OF THE SALIVARY GLANDS IS TO SECRETE A watery liquid which mingles with the food, softens and moistens it, and reduces it almost to a semifluid state, so that it passes easily through the fauces and the esophagus to the stomach. The saliva has other subsidiary uses, which will be considered presently; but this is the most important.

Water is, throughout the three kingdoms of nature, the vehicle of circulation; it is the means of conveying into the veins of animals, the fibers of plants, and the minute interstices of the rocks, the materials needed for their nourishment and growth.

As to its cleansing properties, water corresponds to the truth which distinguishes right from wrong. As to its nutritive and mobilizing properties, it corresponds to the same truth teaching what it is right to do, and thus giving the means of motion to those desires which, without such truth, would lie helplessly inert.

The saliva, therefore, which is almost pure water, having only about one percent of solid material, represents the instruction first given to new spirits as to the world into which they have come, as to what it is allowable and possible for them to do, and as to the state of their friends who have gone before—instruction which gives them freedom to go withersoever they desire.

The fluid is secreted by large glands lying behind and under the lower jaw, and under the tongue, which summon, according to their need, copious streams from the general circulation, which corresponds to fresh information concerning the state and wants of the heavenly man and the world of spirits.

The purer saliva, whose office is to mingle intimately with the food, to dissolve such portions as admit of ready solution, and convey them at once into the circulation, and to soften other portions to a semifluid condition so that they may easily pass to the stomach, corresponds specifically to instruction concerning heaven and heavenly life, the purpose of which is to introduce immediately into heaven those who are fitted for it, and to assist others on the way to heaven.

The viscid element of the submaxillary saliva, and still more evidently the mucus discharged by the follicles of the mouth, has for its specific office to lubricate the food, so that it may pass easily through the esophagus to the stomach; and corresponds to instruction which serves to introduce spirits to societies in the world of spirits, where they remain for further preparation. The salivary glands correspond to societies of spiritual angels who love to acquire and communicate such instruction.

In regard to this instruction, which, it will be observed, is given immediately after the spirit passes the province of the lips, we read as follows:

When the celestial angels are with a resuscitated person, they do not leave him, because they love everyone; but when the spirit is such that he can no longer be in company with the celestial angels, he desires to depart from them; and when this is the case, angels from the Lord's spiritual kingdom come, by whom is given to him the use of light, for before he saw nothing, but only thought. . . . The angels are extremely cautious lest any idea should come from the resuscitated person but what savors of love; they then tell him that he is a spirit. The spiritual angels, after the use of light has been given, perform for the new spirit all the offices which he can ever desire in that state, and instruct him concerning the things of the other life, but so far as he can comprehend them. But if he is not such as to be willing to be instructed, the resuscitated person then desires to depart from the company of those angels; but still the angels do not leave him, but he dissociates himself from them; for the angels love everyone, and desire nothing more than to perform kind offices, to instruct, and to introduce into heaven; their highest delight consists in that. When the spirit thus dissociates himself he is received by good spirits, and when he is in their company, also, all kind offices are performed for him; but if his life in the world had been such that he could not be in the company of the good, then also he wishes to remove from them, and this even until he associates himself with such as agree altogether with his life in the world, with whom he finds his life, and then, what is wonderful, he leads a similar life to what he led in the world. This beginning of man's life after death continues only for a few days. (*Heaven and Hell* §450–451)

In the posthumous treatise concerning the "Last Judgment," pp. 125–133, we have the following account of the reception and instruction of new spirits:

> When a man after death comes into the spiritual world, which usually takes place on the third day after he has breathed his last, he appears to himself in a similar life to that in which he had been in the world, and in a similar house, room, and bedchamber, in a similar dress and covering, and in similar companionship in the house; if he was a king or prince, in a similar palace; if a husbandman, in a similar cottage; rustic things surround the one, splendid the other. This takes place with everyone after death, for the purpose that death may not seem to be death, but a continuation of life, and that the last state of the natural life may become the first of the spiritual life; and that from this he may go on to his goal, which will be either in heaven or in hell. . . . When newcomers into the spiritual world are in this first state, angels come to them for the sake of wishing them a happy arrival, and at first are much amused in conversation with them, since they know that they do not then think otherwise than that they are still living in the former world. Therefore, they ask them what they think about the life after death; and the newcomers answer according to their former ideas; some that they do not know; some that they are ghosts or a kind of ethereal beings; some that they are transparent, aerial bodies; some that they are flying

specters, either in the ether and the air, or in the waters, or in middle of the earth; and some that souls like angels are in the stars; some of the newcomers deny that any man lives after death. After listening to these replies, the angels say, "Welcome! We will show you something new which you have not before known or believed, namely, that every man after death lives as man in a body exactly as he lived before." To this the new spirits rejoin, "This is impossible! Whence has he a body? Does it not lie with all there is of it dead in the grave?" The angels laughingly answer, "We will give you ocular proof of it." And they say, "Are you not men perfect form? Examine and feel yourselves; and yet have left the natural world. That you have not known this till now is because the first state of the life after death is exactly like the last state of the life before death." Hearing this, the new guests are astonished, and exclaim from joy of heart, "Thanks be to God that we are alive, and that death has not annihilated us." I have very often heard newcomers instructed thus as to their life after death, and gladdened by their resurrection.

Then follow examples of instruction by the angels concerning the consummation of the age, the destruction of the world, and the end of the Church; and, presently, leading the new spirits out, the angels showed them the Sun of Heaven, and beautiful representatives of the instruction of angels and spirits from the Lord in the Sun, and of the possible influx of Divine Truth also to man on the earth. And then also they showed how the evil spirits were multiplying in that time, before the Last Judgment, and cutting off the light of heaven from the minds of men on the earth.

All these things are of the instruction given by angels to introduce new spirits into the life of the spiritual world.

Those soluble portions of the food which are in a condition to be readily absorbed correspond to spirits who readily receive instruction concerning heaven and are in a state to conform to it at once. The portions not readily dissolved or absorbed correspond to those who need more gradual initiation.

The small amount of organic substance contained in the saliva has an important subsidiary use in beginning the preparation of some elements of food which are not yet ready for absorption. The sweetness of fruits is in a form that can be absorbed at once. But the sweetness of sugar cane needs a chemical combination with a little more water to be reduced to the same form. Starch and gum also, which are chemically akin to cane sugar, need the same addition to become food like the sugar of fruit. And the organic substance in the saliva, by its very presence, stimulates this chemical change, some portions of the sugar and the starch undergoing the change almost instantly upon coming in contact with it. The chemical union of a little more water with these substances can hardly correspond to anything else than the reception of a little necessary truth into life. And the organic substance from the glands, which stimulates this reception, seems to correspond with the influence of angels who by encouragement or by warning immediately open eyes of some who are already in good to purer truth, and perhaps to humbler acknowledgment than they had been in before.

The slightly alkaline quality of the saliva probably represents the checking of all self-assertion, and the enforcing of the acknowledgment that self is nothing, and the Lord everything, in this kingdom.

By no means the whole of the soluble portion of the food is absorbed in the mouth; a large part, dissolved or dissolving in the saliva, is carried into the stomach; much of it goes even further, into the intestines, before it is absorbed. And in correspondence with this, no doubt many newcomers who are open to spiritual instruction, hasten first to the company of their former friends in the world of spirits, and by a longer way, and through various methods of preparation, are carried into heaven.

The Esophagus

THROUGH THE ESOPHAGUS THERE IS A STRAIGHT ROAD from the mouth to the stomach. Its office is to conduct the food gently and properly from one province to the other. The food does not fall from the mouth into the stomach by mere force of its weight—we can swallow upward nearly as well as downward; as we do in drinking from a brook, and as the grazing animals constantly do. The esophagus takes it in charge, and conducts it to the stomach with uniform motion, warming and lubricating it by the way, and thus preparing it somewhat for digestion, and preventing its doing injury to the stomach by sudden blows or chills. Perhaps it should be mentioned, also, that in the esophagus the food first receives the motion of the heart and lungs, which afterwards is a necessity to its life, as long as it is a part of the body.

The mouth is in the province of the head, which constitutes the third heaven; the stomach is in the domain of the first or natural heaven; and the heart and lungs belong to the second heaven (*True Christian Religion* §119). By angels of the third heaven spirits are first received, that, at their introduction into the spiritual world, they may receive all the care that the kindest and wisest of the angels can give; and, further, that their quality may be carefully discriminated by the most sagacious angels, through whom the whole heaven may be informed of their presence and quality, and exactly such care may be provided for them as they need.

Still another advantage arising from the reception of spirits by these angels, is, that the spirits of infants, and of others who have become innocent as infants, may be received by the shortest way into heaven, being spared unnecessarily harsh treatment, and carrying at once the treasures of their innocent lives to increase the happiness of the heavenly societies to which they belong.

But it is necessary for spirits in whom good is not yet freed evil or falsity, and those in whom evil still assumes the cloak of piety and morality, to have these elements of their natural character thoroughly made known, and to pass through whatever discipline is necessary to make them homogeneous, before the good can be taken up into heaven or the evil cast down into hell; and therefore such spirits pass from the care of angels of the third heaven, under the kind and wise direction of those of the second heaven, into the province of the stomach, on the natural plane.

They do not remain long in company with angels of the second heaven. These serve as friendly guides and introducers; also they initiate the newcomers into the flow of thought and affection of the Greatest Man, which they themselves receive with peculiar fullness by reason of their nearness to and close connection with the heart and lungs of the heavens.

This heavenly rhythmical motion the same angels, in conjunction with those of the diaphragm, impress upon the whole world of spirits; for the esophagus is continued into the stomach, upon which the diaphragm also presses from above; and all their motions they impart in considerable degree to the stomach; and this communication is an important element in the training which spirits undergo to fit them for life in the kingdom of heaven, every fiber of which responds to the throbs of the same heart and the respirations of the same lungs. Not fully do the new spirits receive the influence. This they cannot do till the angelic plane of their minds is opened, and they pass once more through this heaven in the circulation of the lungs and heart—where they become angels, and their angelic faculties are opened—on their way to their own societies. As yet they perceive only the general influence of it, so far as it can affect their natural life.

The Stomach

"The world of spirits is like a forum or place of resort, where all are at first assembled, and is as a stomach in which the food is at first collected; the stomach, moreover, corresponds to that world" (*Apocalypse Revealed* §791).

And again we read,

The world of spirits, which midway between heaven and hell—into which every man first comes after death, and is there prepared—corresponds to the stomach, in which all the things that are put in are prepared, either to become blood and flesh, or to become excrement and urine. (*Apocalypse Revealed* §204)

It is known that nourishment or food is worked over in many ways in the stomach, that its interior things which are good for use may be brought out; namely, which those which go into the chyle, and afterwards into blood; and that the process is continued in the intestines. Such workings are represented by the first discipline of spirits, which is according to their life in the world, that evil things may be separated, and good things, suited for use, may be collected. Wherefore it may be said of souls or spirits soon after decease, or separation from the body, that they come as it were into the region of the stomach, and there are disciplined and purified. They with whom evils have obtained dominion, after they have been disciplined in vain, are borne through the stomach into the intestines, and even to the last, namely, the colon and the rectum, and thence are cast out into the draught, that is, into hell. But they with whom good things have dominion, after some discipline and purification, become chyle, and go into the blood, some by a longer way, some by a shorter; and some are disciplined severely, some gently, and some scarcely at all: these last are represented by the juices of food, which are immediately drunk in by the veins, and carried into the circulation, and even into the brain, and so further. (*Arcana Coelestia* §5174)

Some of these good spirits, as we have already seen, are taken up into heaven before they reach the stomach, by the way of the ducts of the mouth. But some, of equally tender and pure quality, are more closely connected with worldly affairs and worldly people, and, like the juices entangled among coarser materials, are carried into the general place of assembly for new spirits, where they are soon made spiritually free and are conducted by a little longer way into heaven.

In the world of spirits, strictly speaking, to which the stomach corresponds (*Apocalypse Revealed* §791), spirits may remain from a month to thirty years (*Apocalypse Revealed* §866); and here are collected a vast multitude who live and work in societies, as in heaven or in hell. The work done here is that of what Swedenborg calls "the second state after death," that is, the state of the interiors; and consists largely in the opening of the interiors.

> When the first state is passed through, which is the state of the exteriors...the man-spirit is let into the state of his interiors, or into the state of his interior will and consequent thought, in which he had been in the world when, being left to himself, he thought freely and without restraint. Into this state he slides without being aware of it, in like manner as in the world when he withdraws the thought which is nearest the speech, or from which the speech is, towards interior thought, and abides in it; wherefore when the man-spirit is in this state, he is in himself, and in his own very life; for to think freely from his own proper affection is the very life of man, and is himself.
>
> The spirit in this state thinks from his own very will, thus from his own very affection, or from his own very love, and in this case the thought makes one with the will, and one in such a manner that it scarcely appears that the spirit thinks, but that he wills. The case is nearly similar when he speaks, yet with this difference, that he speaks with some degree of fear lest the thoughts of the will should go forth naked, since by civil life in the world his will had contracted this habit. (*Heaven and Hell* §502–503)

In this state the habits of speech and action in which he has presented himself to society are separated from him, as the hulls from wheat, and the cell walls from the starch, sugar, or nutritive juices which they contain; and his interior affections act freely without any artificial cloak. And it is the dissolving of these cell walls and setting free of the contents which is the principal work of the stomach.

The food in the stomach is collected in considerable quantities, and is rolled in a spiral course around the large end of the stomach, and thence to the neighborhood of the pylorus, and back along the upper curve to the esophagus. No doubt this takes place with great variety, and portions may be delayed in their course, and even drawn apart into the little chambers in the lining of the stomach for special treatment. All the while it is being mingled and worked over with the acid gastric fluids, whose function it is to set the purer parts of the food free and to separate them more completely from the gross and worthless.

The gastric fluids are secreted continually during the process of digestion and are continually absorbed again by the coats of the stomach, carrying with them food which they have dissolved and returning again for more. The quantity required for digestion it would be impossible for the body to supply except by this process of re-absorption and repeated secretion. And as in the saliva there is an organic element, the ptyalin, whose office it is to induce the change of starch and sugar into a form which can be assimilated, so in the stomach there is its peculiar organic substance, called pepsin, mingling with the gastic fluids, and quickening the solution of the "proteids," or muscle-making elements of the food.

The food thus massed together is like societies of spirits in similar states; the fluids are instruction concerning good and evil, concerning things that have life and those that are dead and useless, which is to good spirits the means of increased and more joyous activity, and to the evil the means of self-condemnation and rejection.

All who have lived in good in the world, and have acted from conscience, as is the case with all those who have acknowledged a Divine and have loved Divine truths, especially those who have applied them to life, appear to themselves, when let into the state of their interiors, like those who being awakened out of sleep come into the full use of sight, and like those who from shade enter into light: they think also from the light of heaven, thus from interior wisdom, and they act from good, thus from interior affection. Heaven also flows in into their thoughts and affections with interior blessedness and delight, of which before they knew nothing; for they have communication with the angels of heaven. Then also they acknowledge the Lord and worship Him from their very life; for they are in their own proper life when in the state of their interiors; and they likewise acknowledge and worship Him from freedom, for freedom is of interior affection. They recede also thus from external sanctity, and come into internal sanctity, in which essential worship truly consists. Such is the state of those who have lived a Christian life according to the precepts delivered in the Word. But altogether contrary is the state of those who in the world have lived in evil, and have had no conscience, and hence have denied a Divine. . . . By reason of their evil lusts, they burst forth into all abominations, into contempt of others, into ridicule and blasphemy, into hatred and revenge. (*Heaven and Hell* §506)

Physiology says that the starchy elements of the food, and perhaps cane sugar, are not absorbed in the stomach, but, being acted upon by the saliva, and afterwards by the pancreatic and intestinal fluids, are turned into the more readily absorbed sugar, usually called grape sugar, or glucose, in which form they are taken up by the veins and lacteals; that fatty materials pass unchanged into the intestine, where, soon after meeting with the bile and the pancreatic fluid, they are reduced to the form of an emulsion, or milky fluid; the oil being divided into minute particles which are held as if in solution, in a state to be absorbed; and that the fluids of the stomach dissolve only the muscle-making element of food—the lean meat, the cheese of milk, and the gluten of grains. A portion of this, when dissolved, is taken up immediately by the veins and lacteals of the stomach; and a portion, needing further purification by the bile and pancreatic fluid, is carried on for a short distance in the intestine. And, correspondingly, we should expect to find only a small proportion of spirits, and those the most willing and unselfish in their usefulness, taken up directly from the province of the stomach to the places of instruction. The greater part need some further preparation. Most persons, Swedenborg says, are in the lower earth before they are taken up into heaven (*Arcana Coelestia* §4728).

Of starch and fat we will speak hereafter, when we come to the intestines and the pancreas.

Sugar corresponds to spiritual sweetness and pleasantness, which is immediately cheering and encouraging, and, in proper proportion to the more substantial satisfactions of good work, is wholesome mental nourishment. And the nitrogenized elements of food, which make muscle in the body, correspond to the love of useful work. It is to the assimilation of this that the stomach in the spiritual world especially addresses itself, separating it carefully from routine forms and conventionalities, and the many selfish considerations that mingle with everyone's love of work, also from habits of indolence and self-indulgence, and rousing in it the desire to do the use in the Lord's kingdom for which it is fitted, and to learn to do it wisely and well.

The great mass of the good that there is among men consists of various kinds of love of work. It may be largely mixed with love of the world and of various selfish rewards, and widely misdirected by mistaken notions of what is useful, and by foolish requirements of society; yet it exists in some form in every mind that feels unhappy without useful occupation, and prefers good work to large returns: and all such minds are collected and trained and purified in the world of spirits.

The chief acid of the solvent fluids of the stomach is hydrochloric acid, which is the acid of common salt. Salt is a representative of the principle that good and truth need each other and belong together; and the active principle of the salt represents a stimulus to every good to seek its truth, and to every truth to seek its good. The passive or alkaline principle may mean that they can do nothing alone. Solution by means of this active principle must mean the shaking off of all hindrances to the diligent learning to do good or to live the truth. And the organic substance by which this solution is stimulated must represent the personal encouragement or warning of angels who themselves delight in assisting in the union of every good with its truth (compare *Heaven and Hell* §425). The action of the gastric fluids in immediately arresting decay has a correspondence in the fact that a descent into worse evil or greater profanation of good than one was in in the world is not permitted.

By such influence and instruction good spirits are brought into more free and active life and are quickly separated from their worldly habits and desires. And, on the other hand, evil persons, who love self and the world supremely, reject the truth and when they come to those who accept it they repel each other. Swedenborg says of these, "They are generally carried about through a wide circle, and everywhere are shown to good spirits as they are in themselves; at the sight of them good spirits then turn themselves away; and as they turn themselves away, so also the evil spirits who are carried about turn themselves from them to the quarter where their infernal society is, into which they are about to come" (*Heaven and Hell* §511).

Spirits who are good, but have confirmed in themselves some falsity or evil from which they must be freed, also turn away from those who accept the truth, and pass first through another stage of purification.

The truth which is taught in this state, and which is represented by the general digestive fluids of the stomach, has for its purpose to bring the good into spiritual freedom and to separate evil from them. It is not interior spiritual truth; it is religious and moral truth, such as is drawn from the letter of the Scriptures by those who are in the light of heaven and who love heavenly good. Interior truth, teaching more fully about the Lord and heaven and the spiritual sense of the Scriptures, is given to good spirits in their next places of sojourn, described in Swedenborg as the "places of instruction" into which good spirits come in "the third state after death."

How the Lord guides and controls all spirits, even when they seem mixed and confused, is described as follows:

There was a numerous crowd of spirits about me, which was heard as something disorderly and flowing. They complained, saying that now a total destruction was at hand; for in that crowd nothing appeared consociated, and this made them fear destruction. They suppose also that it would be total, as is the case when such things happen. But in the midst of them I perceived a soft sound, angelically sweet, in which was nothing but what was orderly. The angelic companies there were within, and the crowd of spirits to whom appertained what was without order was without. This angelic flowing stream continued a long time, and it was said that hereby was represented how the Lord rules things confused and disorderly which are without from what is pacific in the midst, whereby things disorderly in the circumference are reduced into order, each being restored from the error of its nature. (*Arcana Coelestia* §5396)

The salivary fluids in the Greatest Man are such knowledge of heaven and of the world of spirits as serves to introduce new spirits into societies in the spiritual world. In the minds of men the correspondence of these fluids is with a knowledge of their own states and wants, which is the means of bringing new truth into relation with themselves. If sugar or salt or any other dry solid food be placed upon the dry tongue it is perfectly tasteless; but as soon as the saliva or other watery fluids dissolves a portion of it its quality is perceived. So we may hear new truth without any knowledge or thought of its relation to our own states, or to any human states, and it cannot be otherwise than insipid; but as soon as such knowledge or thought comes into contact with it instantly its agreement or disagreement with the life is felt, and it is received or rejected. Spitting upon anything is therefore a correspondential mode of expressing its utter disagreement with one's states of life.

On the other hand, the spittle of which the Lord made clay, and anointed the eyes of the blind man, represented the simplest truth of His life which, adapted to the states of men, shows the relation between their lives and His and opens their eyes to spiritual things.

After we have once received and accepted a knowledge of what is good and true, which is food for the mind, we may meditate further upon it or we may simply take it home with the determination to live it. The desire to live it, and to incorporate it in our life, will separate the essential goodness from the special forms in which it comes to us and do the work of assimilation as silently as the solvents of the stomach do their work; and we may know nothing of the process but only feel that we are encouraged and strengthened for our duties.

There is a likeness of indigestion when we cram knowledge or terms which we do not understand, and which we long revolve in the memory, vainly trying to get some good out of it. We become weary and disgusted with it and, for a time, with all knowledge.

There was also a likeness of indigestion in the heavens when there long remained and accumulated in the world of spirits those who were good externally and evil internally, and whose internals could not be opened until the time of the Judgment. Then by the solvents of the new truth taught, the externals were broken through, the good internals were gathered into heaven, and the evil were cast down.

THE INTESTINES

WHEN THE WORK OF THE STOMACH IS DONE, AND BY THE dissolving of cell walls the nutritious contents are set free, and as much as possible of the muscle-making elements of the food is dissolved, the work of digestion is continued in the intestines. But in the intestines the modes of action upon the food are changed according to the form and nature of the organ. The food is no longer revolved in a large mass, but is distributed into little pockets or chambers formed by the folds of the lining membrane of the intestine, and receives treatment adapted to the character of its various elements. It is mingled with a variety of pungent fluids, from the liver, the pancreas, and the intestinal glands, and is worked over in little handfuls much more urgently and severely than was possible in the general stomach.

During the process of the stomach digestion the door between stomach and intestine is not wholly closed; but those portions of the food which need the intestinal treatment, and will not be benefited by that of the stomach, are constantly passing out; and some of them, as fat and starch, are quickly changed by the bile and the pancreatic and intestinal fluids, and absorbed by the lacteals from the intestinal wall. A considerable mass, however, remains in the stomach and undergoes its utmost powers of digestion, without perfectly yielding to the influences which would make fluid the good elements and separate them entirely both from the useless and from those that need severer treatment. But when all that the stomach can do is done this large remainder rapidly passes out and all its elements meet the bitter and acrid bile. This precipitates at once the nitrogenized portion of the chyme, and delays it for solution again and absorption, while the other materials pass on—the remaining fat and starch to be converted into an emulsion and sugar respectively, and then absorbed, and the worthless materials to be rejected.

This great mass corresponds to the spirits long delayed in the world of spirits, many of whom are in the main good and charitable, disposed to good uses but confirmed in some falsity, or attached to other persons who appear well as to worship and life, yet in heart love evil of life and the false doctrines that permit it. These need to meet together the sharp corrections of spirits who love to bring out and punish all the evil of heart and thought that they can find, thus thoroughly exposing the wicked and causing them to flee, when the humbled and chastened good, fearing that they also shall be rejected, desire more earnestly to be instructed and taken up into heaven. The solvents of the stomach are mildly acid and perhaps, like the acids of fruit, represent instruction that is altogether pleasant and friendly but stimulating and quickening. The solvents of the intestine are acrid and alkaline, and, like the alkalies used in soap, and formerly used instead of soap, seem to represent reproving, chastening instruction by which good and evil are separated.

Who they are who constitute the province of the intestines in the Greatest Man, may be manifest in some measure from those who relate to the stomach; for the intestines are continued from the stomach, and the offices of the stomach there increase and become more harsh, even to the last intestines which are the colon and rectum. Wherefore they who are in these are near to the hells which are called excrementitious. In the region of the stomach and intestines are they who are in the lower earth, who because they have brought with them from the world unclean things which are fixed in their thoughts and affections, are kept there for some time, until such things are wiped away, that is, are cast aside. After this is done, they can be taken up to heaven. They who are there are not yet in the Greatest Man; for they are like ailments let down into the stomach, which are not introduced into the blood, thus into the body, until they are purified. They who are defiled with more earthly dregs are under these in the region of the intestines; but the excrements themselves which ate discharged correspond to the hells which are called the excrementitious hells. (*Arcana Coelestia* §5392)

There are many kinds of persons who need such discipline; among them are those who have contracted strong personal friendships without regard to the good or evil in one another. These, Swedenborg teaches us,

cannot like others be separated according to order, and assigned to the society correspondent with their life; for they are bound together interiorly as to the spirit, nor can they be severed, because they are like branches engrafted into branches. There-

40

fore if one as to his interiors is in heaven, and the other as to his in hell, they remain fast to each other, much like a sheep tied to a wolf, or a goose to a fox, or a dove to a hawk; and he whose interiors are in hell inspires the infernal things belonging to him into the one whose interiors are in heaven. For among the things that are well known in heaven is also this, that evil may be inspired into the good, but not good into the evil; this is because everyone is by birth in evils. Consequently the interiors are closed in the good that are thus joined with the evil; and they both are thrust down into hell, where the good man suffers hard things, but after a lapse of time is taken out and then first is prepared for heaven. It has been granted me to see such bindings, especially among brothers and relatives, and also between patrons and their dependants, and of many with flatterers, among whom were contrary affections and unlike genius; and I have seen some like kids with leopards, and they were then kissing one another, and swearing to their former friendship. And I then perceived that the good were absorbing the enjoyments of the evil, holding each other by the hand, and together entering into caves where crowds of the wicked were seen in their hideous forms, though to themselves, from the illusion of fantasy, they seemed in lovely forms. But after a while I heard from the good mournful cries of fear, as if on account of snares, and from the wicked I heard rejoicings like those of enemies over spoils; besides other sad scenes. I have heard that the good, when taken out, were afterwards prepared for heaven by reformatory means, but with greater difficulty than others. (*True Christian Religion* §448)

Closely allied to these evil friends, who drag those who are attached to them down with them, seem to be "the judges of friendship and bribes," who could see nothing but what favored their friends, whom Swedenborg saw "in the lower earth, next above hell," and who were afterwards cast out (*Conjugial Love* §231). There also were those called "learned," because they were able by ingenious reasoning to throw doubt upon the real existence of every thing; who also, because they perpetually argue upon the surface of things, from appearances, are likened to "shells around almonds, without kernel," and to "rinds around fruits, without pulp." These likewise were cast out (*Conjugial Love* §232).

A third class seen in the same region were the "confirmators," called "wise" because they could make anything whatever appear to be true, no matter whether it were reasonable or unreasonable, true or false; but they had no genuine wisdom or understanding (*Conjugial Love* §233). All three of these classes would be likely to drag down with them some who were simple minded, or strongly attached to them for various reasons, and to bring them into states of great suffering, from their evil associations in that lower earth.

Of the lower earth, as he usually calls it, Swedenborg says that in the world of spirits it is "next beneath the feet, and the region round about to a little distance; there most persons are after death, before they are taken up into heaven. . . . Beneath it are the places of vastation, which are called pits; below these places, and round about to a great distance, are the hells" (*Arcana Coelestia* §4728). He more commonly speaks of the places of vastation, by which are meant the places of severer trials by which the good are freed from evil clinging to them, as in the lower earth. He says:

> In order that I might see the torments of those who are in hell, and also the vastation of those who are in the lower earth, I was sometimes letdown thither.... I perceived plainly that, as it were, a kind of column encompassed me; that column was sensibly increased, and it was insinuated to me that this was the wall of brass spoken of in the Word, formed of angelic spirits, in order that I might be let down safely amongst the unhappy. When I was there I heard miserable lamentations, and indeed this cry, "Oh God, Oh God, be merciful to us, be merciful to us"; and this for a long time. It was granted to me to discourse with those miserable persons for some time. They complained chiefly of evil spirits, as burning with a continual desire only to torment them; and they were in a state of despair, saying that they believed their torments would be eternal; but it was granted me to comfort them. (*Arcana Coelestia* §699; compare §4940)

Of the purpose of the vastation, he says:

> Man, by reason of actual sin, brings with him into the other life innumerable evils and falsities, which he accumulates and joins together. This is the case even with those who have lived uprightly. Before they can be elevated into heaven, their evils and falsities must be dissipated; and this dissipation is called vastation. There are many kinds of vastation, and the times of vastation are longer and shorter;

some are taken up into heaven in a very short time, and some immediately after death. (*Arcana Coelestia* §698)

There are many who while they were in the world, through simplicity and ignorance, imbibed falsities as to faith, and formed a certain species of conscience according to the principles of their faith; and did not live, as others, in hatred, revenge, and adulteries. These in the other life, so long as they are in what is false, cannot be introduced into heavenly societies, for thus they would defile them; therefore they are kept for some time in the lower earth, in order that they may put off the principles of falsity. The times of their stay there are longer or shorter according to the nature of the falsity and the life contracted from it, and according to the principles confirmed in themselves; some endure hard things in that state, others not hard. These are what are called vastations, whereof much mention is made in the Word. When the time of vastation is over, they are taken up into heaven, and are instructed as novitiates in the truths of faith; and this is done by angels by whom they are received. (*Arcana Coelestia* §1106)

There are some who willingly endure to be vastated, and thereby to put off the false principles which they had brought with them out of the world. (It is not possible for any one to put off false principles in the other life, except after some length of time, and by means provided by the Lord.) During their stay in the lower earth they are kept by the

Lord in hope of deliverance, and in the thought of the end, that thus they may be amended and may be prepared to receive heavenly happiness. (*Arcana Coelestia* §1107)

In those places are they who have ascribed all things to nature, and little to the Divine. I conversed with them there, and when the discourse was concerning the Divine Providence they attributed all things to nature. Nevertheless those there who have led a good moral life, when they have been detained there some time, successively put off those principles and put on principles of truth. (*Arcana Coelestia* §4941)

In the lower earth, beneath the feet and the soles of the feet, are also they who have placed merit in good deeds and works; some of them appear to themselves to cut wood; the place where they are is rather cold, and they seem to themselves to acquire heat by their labor. With these also I conversed, and it was given to ask them whether they wished to come forth from that place. They said, that as yet they had not merited it by labor; but when that state has been passed through they are then conveyed away thence. These also are natural, because to wish to merit salvation is not spiritual. And moreover they prefer themselves to others; some of them even despise others. These, if in the other life they do not receive joy above others, are indignant against the Lord; wherefore when they cut wood it sometimes appears as if somewhat of the Lord was under the wood, and this from indignation. But whereas they have led a pious life, and have acted thus from ignorance, in which there was somewhat of innocence, therefore occasionally angels are sent to them and console them. (*Arcana Coelestia* §4943; also *Arcana Coelestia* §1110; the grass-cutters, *Arcana Coelestia* §1111)

They who came out of the world from Christian lands, and have led a moral life and had some degree of charity toward the neighbor, but have had little concern about spiritual things, for the most part are sent into the places beneath the feet and soles of the feet; and are kept there until they put off the natural things in which they have been, and are imbued with spiritual and celestial things as far as they can be according to their life; and when they have become imbued with these, they are taken up thence into heavenly societies. I have seen them at times emerging, and their joy at coming into heavenly light. (*Arcana Coelestia* §4944; also *Arcana Coelestia* §4950)

All these states of vastation appear to be accomplished in those parts of the lower earth corresponding to the intestines, and from thence the chastened good spirits are taken up as chyle is absorbed by the veins and lacteals. No doubt the modes of correction and vastation are all represented in the methods by which the chyme is sorted, some of which we have briefly touched upon, and others will appear more clearly when we study the liver and the pancreas.

The intestines are generally distinguished into two—the large and the small; and these are each subdivided into three or more. The small intestine is long, much convoluted, and freely supplied with absorbing vessels. Into this the imperfectly digested food first passes from the stomach, and almost immediately meets the bile, the pancreatic fluid, and the intestinal fluids.

By the bile a large part of the muscle-making chyle is immediately precipitated, and thus separated from impurities and held for solution by the pancreatic fluid; also a part of the fat is turned into soap, in which form it is readily absorbed. The pancreatic fluid, besides effecting the solution of the albuminous precipitate, quickly makes to a milky emulsion of the remaining fat, at least in reasonable quantity, and also, with the fluid of the intestinal glands, quickly completes the transformation of the starch into sugar, in which forms respectively both fat and starch are readily absorbed.

The remainder of the chyme, together with such portions of these good materials as have not completed their metamorphoses, passes rapidly on, subjected their metamorphoses, passes rapidly on, subjected to more and more severe treatment, and parting at every turn with its good particles, till by the time it reaches the large intestine, called the colon, there is scarcely anything in it which can serve any good use in the body.

In the colon the residue is no longer treated as food to be redeemed to good uses if possible; but is compacted for rejection, and undergoes the last wringing to rescue from it the small remainder of possibly nutritious fluids.

That any spirits can be saved who, in the corresponding treatment in the lower earth, so long resist both kindness and chastisement, and remain as companions with the wicked until their loathsomeness is so fully exhibited, shows the infinity of the saving mercy of the Lord, which does not permit the least thing in a human spirit to be lost that can possibly be saved to heavenly life. There are spirits, Swedenborg tells us, "who have lived an evil life, and yet have some remains of good concealed in them. These remains cause them to have a little spiritual life after many ages of vastations" (*Arcana Coelestia* §5561).

These, perhaps, are taken up from the province of the colon. Others, corresponding to the contents of the colon, some of whom are saved, are described as delighting in rapine and slaughter, yet having a little humanity (*Arcana Coelestia* §5393).

As to those who correspond to the walls of the intestine, and are a part of the Greatest Man, they must be such as take pleasure in correcting and punishing, yet from justice and for the sake of reformation. They who correspond to the small intestine, especially the upper part of it, from which chyle is most freely absorbed, are especially delighted to rescue the good from the evil, by sharp reproof it necessary, and to introduce them among heavenly companions. But they who are in the large intestine, and especially those who correspond in their uses to the rectum, take pleasure in punishing and confining the evil; yet always with an interior satisfaction in protecting the good from them.

Of course they who have absolutely no love of good, and no childlike remains, but are wholly devoted to self, have no basis for heavenly development. To make angels of them would be to destroy them utterly, and create new spirits. They are not destroyed, but are permitted to enjoy such vile pleasures as they can without injuring other spirits.

They who in the life of the body have made voluptuous pleasures their end, and have loved only to indulge their natural propensities, and to live in luxury and festivity, caring only for themselves and the world, without any regard to things Divine, and void of faith and charity, these after death are at first introduced into a life similar to what they have lived in the world. There is a place in front towards the left, at a considerable depth, where all is pleasure, sport, dancing, feasting, and light conversation; to this place such spirits are conveyed, and then they know no other but that they are still in the world. But after a short time the scene is changed; for then they are carried down to hell. . . for such pleasure, which is merely corporeal, is, in the other life, changed into what is excrementitious; I have seen them there carrying dung and lamenting. (*Arcana Coelestia* §943)

In the other life, the quality of spirits is made sensible by odors; and "they who have indulged in mere sensual pleasures, and have lived in no charity and faith, exhale an odor like that of excrement. The case is the same with those who have passed their lives in adulteries; but the odor of these is still more offensive" (*Arcana Coelestia* §1514).

Those also who have lived in intense self-love, with no charity or humanity towards those who do not favor them, also those who have delighted solely in avarice, or in cruelty or robbery, or mere selfish indolence, or any other form of evil, of necessity are entirely separated from the heavenly man.

In us as individuals, the operation of the intestines, as regards the digestion of food and the absorption of good material, is scarcely felt. And the like is true of the operation of the mind in absorbing strength from the true and good things we learn and adopt. That the process does go on, however, and that we do continue for a time to gather strength from such spiritual food is evident.

But much of the truth we receive is contained in forms and formulas which are themselves of no account; and the mind which is healthily growing in wisdom extracts the wisdom from them, and lets the mere learning pass into oblivion. And, again, the mind is recreated by pleasant natural things, which are correspondences of good affections and thoughts. Music, beautiful scenery and pictures, pleasant food, and other things agreeable to the senses may serve this purpose. A healthy mind loves these for their use, and then lets the sensual impressions pass away; but an unhealthy mind clings to these with a kind of indolent fascination, retaining them in the thoughts long after their use is over, and grows spiritually stupid and unhappy from them.

THE MESENTERY

FROM STOMACH AND INTESTINES THE CHYLE IS ABSORBED both by veins and by lacteals. That which is taken up by blood vessels is carried forward by the portal vein to the liver, there to be sorted, trained to the activities of the body, and distributed in several ways according to its quality. That which is absorbed by the lacteals is carried through a labyrinthine network, knotted by many glands, called the mesentery, and is then collected into a vessel about the size of a finger, situated on the right side of the spinal column, just under the diaphragm, called the receptacle of chyle. Here it is mingled with the lymph returned by the lymphatics from all the viscera of the abdomen and thorax; and then, through an irregular tube called the thoracic duct, it ascends nearly to the neck, emptying usually into the vein that returns the blood from the left arm to the heart.

Of those who constitute this receptacle and duct, Swedenborg says:

> They who constitute this province are of a twofold kind; some are modest enough, some are forward. The modest are they who have desired to know the thoughts of men, with the intent of attracting and binding them to themselves; for he who knows what another thinks is acquainted with his secrets

and his interiors, which cause them to be conjoined together; the end regarded is conversation and friendship. They desire only to know the good things and explore them, and put a good interpretation upon the rest. (*Arcana Coelestia* §5180)

Of a similar quality in general must be the angels of all the lacteals of the mesentery.

We can imagine these gentle angels, loving conversation and friendship, receiving the new spirits, who by various chastenings have come to desire instruction in the truth of heaven and a life according to it, walking with them by intricate ways, calling out their good thoughts, explaining away their troubles, leading them hither and thither according to the wants they discover in them, introducing them to quick and gentle changes of state, that their sympathies may be quickened and variously extended, and bringing them to one gland-like community or another, as it may seem useful to associate them with other new spirits, or to give them the benefit of angels' teaching, and finally escorting them to the great road in which, with thousands of redeemed, rejoicing spirits, they ascend toward the warm heart of the heavens.

This initiation into heavenly companionship and heavenly thought is a preparation of the good for heaven. The mesentery, therefore, corresponds to places of instruction for a part of the new spirits in their progress toward heaven, as is confirmed by the following passage:

It may be known in some measure from the gyres to what province in the Greatest Man, and correspondently in the body, spirits and angels belong. The gyres of those who belong to the province of the lymphatics are slender and rapid as a watery element gently flowing so that scarcely any gyration can be perceived. They who belong to the lymphatics are afterwards conveyed into places which they said have reference to the mesentery, and it was told me that there are as it were labyrinths therein, and that they are next taken away thence to various places in the Greatest Man, that they may serve for use as chyle in the body. (*Arcana Coelestia* §5181)

The winding ways by which men are taught by the Lord, even in this world, are also likened by Swedenborg to these mesenteric paths:

Everyone is from infancy brought into that Divine Man whose soul and life is the Lord; and in Him, not out of Him, he is led and taught from His Divine love according to His Divine wisdom. But as freedom is not taken away from man, a man cannot be led and taught otherwise than according to reception as by himself. They who receive are borne to their places by infinite windings, as by meandering streams, almost as the chyle is carried through the mesentery and its lacteals into its receptacle, and from this through the thoracic duct into the blood, and so to its destination. They who do not receive are separated from those who are within the Divine Man, as the feces and urine are separated from man. (*Divine Providence* §164)

The glands of the mesentery are of great interest in their correspondence. The fibers of the network of lacteals run from one gland to another, having also threads which pursue their course with more directness; so that it is possible for the chyle to pass through several glands, or, perhaps, to enter none at all, on its way to the receptacle.

In the glands it meets arteries and veins and nervous fibers. The arteries bring fresh blood from the heart, and the nerves bring spirit from the brain. The purpose of the glands is evidently to prepare the new chyle more perfectly to enter into the uses of the body; and this purpose they must fulfill by modifying the chyle, either through the forms of their little vessels, or by communication of vital elements to it from the arteries and the nervous fibers; perhaps it performs its office in both ways. "The mesentery elaborates the chyle, and the liver the blood" (*Divine Providence* §336). It is believed also that the white corpuscles, which are an active element in the blood and which are rapidly multiplied after a meal, are formed in part in these glands.

Now the chyle of the Greatest Man is composed of good spirits freed from their association with the evil and form evil influences, tender in feeling, and eager to learn. The blood of the arteries is composed of angelic spirits, prepared for heaven, but not yet fixed in their own societies; also in part, apparently, of "subject" angels sent from their societies for special service elsewhere. And the nerve influence, direct from the brain, is the direct influence or presence of wise angels of the third heaven.

If, then, we should read of good, intelligent spirits, eager to be instructed, being trained to angelic thought under the care of angels and the direct supervision and inspiration of angels of the third heaven, we should conclude with reason that we had found a place marvelously like a mesenteric gland.

In section 132 of the work *Conjugial Love*, we read:

I once conversed with two angels; one was from the eastern heaven, the other from the southern heaven, who ... said, "Do you know anything of the Exercises of Wisdom in our world?" I answered that I did not yet. And they said, "They are numerous, and those who love truths from spiritual affection, or truths because they are truths, and because by means of them is wisdom, come together at a given signal, and canvass and conclude those things which are of more profound understanding." They then took me by the hand, saying, "Follow us, and you shall see and hear; today the signal for meeting is given." I was led across a plain to a hill; and, behold, at the foot of the hill was an avenue of palms, continued even to its top. We entered it and ascended. And on the top or summit of the hill was seen a grove, the trees of which, upon an elevation of ground, formed as it were a theater, within which was a plain surface covered with little stones variously colored. Around it, in a square form, were placed seats, upon which the lovers of wisdom were sitting; and in the middle of the theater was a table upon which was laid a paper sealed with a seal. Those sitting upon the seats invited us to the seats as yet vacant. And I answered, "I was led here by the two angels to see and listen, and not to sit." And then those two angels went into the middle of the plain surface to the table, and loosed the seal of the paper, and read, in the presence of those sitting, the arcana of wisdom written upon the paper, which they were now to canvass and unfold. They were written by angels of the third heaven, and let down upon the table. There were three arcana: First, what the image of the God is? Second, why man is not born into the knowledge belonging to any love, when yet beast and birds, as well the noble is as the ignorable, are born into the knowledges belonging to all their loves? Third, what the tree of life signifies, and what the tree of the knowledge of good and evil, and what the eating from them?

Under these was written, "Conjoin these three into one opinion, and write this upon a new paper, and lay it upon the table, and we shall see it; if the opinion when weighed appears right and just, there shall be given to each of you a reward of wisdom."

These things being read, the two angels withdrew, and were taken up into their own heavens. And then those sitting upon the seats began to canvass and unfold the arcana proposed to them.

After an orderly and enlightened discussion, their conclusions were combined one series, as follows:

That man is created that he may receive love and wisdom from god, and yet in all likeness as of himself; and this for the sake of reception and conjunction; and that therefore man is not born into any love, nor any knowledge, and also not into any power of loving and being wise into himself; wherefore if he ascribes all good of love and truth of wisdom to God, he becomes a living man; but if he ascribes them to himself, he becomes a dead man.

These they wrote upon a new paper, and place this upon the table; and, behold suddenly angels were present in shining white light, and carried away the paper into heaven; and after it was read there, those sitting upon the seats heard thence the words, "Well, well, well"; and forthwith there appeared one thence if flying, and distributed to all the company beautiful rewards of wisdom.

If this admirable exercise did not take place in the mesentery, it certainly illustrates the processes which must there be accomplished.

Other similar lessons are also described by Swedenborg.

Somewhat similar are the schools taught by the ancient wise men of Greece. "All the Athenians," St. Luke tells us, "and strangers which were there, spent their time in nothing else but either to tell or to hear some new thing." (Acts 27:21)

In the neighborhood of Athens also were the schools of philosophy taught by Pythagoras, Socrates, Plato, Aristotle, and many others, in which, from the new things told, wise lessons of morality or philosophy were deduced; and from which have come down to us, in the form either of allegory or of direct instruction, almost all the remains we have of the wisdom of the Ancient Churches.

The desire of these wise men to learn new things, and to instruct in true wisdom, was not diminished but increased and enlightened by their change to the spiritual world. It is not, therefore, a matter of surprise to find them, in Swedenborg's descriptions, receiving modest and intelligent newcomers with the greeting, "What news from the earth?"—inquiring especially about the thoughts of men concerning eternal life, and then wisely instructing the spirits in the nature of heavenly life and happiness.

These things are set forth at length in *Conjugial Love* §151–154, §182, and §207.

THE LIVER

THAT PART OF THE CHYLE WHICH IS TAKEN UP BY THE lacteals is initiated into the quick and gentle flow of the mesentery, is modified, and, as it were, instructed in the mesenteric glands, and then is carried to the receptacle of chyle, and through the thoracic duct and the left subclavian vein to the heart.

The portion of the chyle which is taken up from the stomach and intestines by the veins, is collected in the great portal vein, where it mingles with the blood returned from all the viscera of digestion, and then by the portal vein it is conducted for its training, instruction, and purification to the liver.

The portal vein enters the liver side by side with the hepatic artery, which brings fresh blood from the heart artery which brings fresh blood from the heart; the bile duct, which returns its peculiar secretion to the intestines; and a coating of cellular tissue which appears to be the origin and home of a host of lymphatic vessels.

These proceed together, dividing and subdividing again and again, till their minute twigs enclose in their embrace minute little lobes or lobules. The walls of these lobules are composed of small tubes running inward, and lined with cellular matter peculiar to the organ.

To these the portal vein and the hepatic artery offer their burdens of chyle and blood, both fresh and refuse;

and the tubuli, with sensitive perception adapted to their use, drink in from them the harmonious elements which will combine in a rich, wholesome current for the use of the body, and this they offer to the open mouths of the hepatic veins. These veinlets open in the cavities of the lobules, and there receive, and thence convey to the vena cava, for the heart, whatever the liver may present to them. The lighter portion of the chyle and lymph, not needed for the present use of the blood, flows quickly on its pleasant lymphatic path, and joins its companions in the chyle receptacle. The hard and obstinate particles which cannot conform to the requirements of the tubuli, and would be of no use elsewhere in the body, are remanded to the bile ducts and the gall bladder; the worst of them to be cast out, the better for a low use in the intestines.

There are gyres into which recent spirits must be inaugurated, that they may enter into consociation with others and may speak and think together with them. There must be concord and unanimity of all, in the other life, that they may be one; as all things in man, which, although they are everywhere various, yet by unanimity make one, so in the Greatest Man. For this end the thought and speech of one must agree with that of others. It is a fundamental thing that the thought and the speech should in themselves be in concord in every member of a society; otherwise something discordant is felt as a harsh noise which affects the minds of others. Everything discordant also is disunient and is an impurity which must be rejected. This impurity from discord is represented by impurity with the blood and in the blood from which it must be defecated. This defecation is effected by vexations, which are nothing else than temptations of various kinds, and afterwards by introduction into gyres. (*Arcana Coelestia* §5182)

As there is a flow of thought and affection in every heavenly society peculiar to itself, so there are forms and motions in every organ of the body peculiar to itself, to which all fluids and particles which are introduced must conform, or they will be immediately rejected. If they do not agree with the little tubes, either in size or shape, or do not flow readily or smoothly through their windings, the tubes refuse to admit them, or contract and expel them. And in this they are guided by an exquisite, unerring sensitiveness, given them continually in kind and degree adapted to their use.

The liver may be regarded as a large gland whose primary use it is to prepare good blood for the general uses of the body. It receives its supplies from the portal vein which brings new chyle and older blood from the abdominal viscera, and from the hepatic artery which brings fresh blood and old from the heart. It selects from these the materials demanded by the wants of the body, examines them thoroughly, carefully strains and sorts them, makes intimately acquainted and combines the new and the old, and thus mingles wisely a stream rich and wholesome and suited to its use, which it sends through the hepatic veins and the vena cava to the heart. A secondary secretion of fresh, lively fluid, suited to replenish the streams returning from the left side of the head and the left arm, it sends thither through the lymphatics and the thoracic duct. And a third secretion of materials, not suited to the general circulation, but still capable of doing service in the digestion of new food, it dispatches to the intestines through the hepatic duct and the gall bladder.

It is also regarded as an important function of the liver to reduce the surplus of sugary material, not immediately needed in the work of the body, to a starch-like condition, in which form it is called glycogen, and store it up until it is wanted for use. In the form of glycogen it remains unchanged until it is summoned, and then is quickly changed again into sugar. While it is proper to mention this use here, the consideration of its significance will be deferred till we study the omentum.

The noble use of the liver to the body corresponds to a noble spiritual use of a vast province to the heavens. The province is large; for the liver is larger than any other viscus, if we except the whole mass of the intestines. And its use is to assimilate to the life and uses of the heavens newly arrived spirits, especially those with a zeal for usefulness; to instruct, also, and expand the minds of others drawn from various provinces of the heavens; and to separate from the system perverse individuals and affections.

It has been given me to perceive the gyres of those who belong to the provinces of the liver, and this for a space of hours. Their gyres were gentle, flowing around variously, like the operation of that organ. They affected me with great delight. Their operation is diverse, but it is in general orbicular. That their operation is diverse is represented also in the functions of the liver, that they are diverse; for the liver draws to itself the blood, and separates it; pours the better part into the veins, that of a middle sort it remands to the hepatic duct, and the vile it leaves to the gall bladder.

(It is thus in adults; but in embryos the liver receives the blood from the mother's womb, and purifies it; the purer part it infuses into the veins, that it may flow by a short way to the heart. It then acts as a guard before the heart.) (*Arcana Coelestia* §5183)

By the liver is signified interior purification; for the liver purifies the blood, but the intestines those things of which the blood is composed.... In other cases by the liver is signified the external good of innocence, such as appertains to infants; by reason that infants, before the rest of the viscera are fully formed to their use, as is the case when they are embryos, are nourished through the liver; for all the nutritious juice is brought thither through the placenta and the navel from the womb of the mother; this juice corresponds to the good of innocence. (*Arcana Coelestia* §10031)

A part of the spirits newly received into the spiritual world are conducted into heaven by the way of the lacteals, being trained in the flow and varieties of heavenly thought and affection in the devious paths of the mesentery, and examined and instructed in the schools represented by its glands. Another, and probably the larger, part ascend by the way of the veins—not yet fairly in the circulation, for they have yet to be trained and instructed in the province of the liver and then received and sent forth by the heart.

As the treatment received by these two portions of the chyle is so different, it may be well to consider briefly the materials of which they consist. Nearly all the elements which enter into their composition they have in common, with the marked exception of the red globules which are already in the veins. There are white globules in the lacteals as well as in the vein, and even imperfect red globules soon appear. The chief difference seems to be in the proportions in which they are mingled. There are fibrine and fat, sugar, water, and salts, in both; but very much more of fibrine and sugar in the veins, and very much more of water and fat, and probably of some salts, in the lacteals. From the comparative redness and solidity of the contents of the veins, it would appear that they represent those who are more in the love of goodness and of usefulness, which love is especially represented by the fibrinous, muscle-making element of the blood; the sweetness of the stream also represents the sweetness of character of those who have suffered hard things, and perhaps the enjoyment in the love of goodness in those in whom this love has been purified. And from the whiteness and wateriness of the contents of the lacteals, it seems plain that they represent those who are more in the love of truth and the good life which truth teaches. The considerable quantity of fat contained in the lacteals may seem to conflict with this, since fat has a celestial meaning. But the spiritual—that is, the kindness and goodwill of those who are in the love of truth; as the butter of milk represents the mother's love for the children whom she teaches.

It seems safe then to conclude that they who ascend by the portal way to the province of the liver are those who are especially in the love of goodness, and in the desire to be trained and instructed in angels' uses. They walk in company with those who have been sent to assist in the preparation of new spirits, and who now, delighted with their docile companions, discourse with them of heavenly employments, inspire into them their own love of use, and enter, together with them, the great province of instruction.

Thither come also, by the way of the heart, other new spirits who have entered the circulation by shorter ways, and angels from all provinces of the body who need to be relieved of opinions and feelings too narrow for their present uses, and initiated into broader views and quicker sympathies; and possibly also some spirits who, by reason of their urgency, have been permitted to enter heaven unprepared, and by this way are cast out, if evil, or have an opportunity for instruction if good (*Apocalypse Revealed* §611). Perhaps it is not by chance that Swedenborg describes some of both of these kinds in the midst of his description of the places of instruction (*Heaven and Hell* §518).

"The third state of man, after death," Swedenborg says, "is a state of instruction; this state appertains to those who come into heaven and become angels, but not to those who come into hell, since these latter cannot be instructed" (*Heaven and Hell* §512). We should, therefore, look for the places of instruction in some province through which the chyle passes after it is separated from worthless materials in the proper digestive organs, and before it reaches the heart. The only organs thus situated are the mesentery and the liver. The province of the mesentery appears to serve for this use, or at least for initiation into exercises of wisdom for a part of the new spirits; but the chief places of instruction and of introduction to heavenly uses evidently must be situated in the province of the liver.

Those places of instruction are to the north, and are various, arranged and distinguished according to the genera and species of heavenly goods, that each and every person may there be instructed according to his particular temper and faculty of reception. Those places extend in all directions there to a considerable distance. The good spirits who are to be instructed are conveyed thither by the Lord, when they have passed through their second state in the world of spirits, *but still not all*; for they who had been instructed in the world were there also prepared by the Lord for heaven, and are conveyed into heaven by another way; some immediately after death; some after a short stay with good spirits, where the grosser thoughts and affections which they contracted from honors and riches in the world are removed, and thus they are purified; some are first vastated, which is effected in places under the soles of the feet, which are called the lower earth, where some suffer severely; these are they who have confirmed themselves in falsities, and still have led good lives; for falsities confirmed inhere with much force, and until they are dispersed truths cannot be seen, thus cannot be received. (*Heaven and Hell* §513)

All who are in the places of instruction have distinct habitations there; for everyone as to his interiors is connected with the society of heaven to which he is about to come; wherefore since the societies of heaven are arranged according to a heavenly form, so likewise are the places where instructions are given; it is on this account that when those places are inspected from heaven, there appears then as it were a heaven in a lesser form.

They extend themselves there lengthways from east to west, and breadthways from north to south; but the breadth to appearance is less than the length. The arrangements, in general, are as follows: In front are those who died infants, and have been educated in heaven to the age of first adolescence, who, after completing the state of their infancy with the females appointed to educate them, are brought thither by the Lord and instructed. Behind them are the places where they are instructed who died adults, and who in the world were in affection for truth from the good of life. Behind them are they who have professed Mohammedan religion, and in the world have led a moral life. . . . Behind these, more to the north, are the places of instructions of various Gentile nations, who in the world have led a good life in conformity with their religion. . . . These in number exceed all the rest; the best of them are from Africa. (*Heaven and Hell* §514)

They who have been educated from infancy in heaven are here instructed by angels of the interior heavens; they who have died adult mostly by angels of the lowest heaven; Mohammedans by angels who once were Mohammedans; and gentiles by their respective angels (*Heaven and Hell* §515). But the "instructions differ from instructions on earth in this respect, that knowledge is not committed to memory, but to the life." "The affection for truth for the sake of uses of life is continually inspired; for the Lord provides that everyone may love the uses suited to his particular genius, which love is also exalted by the hope of becoming an angel." "Truth is thus implanted in use, so that the truths which they learn are truths of use. Angelic spirits are thus instructed and prepared for heaven" (*Heaven and Hell* §517).

It may have nothing to do with the four departments of the places of instruction, that there are two larger and two smaller lobes of the liver; but it may be worth bearing in mind. Undoubtedly it is true that the lobes have their respective characteristics, and draw from the supplies accordingly, and furnish correspondingly varied products.

> After the spirits have been prepared for heaven in the above-mentioned places by instructions, which is effected in a short time, by reason that they are in spiritual ideas which comprehend many things together, they are then clothed with angelic garments, which for the most part are white, as of fine linen, and thus they are brought to the way which tends upwards toward heaven. (*Heaven and Hell* §519)

> There are eight ways which lead from the above places to heaven, and by which the novitiate angels are introduced, two from each place of instruction, one going up towards the east, the other to the west; they who come into the Lord's celestial kingdom are introduced by the eastern way, but they who come to the spiritual kingdom are introduced by the western way. The four ways which lead to the Lord's celestial kingdom appear adorned with olive trees and fruit trees of various kinds; but those which lead to the Lord's spiritual kingdom appear adorned with vines and laurels. This is from correspondence, because vines and laurels corre-

spond to the affection for truth and to its uses, whilst olives and fruits correspond to the affection for good and its uses. (*Heaven and Hell* §520)

May not this distinction be represented in the body by the distinction between the veins and the lymphatics of the liver. For these are the only two kinds of vessels by which there is ascent to the heart; they both go from every part of the liver, and also from every gland in the mesentery; and the lymphatics do go up to the left, and the veins to the right.

The rejoicing of the new angelic spirits in their salvation from evil, and their enjoyment in the uses of heavenly life, may be represented in the abundant sugar which is found everywhere in the liver and in the fresh blood which it sends to the heart. The warmth of the liver, said to be greater than that of every other organ in the body, may represent that supreme exaltation of love which angels feel in initiating new spirits into heavenly joys.

But, besides the angelic spirits who ascend from the places of instruction, rejoicing in new life, there are some, corresponding to the bile, who reject the wise and kindly instruction given in this province, adhere obstinately to their own opinions, are embittered because they are not received into heaven by reason of the natural depravity which they have done nothing to overcome, and therefore delight to find fault and to punish (*Heaven and Hell* §518). (Compare *Apocalypse Revealed* §611 and §839, where is described the casting down of such in the neighborhood of the places of instruction of good boys.) These are permitted to go by the way of the hepatic duct to the intestines, where they may do a use in exposing evil, and in the vastations of the good who have some confirmation of evil and falsity; and as they go they are warned and threatened and guarded lest they should punish more than is useful (*Arcana Coelestia* §5185). Perhaps the best of them, who love to punish for the sake of rescuing the good, may return with them to the safe places of instruction, and again go forth upon similar errands; as the better elements of the bile are absorbed by the veins and lacteals, and are again separated by the liver. Possibly some such may be said to be subjects of the liver sent to perform this use, as the solvents of the stomach were said to be subjects of that organ.

Swedenborg believed that the worst of the bile was deposited in the gall bladder; and either this is true, or the bile after it is carried there is severely wrung out, the lighter portions being carried away by veins or lymphatics, and the denser and bitterer portion being left, of course to be discharged into the intestine at suitable times. The bladder itself is tough and membranous; its inner surface being wrinkled and knotted. Its neck is furnished with a spiral staircase, by which bile is assisted in passing up from the hepatic duct as by the turns of a hollow screw. Through the same spiral way, by a reversal of the turns, the bile descends to the intestine. And possibly is exercised by being driven alternately one way and then the other, which exercise well corresponds with the mode of discipline described by Swedenborg as peculiar to the province.

Swedenborg describes those who are represented by the bile as loving to punish; the worst of them hardly being willing to desist. He says, "their delights are in punishing, and thus doing good; nor do they abstain from filth" (*Arcana Coelestia* §5185). Those in the bladder itself cooperate in the use, moderating and restraining too great severities, and perhaps quickening the slow in the manner presently described. Of those in the gall bladder, he says:

They are those who in the life of the body have despised what is honorable and in some degree what is pious, and also who have brought them into discredit. (*Arcana Coelestia* §5186)

A certain spirit came to me inquiring whether I knew where he might stay. I thought that he was honest, and when I told him that possibly he might stay here, the vexatory spirits of this province came, and vexed him miserably, which I was sorry for, and in vain desired to prevent. I then observed that I was in the province of the gall bladder. The vexatory spirits were of those who despised what is honorable and pious. It was given to observe one kind of vexation there, which was a compulsion to speak with a rapidity exceeding that of the thoughts, which they effected by an abstraction of the speech from the thought, and then by compulsion to follow their speech, which is done with pain. By such vexation the slow are inaugurated into greater quickness of thinking and speaking. (*Arcana Coelestia* §5187)

From the *Spiritual Diary*, §1012–1014, it would appear that in general it is the sprits who have despised spiritual and heavenly things who are thus dealt with, and who are represented by the bile. Excessive slowness has the effect of unwillingness and sullenness; if it can be overcome by temporary suffering the subjects will be forever happier and more useful.

Perhaps some who intend well in the main, but are obstinately slow—too slow to be initiated into the gyres of the liver—are brought here for a time, and then are again taken up by the lacteals, more willing to be instructed, and themselves giving useful warnings to others.

The influx from the province of the liver of the Greatest Man into our minds must produce a desire and capacity, first, to assimilate the knowledge we have loved and received to the uses of our life. As particles of fat and mucilage and gluten cannot always remain in the circulation as fat and mucilage and gluten, but must be combined with the fluids of the body into one homogeneous fluid, ready to turn its hand to any use that may be required of it, so the knowledge of good works that others do, of the goodness of the Lord and of the uses that He desires us to do, cannot remain in the mind in those forms, but must be transformed into thought and love of what it is good and right for us to do, and so enter the life current of our will. And this initiation of new ideas and intentions into the life of the spirit is done to a great extent in the province of the mind corresponding to the liver.

A secondary, though very important, effect of that influence is to separate and expel from the current of our thoughts, ideas and opinions which prevent harmonious cooperation with others, especially such as are self-asserting, bitter, and fault-finding. If the liver of the body does not act efficiently, and separate such effete materials, the body becomes heavy and sleepy, suffers much pain and general discomfort, and digests new food imperfectly, or rejects it altogether. And if the corresponding mental faculty does not faithfully do its duty in removing vain regrets and bitter fault-finding, the mind loses its living relation to present circumstances; it adheres tenaciously to its own ways and opinions, refusing new ideas and affections, and becomes morose, stupid, and miserable.

The Spleen and the Pancreas

Close under the lower ribs, on the left side of the body, just outside the stomach, lies the spleen—a body about the size of the thick part of the hand, though nearly twice as thick; of soft, spongy structure, composed of what is called the spleen pulp, together with very numerous arteries, veins, and lymphatics. The spleen receives a considerable quantity of blood through the splenic artery, and returns it though the splenic vein more fluid and lively than when it came. It sends also a considerable quantity of lymph by the lymphatics through the omentum to the chyle receptacle; but discharges no other peculiar secretion.

Its purpose is to modify the blood and prepare it for the winnowing of the liver, whither the blood returned by the spleen is immediately sent through the portal vein. At the extremities of the arteries in the spleen, the blood appears to circulate among the cells of the pulp, unconfined by the usual capillary walls, and to be collected from this pulp circulation by the veins. During this process the mischievous adhesions among its particles are broken up, the worn-out globules are disintegrated, the worthless particles are set free, so as to be easily sifted out by the liver, and the good elements also are set free, so that they may meet and combine with the new chyle with more ready sympathy and greater power for usefulness. All the lymph that can be spared is sent off to the receptacle; for the good blood is on its way to meet the new chyle, which will need all its power of absorbing and assimilating.

Huxley says that the blood returned from the spleen "is found to contain proportionally fewer red corpuscles and more fibrine than that in the splenic artery; and it has been supposed that the spleen is one of those parts of the economy in which the colorless corpuscles of the blood are especially produced." Probably some of the worn-out red corpuscles are really destroyed by the action of the spleen. It would naturally contain a larger proportion of fibrine, because the lymph is so largely withdrawn, and also because the colorless corpuscles seem to have the power of converting the albuminous materials, dissolved in the blood, into coagulable fibrine, ready to be built into the tissues of the body. Hence also these corpuscles are especially wanted in the work of receiving and initiating new blood. It should be added that the spleen increases in size immediately after taking food, and continues swollen and active during the process of digestion.

The office of the spleen is supplemented by that of the pancreas. As the splenic artery runs along behind the stomach towards its goal, it sends little branches continually to a long, thin gland called the pancreas, whose shape is likened by several authors to that of a dog's tongue. The pancreas also receives supplies from two other abdominal arteries.

The quality of the blood drawn from the arteries by the pancreas may be inferred from the products which it makes of it. These are, first, a thin, watery, alkaline fluid called the pancreatic fluid, or, by Swedenborg, and other old authors, the pancreatic bile, which is discharged into the small intestine through the same orifice with the hepatic bile; second, a purified blood which it presents to the splenic vein as this brings back the fluid blood from the spleen; and third, the lymph and fatty particles which it withdraws as much as possible from the other secretions to fit them for their uses, and dispatches to the mesentery, and probably at times to the omentum (*Animal Kingdom* §228).

The blood returned from the pancreas unites with that from the spleen, and together they proceed to the portal vein and the liver, to be there strained and purified, and then to unite with the new chyle and initiate it into the uses of the blood.

The pancreatic fluid, in its humbler way, enters upon a lower part of the same use; for it proceeds immediately to the intestine, where it performs a prominent part in the digestion of fats and also of starch. Of the fats it quickly forms an emulsion, which is then readily absorbed by the coats of the intestine, and is conducted away by the lacteals and veins. And it assists greatly in transforming the rigid, insoluble starch into soluble sugar, which is taken up principally by the veins. Thus the spleen and the pancreas join hands to assist the liver in the work of preparing a stream of good blood for the general uses of the body, and initiating the new chyle into those uses.

The spiritual uses of the correlative provinces in the Greatest Man must correspond to these natural uses. It is not for a moment to be supposed that any angel who has been received into heaven ever becomes useless and is cast down (*True Christian Religion* §341). The correspondence of the continual renovation of the tissues and the blood globules of the body is with the continual purification of forms of thought and affection in the heavens. "It is a known truth," Swedenborg says, "that heaven is not pure before the Lord; it is true, also, that angels are in continual progress towards perfection" (*Arcana Coelestia* §2249).

It is worthy of notice, yet it is altogether unknown in the world, that the states of good spirits and angels are continually changing and being perfected, and thus they are carried on into the interiors of the province in which they are, thus into nobler functions; for there is in heaven a continual purification, and, so to speak, a new creation; but still it is true that no angel will ever attain absolute perfection to eternity; the Lord alone is perfect; in Him and from Him is all perfection. (*Arcana Coelestia* §4803)

The worn-out elements of the heavens, therefore, are not the angels, but their inadequate forms of thought and states of feelings. The plan of the heavens is constantly being enlarged by the addition of new members; and these members bring states of life which are new; consequently the angels must have constantly expanding sympathies, and enlarging ideas of their mutual relations and uses. Any who suffer themselves to be hindered in their usefulness by too strong attachments to persons and ways, or by too limited views or set opinions, need to be brought within the influence of the province of the spleen, that their states of life may be taken out of their routine and thoroughly examined. With gentle reproof those natural limitations are there broken, and they are prepared to receive broader views, and more comprehensive, freer affections, more fit for their uses. Sullen, disappointed feelings, and whatever selfish affections there may be mingled with the good, are there exposed and loosened; and if any cling to such feelings, or if evil persons have forced themselves into the company of the good, they are detached and sent on to the places of instruction, whence they are at once cast out for the sterner warnings of the gall ducts, where all such bitterness is rendered harmless. Before the Last Judgment there were many evil spirits, especially of the dragonists, who thus intruded themselves; so that Swedenborg says the province of the spleen was crowded with them (*Spiritual Diary* §1005). But the good angels who receive well the mild discipline of the spleen, made gentler, happier, and more ready for extended sympathy and good use, are gladly received in the province of the liver, and are entrusted with the care and instruction of new spirits just entering upon the life of heaven. This expansion of thought and plan and sympathy is continually needed by the whole heaven, especially in the process of assimilating new spirits; and to obtain such expansion, probably angels from all parts of the heavens are continually descending to the places of instruction where new spirits are received. Therefore also the spleen, as well as the liver, is in its highest activity during the process of digestion.

The pancreas, for its part of the work, separates from the currents of thought, or of spirits or angels, who come to it, those who are censorious, and unnecessarily disposed to correct others; and sends such to the intestines, where such work is needed.

No doubt, in both these organs, a similar work is done for those not so much in the love of practical uses as in that of intelligent thought and conversation, who are represented by the lymph. These, too, in the gyres of the pancreas and the spleen are winnowed of the love for mere pleasant, idle talk, and also of that for censorious and acrimonious discussion; and made more intelligent by the purification, and more ready to do kindly uses as guides and instructors, they are permitted to offer themselves in such capacity to the novitiates ascending through the lacteals and the receptacle.

Enough perhaps has been said of the muscle making elements of food, the digestion of which is begun in the stomach and completed in the intestine. Their correspondence, it will be remembered, is with the love of useful work; the stomach digestion of them seems to correspond to the freeing of them from externals of form and routine, that the inner love of usefulness may appear; and the subsequent digestion in the intestines seems to represent the purification of this love.

It remains to speak of the digestion of fats and starch, which takes place chiefly in the intestine.

No doubt some delicate oils are absorbed from the stomach, and even from the mouth. The grosser kinds, as butter and the fat of meat, pass on to the intestine, and meet the acrid biles, by which they are emulsified, and made ready for absorption by the lacteals. They seem to correspond to natural goodness and kindness which has paid little attention to spiritual things, and needs a sharp warning to arouse a sense of need of instruction. Possibly they are those who are described by Swedenborg as follows:

> They who came out of the world from Christian lands and have led a moral life, and had somewhat of charity towards their neighbor, but have had little concern about spiritual things, for the most part are sent into the places beneath the feet and the soles of the feet; and are there kept until they put off the natural things in which they have been, and are imbued with spiritual and celestial things as far as they can be, according to their life; and when they have become imbued with these, they are elevated thence into heavenly societies. I have at times seen them emerging, and their joy at coming into heavenly light. (*Arcana Coelestia* §4944)

To such good but careless spirits the sharp censoriousness of the pancreatic spirits brings a sudden and wholesome awakening, one effect of which is to fill them with anxiety to be instructed, in which state they are ready to be taken up, and introduced into various exercises of spiritual wisdom.

A similar use to that which the bile and pancreatic fluid do for oils is done for starch by the pancreatic and intestinal fluids. Starch is exclusively a vegetable product, nearly resembling oil in its elements, but in a stiff, insoluble form. It is also like cane sugar in its composition, and needs only a slight modification to become like the sugar of fruits. Fruits correspond to works of affection, and their sugar to the enjoyment in them. Grains correspond to the duties of life, and their starch, which is in the place of sugar, to the satisfaction in good, faithful work. This has some sense of merit and virtue in it, which needs to be chastened and humbled, in order that it may work gently and sweetly with other people; and this no doubt is represented by the turning of starch into easily soluble sugar by the action of the harsh pancreatic and intestinal fluids.

They who receive this treatment, perhaps, are the spirits who, conscious of their own merit, saw wood in stern, puritanical style, wanting no assistance, determined to earn their own salvation; and indignant with the Lord that they do not receive more of heavenly joy than other men (*Arcana Coelestia* §1110, §4943).

Some, however, who are represented by the starch of wheat and rice, must be innocent and easily instructed, with a childlike sense of well-doing, only needing to have it clearly shown to them what they are in themselves, and how mercifully the Lord has dealt with them.

As the use of the spleen is to prepare the blood so that in the liver the pure, living portion may unite readily with the new chyle, and the hard, unelastic particles may be separated and rejected, the spiritual work of the spleen of the mind is to examine the thoughts of the heart, and prepare them to unite readily with new ideas, affections, and satisfactions which come to us in our work and social intercourse with the community. In the spleen of the mind the thoughts are drawn out into a quiet chamber, apart from the busy circulation, and there the feelings and opinions that are beginning to make trouble are candidly inspected, and those elements which do not agree with the practical life of charity are detached from those that are alive and willing, and are made ready for speedy rejection. Their hold upon the mind is loosened, so that when the opportunity for usefulness comes they are immediately given up.

Minds in which this work is not well done, which adhere tenaciously to bygones, and therefore do not come into pleasant relations with new things that are both true and good, but are disposed to complain of evils which arise simply from their own lack of sympathy and charity, are popularly called "spleeny"; perhaps from a common perception or tradition of the uses of the spleen surpassing the medical science of the present day.

The pancreas joins in the work of the spleen by setting aside from the current of thought, in regard to the good and true things we are loving and receiving, all that is unnecessarily acrimonious and severe, reserving this for the complacent enjoyment of natural kindliness, and the sense of superior merit and virtue, which need some rebuke, and sending forward sympathetic and friendly feelings which will enter heartily, without censoriousness, into good uses.

The Omentum

The great omentum is a thin membranous bag, quilted as it were into little pockets which are filled with fat; the whole suspended from the stomach and the transverse colon, and overhanging the intestines like an apron. A smaller and more delicate omentum is stretched between the stomach and the liver. And other still smaller omenta and epiploic appendages, all containing deposits of fat, occupy various crevices among the abdominal viscera.

Through these omenta arteries ramify, which, when there is a superfluity of fatty material in the blood, deposit it in these convenient places, from which it may as readily be absorbed again in time of want. From their close relation to the lacteals, the mesentery, and the lymphantics of the liver, pancreas, and spleen, it is probable that they receive temporary deposits from all these sources.

And these deposits they hold subject at all times to the demands of the liver, the great purveyor for the body; for this purpose sending all their veins to the portal vein which carries to the liver its supplies.

That the omentum has other secondary uses Swedenborg explains; as protecting the viscera from changes of temperature, and distilling an oily vapor to lubricate the surfaces of the viscera, which are perpetually in motion over one another. But its chief use is this, of gathering in the superflous elements of the nutrition of the body, which otherwise must be cast out; and then, in time of need, furnishing freely from its stores whatever is wanted. The omenta, and also the other smaller reservoirs of fat, all share in this use.

In the liver itself the surplus of sugar, or of starch which had been converted into sugar, is reduced to a form of starch called glycogen, and is stored for use as it is wanted. In the omentum fatty elements are similarly stored, and both deposits are reserves which can be drawn upon at any time for the uses of the body.

In the chapter on the saliva it was shown that the change from starch to soluble sugar consists in the chemical combination of a little more water with the starch; and that in the application to the heavens this corresponds to the reception by new spirits of the knowledge that opens to them the way to heaven. So, in the reverse of the process, the reducing the sugar again to starch is equivalent to saying, "Wait a little; the place for you will be ready presently; be content and wait patiently without thinking of particular uses in heaven, until the Lord calls you." The fat deposited in the omentum is similarly reduced from the active state of an emulsion to a passive, waiting state, which would represent a return from more active spiritual to quiet, natural states. Therefore Swedenborg speaks of the omenta as representing exterior and interior natural good. As this function of the liver and the omentum is a permanent one, it seems possible that spirits are frequently detained in such quiet states for a while, perhaps until they can join friends who come later from the earth, or until the occasion for their full cooperation with angels is fully come.

Unless specially instructed, we should not know that there could be in the spiritual world quiet resting places for good spirits, where they may live happily until their final homes are prepared for them. But John says:

I saw under the altar the souls of them that were slain for the Word of God, and for the testimony which they held; and they cried with a loud voice, saying, "How long, O Lord, holy and true, dost thou not judge and avenge our blood on them that dwell on the earth?" And white robes were given unto every one of them; and it was said unto them, that they should rest yet for a little season, until their fellow servants also and their brethren, that should be killed as they were, should be fulfilled. (Revelation 6:9–11)

These souls, Swedenborg says, were good spirits

who were hated, reproached, and rejected by the evil on account of their life according to the truths of the Word, and their acknowledgement of the Lord's Divine Human, and were guarded by the Lord lest they should be led away. . . . As they were under the altar it is manifest that they were guarded by the Lord; for all who have lived any life of charity are guarded by the Lord lest they should be hurt by the evil; and after a last judgment when the evil have been removed, they are released from the guards, and are taken up into heaven. After the last judgment I often saw them sent forth from the lower earth and transferred to heaven. (*Apocalypse Revealed* §325)

The place where they were kept concealed is called the lower earth, which is next above the hells, under the world of spirits; and there by communication with heaven and by conjunction with the Lord they are in safety. There are many such places; and they live there cheerfully among themselves and worship the Lord; nor do they know anything about hell. They who are there are from time to time taken up by the Lord into heaven after a last judgment; and when they are taken up those who are meant by the dragon are removed. It has very often been given me to see them taken up and consociated with the angels in heaven. (*Apocalypse Revealed* §845)

Before the Last Judgment there were fictitious heavens which at the time of the judgment passed away. They who constituted this heaven

were seen upon mountains, hills, and rocks in the spiritual world, and hence they fancied themselves to be in heaven; but they who thus constituted this heaven, inasmuch as they were only in an external moral life, and not at the same time in internal spiritual life, were cast down, and then all those who were reserved by the Lord, and concealed here and there, for the most part in the lower earth, were raised up and translated into the same places, that is, upon the mountains, hills, and rocks where the former heavens had been, and from these a new heaven was formed. They who had thus been reserved, and were then raised up, were from those in the world who had lived a life of charity, and were in spiritual affection for truth . . . The elevation of such into the places of those who constituted the former heavens has been often seen by me. (*Apocalypse Explained* §391; see also §392)

The reason that the evil were so long tolerated upon the high places, and the good so long detained under heaven, was in order that both might be fulfilled or completed, that is, that the good might amount to such a number as to be sufficient to form a new heaven, and also that the evil might fall down of themselves into hell. (*Apocalypse Explained* §397)

They who were under the altar received white robes, because those robes represented the presence of the Lord with the Divine truth around them; and the Lord by the Divine truth protects His own, for He surrounds them with a sphere of light from which they have white robes; and when they are thus encompassed, they can be infested no more by the evil spirits who before infested them, in consequence of which they were hid by the Lord. The case is the same also with those who are raised by the Lord into heaven, who are thus clothed with white robes, which is an indication that they are in Divine truth, and so in safety. (*Apocalypse Explained* §395)

Very similar things are said of those who were preserved in the safe places of the lower earth at the time of the first coming of the Lord, and who were then raised up by Him into the spiritual heaven (*Arcana Coelestia* §6854, 7090, 8054).

Such quiet places, where hell is not known, and where the good dwell cheerfully together, cannot be in the intestines, through which evil is continually passing, and where painful vastations are always going on. But the omentum covering the intestines, and the various deposits among them, are in nearly the same situation relatively to the stomach, and though very near the evil may not be at all disturbed by them.

The deposits in the liver, also, though so near the evil in the gall bladder, are perfectly protected from them, and may well represent a peaceful, gentle life in waiting for freer opportunities.

Apparently the deposits in the omenta represent spirits like those carried by the way of the mesentery; and the deposits in the liver other spirits like those carried in the portal vein.

The province of the liver cannot strictly be regarded as in "the lower earth," since it is above the plane of the stomach. But Swedenborg's expression is, that those who are reserved are "in great part," or "mostly" (*plerique*) in the lower earth; which implies that they are partly elsewhere.

The great omentum I understand to be "the fat covering the intestines" in the Jewish sacrifices; and the smaller omentum, "the fat upon the liver"; of which last, Swedenborg says that it corresponds to a nobler, more interior good than the other, because it is connected with a nobler organ (*Arcana Coelestia* §10031).

In an individual man the omenta must correspond to a memory of natural and spiritual good which is reserved for times of temptation and want.

THE SUPRARENAL CAPSULES

THESE ARE TWO CONICAL CAPS UPON THE TWO KIDNEYS. In embryos these capsules are as large as the kidneys; but after birth they diminish considerably.

They consist of a yellowish, cortical substance, composed of parallel tubes perpendicular to the surfaces, which are ramifications of superficial arteries, and lead inwards; and an inner, dark red, soft substance, in the cavity of which open the mouths of a vein much larger than the capsular arteries. They lie on either side close to the aorta, which brings the blood directly from the heart, and the vena cava, which returns it directly to the heart; and at the point whence the arteries which supply the principal abdominal viscera go off from the aorta.

Branches from several of these arteries ramify upon the capsules, as well as two small arteries of their own direct from the aorta. And one important use which they serve is to draw off and return immediately to the heart as much of the pure, good blood as is not needed by the lower viscera; so that none shall be wasted or compelled to serve in unnecessarily low offices.

The capsules are embedded in a mass of fatty, cellular tissue, by which they are connected with the kidneys and with the cellular coat of the peritoneum, which lines the whole abdomen. Through this cellular tissue circulates a useful serum derived from its arteries which is absorbed and again mingled with the blood by the capsules. This is the cause of the large size of their veins compared with that of their arteries. The reason that the capsules are so large before birth is that the streams of serum which after birth become defiled, and are sorted and purified by the pancreas, kidneys, and other viscera, in the innocent state before birth are not foul, but circulate in the viscera, forming them for their future uses, and are by no means to be cast out as worthless; nor, indeed, are means of casting them out yet provided; but they are gathered in and restored to the circulation by the capsules—now necessarily large, soft, and active.

These two uses, explained at length by Swedenborg in the *Animal Kingdom*, are thus described in the *Arcana*:

> There are also kidneys which are called succenturiate kidneys, and also renal capsules. Their office is not so much to secrete the serum, but the blood itself, and to transmit the purer blood towards the heart by a short circle; thus to prevent the spermatic vessels, which are in the neighborhood, from carrying off all the purer blood; but they perform their principal service in embryos and in newborn infants. (*Arcana Coelestia* §5391)

And concerning those who constitute that province in the Greatest Man, we read,

> There are chaste virgins who constitute that province in the Greatest Man; prone to anxieties and timid lest they should be disturbed, they lie quiet on the left part of the side beneath. If anything be thought concerning heaven, and anything con-

cerning their change of state, they become anxious and sigh, of which it has sometimes been given me to be very sensible. (ibid)

Their use is to prevent the thoughts from descending to ultimates and to things unclean, and to turn and return all thoughts to heavenly things in which they take delight. It is to be noticed that they lie just below the diaphragm, and stop the thoughts from descending further.

It is not to be supposed that the same virgins occupy the province perpetually; but a succession as they approach a marriageable age. No doubt there are with them persons of both sexes who are in the love of educating those in such states; so that it is a province for the education of girls of a certain age. "They become anxious and sigh when heaven is thought of," because they fear lest they shall not be prepared for heaven, and fear also a loss of the influx of heavenly thoughts which are their life; "they are troubled when anything not heavenly is thought of," and love especially innocent thoughts like those of infants (*Spiritual Diary* §968–972).

The corresponding province in the mind everyone may detect in the conscientious faculty which anxiously prevents the thoughts from descending, and brings them back to pure interior subjects. It is the instinct of delicacy and modesty, regulating the flow of thought. The unusually large supply of nerves to the capsules has a correspondence with sensitiveness of this kind.

It is by virtue of this faculty that what Swedenborg calls "the chaste love of the sex" is possible; for it makes of the closure of the thorax a tight compartment which can be filled full with affection and pure and friendly thought between the sexes, without descending (compare *Conjugial Love* §44).

Immediately after passing the capsular arteries, the great stream of blood in the aorta is drawn upon by the renal arteries for the impure serum which is to be rejected by the kidneys. And, in like manner, after the capsules of the mind have done their duty in turning the thoughts upwards impure thoughts are quickly excreted and rejected.

The Kidneys

Under the renal capsules, separated only by them from the diaphragm, on either side of the vertebral column, toward which their concave faces are turned, and lying about two hand-breadths apart, are the kidneys.

Into their concave sides the large renal arteries enter, beginning their divisions and subdivisions even before they reach the surface of the kidneys, and continuing them rapidly till their little branches ramify all over the exterior of the organs in company with equally minute veins. In close contact with these capillary vessels are multitudes of little glands and much convoluted tubes which form a layer about the kidneys and are continued into larger tubes. These larger tubes pass inwards, uniting as they go, and terminating in little papillae, through which the excretion of the kidneys is discharged into the basins at the head of the ureters.

The arteries come off from the aorta just below the branches which supply the stomach, liver, spleen, and the mesentery, and the suprarenal capsules. These have withdrawn a considerable proportion of the thick and the fresh blood, and have left the stream polluted with an unwonted proportion of watery materials and superfluous salts. These the renal arteries suck in as their prey, and send it whirling through their capillaries, into the convolutions of the renal glands and tubes, over pathways and through gates which none but the elastic living particles can pass, and from which the stale dying particles, slow and reluctant even with sharpest urging, are ignominiously rejected (*Animal Kingdom* §288).

The living, purified blood returns through the veins and lymphatics to the heart. The worthless serum is caught by the tubes which form the principal substance of the kidneys, and discharged through their papillae into larger cavities, whence it is expelled by contractions of the kidneys into the ureters, and conducted to the bladder. The attitude of all the parts towards it is that of expulsion (*Animal Kingdom* §290).

Of those in the other life who belong to these province we read as follows:

> They who constitute the province of the kidney, ureters, and bladder, in the Greatest Man, are of such a genius that they like nothing better than to explore and search out the quality of others, and there are also some who desire to chastise and to punish, if only there be some justice in it. The functions also of the kidneys, ureters, and bladder are such; for they explore the blood thrown into them to see if there be any useless and hurtful serum there, and also they separate it from the useful, and afterwards chastise it, for they drive it down towards the lower regions, and in the way and afterwards they agitate it in various ways. These are the functions of those who constitute the province of those parts. But the spirits and societies of spirits to which the urine itself, especially fetid urine, corresponds are infernal; for as soon as the urine is separated from the blood, although it is in the little

tubes of the kidneys, or within in the bladder, still it is out of the body, for what is separated no longer circulates in the body, hence it contributes nothing to the existence and subsistence of its parts.

I have often observed that they who constitute the province of the kidneys and ureters are quick to explore and search out the quality of others, what they think and what they will, and that they are in the desire of finding occasion to condemn, for the end especially that they may chastise; and I have spoken with them concerning that desire and that end. Many of that kind, in the world, when they lived there, were judges; and then rejoiced in heart when they found cause which they believed to be just to fine, chastise, and punish. The operation of such is felt at the region of the back where are the kidneys, ureters, and bladder. They who belong to the bladder extend themselves towards hell (*gehennam*), where also some of them sit as it were in judgment.

The modes in which they explore or search out the dispositions of others are very many, but it is permitted to present only the following. They induce other spirits to speak, which is done in the other life by influx, which cannot be described intelligibly; if then the induced speech is easily followed, they judge from it that the spirits are such; they induce also a state of affection. But they who explore thus are among the grosser of them; and others otherwise. There are some who as soon as they approach perceive immediately the thoughts, desires, and acts of another, also what he has done that he is ashamed of. This they seize upon, and, if they think there is just cause, they also condemn. It is wonderful in the other life, which scarcely any one in the world can believe, that as soon as any spirit come to another, and still more when he comes to a man, he instantly knows his thoughts and affections, and what he then was doing, thus all his present state, altogether as if he had been long with him, so perfect is the communication. But there are differences in these apperceptions; some perceive interior things, and some only exterior; these if they are in the desire of knowing explore the interiors of others by various methods.

The modes in which they punish who constitute the province of the kidneys, ureters, and bladder in the Greatest Man are also various; for the most part they remove joyous and glad things, and induce such as are joyless and sad. By this passion those spirits communicate with the hells; but by the justness of the cause, which they seek for before they punish, they communicate with heaven. Wherefore they are kept in that province. (*Arcana Coelestia* §5381–5384)

There is an evident correspondence between the mode of exploration here mentioned, and the most evident mode of the kidneys—the flow of speech induced by the spirits corresponds to the currents induced in the little tubes, the forms of speech corresponding to the forms of the tubes. The forms no doubt are heavenly forms, and all who love heavenly thought flow into them readily and gladly, while those who are gross and selfish and worldly flow into them unwillingly, if at all, and are quickly condemned and cast out.

From these things it may appear what it signifies that it is said in the Word that Jehovah searches and tries the reins and the heart; also the reins chasten, as in Jeremiah, "Jehovah that triest the reins and the heart" (11:20). And again, "Jehovah that triest the just and seest the reins and the heart" (20:12). In David, "The just God trieth the hearts and reins" (Psalms 7:9). And again, "O Jehovah, try my reins and my heart" (26:2). "Thou hast possessed my reins" (139:13). In John, "I am He Who trieth the reins and the heart" (Revelation 2:23). By the reins there are signified spiritual things, and by the heart celestial; that is, by the reins are signified those things which are of truth, and by the heart those which are of good. The reason is because the reins purify the serum, and the heart the blood itself; hence by trying, examining, and searching the reins is signified trying, examining, and searching the quantity and quality of truth or the quantity and quality of faith in man. That this is signified is also evident in Jeremiah, "Jehovah, Thou art near in their mouth, but far from their reins" (12:2). And in David, "Behold, Thou desirest truth in the reins" (2:8). That chastening also is attributed to the reins, is also evident in David, "My reins chasten me in the nights" (16:7). (*Arcana Coelestia* §5385)

With the heart, as an organ of purification, are included the liver, gall bladder, spleen, and pancreas, which unite with it in preparing the blood for the body. Even the mouth and the stomach belong to it as to this use (*Spiritual Diary* §1010; *Arcana Coelestia* §4791). By the mental faculties corresponding to this series of organs, the spirit should be freed from narrow, selfish, indolent feelings and thoughts, also such as are vile and cruel, all of which are opposed to a life of charity. But the reins of the mind expose and separate from the current of thought false things, and such as being merely and pertinaciously natural prevent the mind from thinking spiritually; also fallacious and deceitful reasonings, excuses, and pretences, designed to cloak a fault or a malicious intention.

The love and the power to discern these things and separate them from our thoughts flow into our minds from the corresponding provinces of the Greatest Man. The angels of these provinces love to remove such things from heaven and from humanity, and wherever it will be received they give the ability. We receive it from them when we discern and condemn in ourselves anxious thoughts that are opposed to the Divine Providence, unjust or fraudulent thoughts in relation to one another; and, in general, any falseness toward God or man.[1]

---

1. Certain pirates and other deceitful and fraudulent persons corresponding to urine are described in *Arcana Coelestia* §5387–5390; the ways to hell by the bladder and by the intestines in *Arcana Coelestia* §5380.

The Peritoneum

The peritoneum is an extensive membrane, thick, soft, elastic, and on its inner surfaces very smooth, lining the walls of the abdomen, and by many folds and pockets investing its viscera. It unites in a common bond all the organs whose use it is to receive new elements for the nourishment of the body, to digest, strain, and prepare them for use, and to cast out all that refuse to be assimilated to the elements of the body; also to purify and sort the blood itself, restoring to the circulation, purer, cleaner, and more lively, whatever is capable of restoration, and straining out and rejecting whatever is worthless.

All these uses are parts of one use—the proper nourishment of the body—and the organs which perform them are combined in relations of mutual help and support by the peritoneum. Besides serving as a common bond, the peritoneum communicates to all the abdominal viscera the alternate expansions and contractions of the thorax, which are essential to the proper functions of every viscus, and are received by the peritoneum through the diaphragm.

It covers and adheres closely to nearly the whole of the underside of the diaphragm; it applies its cellular coat to the liver, investing it closely, and even following the blood vessels through its substance—its smooth, serous coat making easy the gentle, hepatic motions, and its connections with the diaphragm helping to support the liver in its proper place. As it passes to the stomach, it embraces the small omentum between its layers. It environs the stomach with a smooth, elastic coat, essential to its free movements. It encloses in its duplicature the great omentum, protecting it perfectly from the intestines, which lie immediately behind it. It sheathes the spleen and the pancreas; embeds the kidneys, the renal capsules, and the receptacle of chyle, in its thickened, cellular coat. It surrounds the great, unruly colon, and holds it firmly in its place. It covers the small intestines, and within its folds offers a secure asylum for the mesenteric vessels and glands. It presses upon the bladder and the rectum, perhaps surrounding them with its cellular tissue, ready to concentrate all the power of the viscera upon them, and to assist in expelling their contents. It covers the uterus with a firm, elastic coat, and even extends a partial covering to the testicles. And it lines the whole of the front abdominal wall with a polished surface, within which the viscera move with perfect freedom, each according to its own nature.

The peritoneum, with its contents, may be regarded as a single organ, the purpose of which is to prepare and purify nourishment for the body. Materials it receives through the esophagus and the aorta; these it digests, strains, and sorts, like one large, complex gland, sending its profitable results to the heart through the vena cava and the thoracic duct, and discharging the unprofitable through the rectum and the bladder. And the various abdominal viscera, by the aid of the peritoneum, are enabled to act as one organ, harmoniously, and with mutual support; no part either unduly exalting itself, or lying idle through lack of its proper stimulus of supply, demand, and alternate motion.

With this knowledge of the peritoneum, we are prepared to see the truth of Swedenborg's description of the good spirits in the corresponding province of the Greatest Man:

> Certain spirits came to me, but they were silent; still they afterwards spake with me, yet not as many, but all as one. I perceived from their discourse that they were such that they wished to know all things, and desired to explain all things, and thus to confirm themselves that it is so. They were modest, and said that they do nothing of themselves but from others, although it appears that it is from them. They were then infested by others; it was said that it was by those who constitute the province of the kidneys, ureters, and bladder. They answered them modestly, yet still they infested and attacked them; for such is the nature of those related to the kidneys. Wherefore, because they could gain no advantage against them by modesty, they resorted to something which was according to their genius, namely, to expanding themselves and thus terrifying. Hence they seemed to become great, but only as one, who so enlarged his body that, like Atlas, he seemed to touch the heaven. There appeared a spear in his hand, but still he did not wish to do any harm except to terrify. In consequence the kidney spirits fled away. Then there appeared one who pursued them in their flight, and another who flew from in front between the feet of that great one; and also that great one seemed to have wooden shoes which he threw at the kidney spirits. It was told me by the angels that those modest spirits who so

enlarged themselves were they who relate to the peritoneum. The peritoneum is the common membrane which encompasses and includes all the viscera of the abdomen, as the pleura all the viscera of the thorax; and because it is so extensive and respectively large and also expansible, therefore it is permitted them, when they are infested by others, thus to present themselves great in appearance, and at the same time to strike terror, especially towards those who constitute the province of the kidneys, ureters, and bladder; for these viscera or vessels lie in the folds of the peritoneum, and are compelled by it. By the wooden shoes were represented the lowest natural things, such as the kidneys, ureters, and bladder absorb and carry off.... In saying that they do nothing of themselves, they also resemble the peritoneum, which likewise is such. (*Arcana Coelestia* §5378)

It was also shown representatively how the case is when they who constitute the colon intestine infest those who are in the province of the peritoneum. They who constitute the colon are puffed up, as the colon with its wind. When they wished to assail them, it appeared as if a wall were in the way; and when they endeavored to overturn the wall there rose up always a new wall; and thus they were kept away from them. (*Arcana Coelestia* §5379)

The spirits of the peritoneum must be numerous, closely connected, and of such a nature that the impressions made upon any of them are communicated to all. Being intimately connected with the spirits who constitute the other abdominal provinces, and receiving impressions from them, they react upon them all, supporting them in their work, providing safe conduct from one province to another, conveying information of the common weal to all the parts, and uniting the efforts of all to furnish for the whole heaven good and well-instructed accessions, freed from the idle, vicious, and corrupt. They have no independent plans and wishes of their own, but have a strong love for all who are engaged in this use; and by holding to them all with generous and just appreciation, they compel them to work together as a band of brothers for a common purpose.

They combine all the parts of the great province whose function it is to prepare new spirits for heaven, and to separate from the heavens the evil. It is a work not of the most elevated kind, being mostly performed upon the interior natural plane; but it is a work of vital importance to the whole heaven and to every society of it.

THE HEART AND THE LUNGS

THE HEART IS THE MOTIVE POWER BY WHICH THE BLOOD is sent on its errands of usefulness to all parts of the body. Towards the heart varied streams of fluid from all directions wend their way. From the liver comes a great stream of purified, sugary fluid, gathered from the digestive organs, and loaded with nutritious elements from the food, selected and sorted and partly trained to the motions of the body, ready to be put to useful service. Other great streams descend from the head, bringing, as Swedenborg believed, the freshest results of spirit and lymph from the laboratory of the brain; and side by side with one of them flows the stream of chyle and lymph brought up from the receptacle by the thoracic duct. And besides all these elements, there are the weary currents returning from the limbs and from the muscular system of the whole body, bringing the results of labor and experience, and greatly in need of straining and replenishing.

A motley throng of materials, unacquainted, unaccustomed to one another's ways and qualities, yet of abundant goodwill and ability to serve, are brought by various channels to the heart, and from them the heart is expected to prepare and send forth a fresh, lively, elastic, homogeneous blood, ready for any good, human use which may be required of it.

In order that it may rightly perform this excellent use, the heart needs the lungs as a means of discriminating among the materials furnished to it, separating those vapors and aerial elements that are unserviceable, and receiving others that are serviceable; and it consociates the lungs with itself in its work, submitting to their discernment, for correction or encouragement, every particle of blood that it receives.

The heart is composed of four chambers; the upper pair thin, the lower, thick and muscular. The upper two serve as reception rooms in which the blood may be received and collected during the contractions of the lower pair. The blood comes up through the veins in a quiet, steady current; but of necessity it is driven out of the heart in pulses. Therefore lest the veins should be burst by the closing of the doors during the contractions of the heart, anterooms are provided, in which the blood can accumulated, ready to fill the stronger chambers instantly when the doors are opened with cordial invitation.

The first anteroom is called the "right auricle," and the first propelling chamber the "right ventricle." To the auricle come first all the streams that enter the heart; and after mingling there a moment they are passed on to the ventricle with gentle urgency, and thence with a strong impulse are sent through the pulmonary arteries to the capillaries of the lungs. These capillaries ramify in the walls of air chambers at the extremities of the bronchial tubes.

Of exquisite thinness though the walls of these air chambers are, they still are double, and find room between their layers for the minute blood vessels, which thus spread out, almost in contact with the air, all the treasures of the heart. With a wise discernment all their own, the delicate membranes, in accordance with the desires of the blood, absorb for its benefit pure oxygen, and a considerable amount of fragrant exhalations and vapors which serve to enrich the blood; and, on the other hand, they invite the blood to give up and reject the fouler, grosser gases and vapors with which it came laden, which they then pass out to the general atmosphere.

Brighter in color, more lively in motion, and rather less in bulk, the blood returns from the lungs, through the pulmonary veins, to the left auricle of the heart, where it waits a moment for the doors of the ventricle to open. Then invited by the ventricle, it presently is sent forth upon its manifold errands of usefulness, with a strong, sustaining impulse which follows it, and whose repetitions are forcibly felt in all the capillaries of the body. Nor is it now in itself an unwilling, sluggish stream. It responds to the impulse of the heart with an elastic bound, and as it goes forward it presses upon the door of every gland and cell and muscular fiber, for opportunity to do good. Neither does it ask in vain; but is everywhere received with welcome according to its quality and the uses that are needed in the several provinces.

Every part of the body is hungry for the materials necessary for its own nutrition, or for the exercise of its functions; and in various ways it makes it s hunger felt, even to the desire of the body for food. It is difficult not to believe that this hunger makes an effective requisition both upon the reserved supplies in the body and upon the newly prepared nutriment; and that when the heart dismisses its richly endowed companies, containing so many elements eager for opportunities to employ their faculties, straightway each is drawn and invited towards the organ that needs it most; that the noblest blood ascends to the head; that streams rich with fibrinous elements hasten to the muscles of the body and limbs; that the more sluggish, adhesive blood descends to the spleen, and that which is poor and serous to the kidneys; and that thus to every member and gland the elements best suited to it are dispatched by the impulse given from the heart, supplemented and directed by the organ itself.

We have followed the good spirits from the earth through their introduction into the spiritual world; and the subsequent opening of the interiors of their minds, and the separation from evil; and then through the places of instruction in which they are prepared for heaven. After this state is completed, Swedenborg says, "they are then clothed with angelic garments, which for the most part are white as of fine linen, and thus they are brought to the way which tends upwards towards heaven, and are delivered to the angel guards there, and are afterwards received by other angels, and are introduced into societies, and into many gratifications."

The "angel guards there," I understand to be at the doors of the heart; the "other angels" by whom they are received, and the societies into which they are introduced, seem plainly to be those of the chambers of the heart and the lungs; and the gratifications there enjoyed are those of angels' love and wisdom.

"Next," Swedenborg continues, "everyone is led by the Lord into his own society, which also is effected by various ways, sometimes by winding paths. The ways by which they are led are not known to any angels, but to the Lord alone. When they come to their own society their interiors are then opened; and since these are conformable to the interiors of the angels who are in that society, they are therefore instantly acknowledged and received with joy" (*Heaven and Hell* §519; see also *Arcana Coelestia* §1381).

To the heart of the heavens the new spirits come rejoicing in their salvations, and in the wonderful things which
they have learned of heavenly life. And there they find
themselves in the very center of the angels' sense of the
goodness of the Lord, and of their desire to do good from
Him. Angels who are like love itself in form, receive them
with affection so innocent and warm that their own hearts
are melted, and they too are filled with a sense of the infinite goodness of the Lord as strong as they can bear; and
at the same time with an equally strong desire to do good
in every possible way to others, because this is the nature
of the love which they receive from the Lord.

But first the love inspires them with desire to know
what they may do, and to find the means of doing good
wisely; by the love itself, whose influence they receive, they
are urged to the province of the lungs, into the society of
angels who introduce them into the very wisdom of heavenly life, and "into interior perception and heavenly freedom" (*Arcana Coelestia* §3894 ½). These are angels who
are in clear perception of wisdom from the Lord, who perceive instantly the quality of every affection, and its agreement or disagreement with the pure truth by which the
Lord which guide the life of the heavens. Such perceptions
they communicate to the angelic spirits who come to
them, opening the inner joys and possibilities of usefulness of the heavenly love which is given them, and causing them to see and reject whatever of grosser, natural
thought and desire still clings to them. And then again
they return with new intelligence and zeal into a state of
love for the goodness of the Lord, and for doing good
from Him; coming now under the influence of those who
receive most fully the Lord's love for the whole heaven and
for every part of it, and His desire to do good to all. Under

their influence, inspired from their love with the desire to do all that they are capable of doing to bless at least a few in their Father's heaven, the angelic spirits once more go forth from the heart of the heavens to find their home and their use. Towards those who are interiorly in similar good, and who therefore will most enjoy what they can bring them, the interiors of their life are irresistibly drawn; and to them they go infallibly, the Lord opening the way. Arriving at the gates of their own society, they are recognized as members of the society who have been already doing its work upon the earth, of whose coming the society was warned by the angels of the tongue on their very first entrance into the spiritual world, whose approach they have assisted in every possible way, and whom they now welcome as brothers and sisters, sharing with them all their joys, The new angels in turn recognize the life of the society as that which has given them their inmost satisfaction upon earth, though then perceived obscurely— the life for which they have interiorly been yearning, and which now fills their cup to overflowing, more than satisfying their desire. The angels, too, seem like brothers and sisters, who come to them at once as their dearest friends. But they have not come merely to receive; the impulse of the heart of heaven is upon them still. Friends and homes and every good thing that love can suggest are provided for them; but the best thing of all is good work, helpful to all these kind friends, perfectly suited to their capacities, which they find waiting for them to do.

And not only the pulses of the heart, the respirations of the lungs, too, follow into every home in the heavens.

For the lungs by their respiration act upon the ribs
and the diaphragm, and through these, by means

of ligaments and through the peritoneum, upon all the viscera of the body throughout, and likewise upon all its muscles, and not only involve, but also thoroughly enter them, and so thoroughly that there is not the smallest part of the viscera nor of a muscle, from the surface to the inmost, which does not derive something from the ligaments, consequently from the inspiration. . . . The heart itself, besides its own, has also a pulmonary motion; for it lies upon diaphragm and in the bosom of the lungs, and coheres and is continued to them by its auricles. In like manner also what is respiratory passes into the arteries and veins. . . . From these considerations an attentive eye may see that all living motions, which are called actions, and exist by means of muscles, are effected by the cooperation of the motion of the heart and of the motion of the lungs which is in each, both the general motion which is external, and the particular motion which is internal; and he who is clear-sighted may also discover that these two fountains of the motions of the body correspond to the will and the understanding, since they are produced from them. This has been also confirmed from heaven, where it was given me to be present with the angels, who presented this to the life. They formed a likeness of the heart and a likeness of the lungs, with all the interior and exterior things of their contexture, by means of a wonderful and inexpressible flowing into circles, and they then followed the flow of heaven; for heaven has a tendency to such forms, by virtue of the influx of love and wisdom from the Lord. Thus they represented all the particulars which are in the heart and all the particulars of the lungs, and likewise their union, which they called the marriage of love and wisdom. And they said that the case is similar in the universal body and in each of its members, organs and viscera, with the things which are of the heart therein and which are of the lungs therein; and that when they do not both act, and each take its turn distinctly, there cannot be any motion of life from any voluntary principle, nor any sense of life from any intellectual principle. (*Apocalypse Explained*, vol. 6, "On Divine Love and Divine Wisdom" §91)

With every society and every angel of heaven, in correspondence with these things, the impulses of the heart of heaven continually inspire love from the Lord; and the respirations of the lungs of heaven constantly interpret this love in forms of useful love to the neighbor. For the heart supplies the fluid and the pressure by which every gland and fiber is filled; and from the lungs is continued the sheathing by which the quality of the fluid received is determined, and the alternate motion of expansion and contraction by which reception is effected; and the sheaths of the fibers are continued into the tendons by which all motion is directed (*Apocalypse Explained*, vol. 6, "On Divine Love and Divine Wisdom" §122).

Swedenborg says:

It was given me to perceive the general operations of heaven as manifestly as any object is perceived by any of the senses. There were four operations which I then perceived. The first was into the brain at the left temple and was a general one as to the organs of reason; for the left part of the brain corresponds to things rational or intellectual, but the right to affections or things voluntary.

The second general operation which I perceived was into the respiration of the lungs, which led my respiration gently, but from within, so that I had no need to draw breath, or respire, by any exertion of my will. The respiration itself of heaven was then manifestly perceived by me. It is internal, and on that account imperceptible to man; but by a wonderful correspondence it flows into man's respiration, which is external, or of the body, and if man were deprived of this influx he would instantly fall down dead. The third operation which I perceived, was into the systole and diastole of the heart, which had, on the occasion, more of softness with me than I had ever experienced at any other time. The times of the pulse were regular, about three within each turn of respiration; yet such as to terminate in and regulate the lungs and what appertains to them. How the alternate changes of the heart insinuated themselves into the alternate changes of the lungs, at the close of each respiration, I was in some measure able to observe. The alternations of the pulse were so observable that I was able to count them; they were distinct and soft. The fourth general operation was into the kidneys, which also it was given me to perceive, but obscurely. From these things it was made manifest that heaven, or the Greatest Man, has cardiac pulses, and that it has respirations; and that the cardiac pulses of heaven, or the Greatest Man, have correspondence with the heart, and with its systolic and diastolic motions, and that the respirations of heaven, or the Greatest Man, have correspondence with the lungs and their respirations; but that they both are unobservable to man, being imperceptible, because internal. (*Arcana Coelestia* §3884)

On another occasion, he says:

It was given me to observe the general respiration of heaven, and what its nature was. It was interior, easy, spontaneous, and corresponding to my respiration as three to one. It was also given me to observe the reciprocations of the pulses of my heart. And then I was informed by the angels that all and each of the creatures on the earth derive thence their pulses and their respirations, and that the reason why they take place at dissimilar moments is because both the cardiac pulse and the pulmonary respiration which exist in the heavens, pass off into something continuous, and thus into effort, which is of such a nature as to excite those motions variously according to the state of every subject.

But it is to be known that the variations as to pulses and as to respirations in the heavens are manifest, and that they are as many as all the societies; for they are according to the states of thought and affection with the angels, and these are according to their states of faith and love; but with respect to the general pulse and respiration, the case is as above described.

In heaven, or in the Greatest Man, are two kingdoms, one of which is called celestial; the other, spiritual. The celestial kingdom consists of angels who are called celestial, and these are they who

have been in love to the Lord, and thence in all wisdom; for they are in the Lord, and are thereby in a
state of peace and innocence, more than others.
They appear to others like infants, for a state of
peace and innocence presents that appearance.
Everything there is as it were alive before them; for
whatever comes immediately from the Lord is
alive. This is the celestial kingdom. The other kingdom is called spiritual. It consists of angels who are
called spiritual; and they are those who have been
in the good of charity toward the neighbor. They
place the delight of their life in this, that they can do
good to others without recompense; it is recompense to them to be allowed to do good to others.
The more they will and desire this, in so much the
greater intelligence and felicity are they; for, in the
other life, everyone is gifted with intelligence and
felicity are they; for, in the other life, everyone is
gifted with intelligence and felicity from the Lord
according to the use which he performs from the
affection of the will. Such is the spiritual kingdom.
They who are in the Lord's celestial kingdom
belong all to the province of the heart; and they
who are in the spiritual kingdom belong all to the
province of the lungs. The influx from the celestial
kingdom into the spiritual is similar to the influx of
the heart into the lungs, as also to the influx of all
things which are of the heart into all which are of
the lungs; for the heart rules in the whole of the
body and in all its parts, by the blood vessels, and
also the lungs in all its parts by the respiration.
Hence there is everywhere in the body as it were an
influx of the heart into the lungs, but according to

the forms there, and according to the states. Thence exists all the sensation as well as all the action which are proper to the body. (*Arcana Coelestia* §3885–3887)

The correspondence of the heart and the lungs in an individual man is with his love of doing and his love of wisdom; or, with his will and his understanding. "In the spiritual world," Swedenborg tells us, "the quality of one's faith is known by his breathing, and the quality of his charity by the beating of his heart" (*Doctrine of Faith* §19).

Every man naturally loves to live a selfish and worldly life, and also to think things that agree with such a life. But by instruction everyone becomes capable of thinking what is truer and better; and if he takes home such thoughts to his heart, he makes his love wiser and better. By wisdom he cleanses his love from its foulness and grossness, and introduces it to spiritual and celestial delights; therefore by wisdom, if it be applied to the love, the love itself becomes spiritual and celestial (*Divine Love and Wisdom* §422).

Of this, Swedenborg writes as follows:

Man is born into evils, and hence he loves corporeal and worldly things more than celestial and spiritual things; consequently his life, which is love, is depraved and impure by nature. Everyone may see from reason that this life cannot be purified except by understanding; and that it is purified by spiritual, moral, and civil truths, which constitute the understanding. Wherefore, also, it is given to man to be able to perceive, and to think affirmatively such things as are contrary to the love of his will, and not only to see that they are so, but also, if he looks up to God, to be able to resist, and thereby remove the depraved and filthy things of his will, which is the same thing as being purified. This may also be illustrated by the defecation of the blood in the lungs. That the blood admitted there from the heart is defecated, is a thing known to anatomists from this consideration, that the blood flows from the heart into the lungs in greater abundance than it flows back from the lungs into the heart; also that it flows in undigested and impure, but flows back refined and pure; also that in the lungs there is a cellular texture into which the blood of the heart presses out by separation its useless particles, injecting them into the little bronchial vessels and ramifications; also that ... the vapor in breathing is from that source. From which considerations it is evident that the feculent blood of the heart is purified in the lungs. By these considerations what was said just above may be illustrated, inasmuch as the blood of the heart corresponds to the lobe of the will, which is the life of man, and the respiration of the lungs corresponds to the perception and thought of the understanding, by which purification is effected.

The life of the understanding also perfects and exalts the life of the will, because the love of the will, which constitutes man's life, is purged from evils by means of the understanding, and man, from being corporeal and worldly, becomes spiritual and celestial, in which case the truths and goods of heaven and of the church are grafted in his affection, and nourish his soul; thus the life of his will is made new, and from it the life of his understanding becomes new, so that each is perfected and exalted. This is effected in the understanding and by it; but from the will; for the will is the man himself. This likewise is confirmed by the correspondence of the lungs and the heart; for the lungs, which correspond to the understanding, not only purge the blood of its feculent particles, as was before observed, but also nourish it from the air; for the air is full of volatile elements and odors homogeneous with the matter of the blood; and there are likewise innumerable plexuses of the blood vessels in the pulmonary lobules, which, according to their wont, absorb the neighboring waves, in consequence whereof the blood becomes fresh and bright, and is rendered arterial, such as it is when conveyed from the lungs into the left ventricle of the heart. That the atmosphere nourishes the pulmonary blood with new aliments is evident from much experience; for there are some breezes which are injurious to the lungs, and some which recreate them, thus some which are hurtful, and some which are salubrious. ... From these considerations it is evident that the pulmonary blood derives nourishment also from the atmosphere. Thus also the life of the understanding perfects and exalts the life of the will according to the correspondence. (*Apocalypse Explained*, vol. 6, "On Divine Love and Divine Wisdom" §120–121)

But if the love refuses to take to itself the admonitions and friendly counsel of wisdom, preferring filthy ideas and gross thoughts, it makes of the understanding a mere purveyor of these things, and drinks them in, to its own further defilement.

And then, in correspondence with this, the man at least in the spiritual world loves to breathe into his lungs the vile odors that correspond to such thoughts, and to defile his blood with them. Of this, Swedenborg teaches:

> That the blood in the lungs purifies and nourishes itself correspondently to the affections of the mind, is not yet known, but it is very well known in the spiritual world; for the angels in the heavens are delighted only with the odors that correspond with their love of wisdom, whereas the spirits in hell are delighted only with odors that correspond with love opposed to wisdom; the latter odors are stinking, but the former odors are fragrant. That men in the world impregnate their blood with similar things, according to correspondence with the affections of their loves, follows of course; for what a man's spirit loves, that, according to correspondence, his blood craves and attracts in respiration. From this correspondence it follows that a man is purified as to his love, if he loves wisdom, and that he is defiled if he does not love her; all a man's purifications being effected by the truths of wisdom, and all his defilement by the falses that are opposed to them. (*Divine Love and Wisdom* §420; see also the end of *Divine Providence*)[1]

---

1. For "animal heat," compare Dalton, p. 257, and *Divine Love and Wisdom* §379. For the "blood globules," see Littell, 1477. For details of the conjunction between heart and lungs, and their correspondence, see *Divine Love and Wisdom* §404.

THE NOSE

THE LUNGS ABSORB AERIAL FOOD COMPOSED OF PURE AIR
and the exhalations and odors of innumerable mineral,
vegetable, and animal bodies. This food is even more
important to the life than the grosser food which is
received through the stomach. If the supply be cut off
even for a few minutes, the body dies; though it will
endure privation from solid and liquid food as many days.
The aerial food is also varied in quality very much more
than the other; and the state of the body, especially of the
brain and the delicate fluids, depends noticeably upon
that quality—upon the cleanness or uncleanness of the
atmosphere, and upon the odors and exhalations which
it bears in it—whether they be fresh, rich, and stimulating, or corrupt, foul, and stupefying.

At the entrance of the passage to the stomach the
mouth stands guard, with its sense of taste. And at the
entrance to the lungs the nose is stationed, instructed in
its use, and intelligent through its sense of smell.

The mouth tastes the liquid food that is brought to it,
and dissolves in its own fluids portions of the solid food
that it may taste them also; the purest and most accept-
able portions it drinks in through its own little tubes and
veins, and forewarns the whole digestive apparatus of the
nature of the coming aliment, that it may open its pores
to receive it freely. It also closes to refuse admittance to

such as is excessively distasteful, or rouses the stomach to reject that which may be swallowed. And so the nose tastes the atmosphere with the various aliments contained in it, dissolving a part in its own fluids, and absorbing a small part of them, at the same time notifying the lungs of the quality of the approaching breath, and preparing all the air cells to receive it rightly. The tongue, "as an organ of taste," Swedenborg tells us, "corresponds to the natural perception of good and truth, but the smell corresponds to spiritual perception" (*Apocalypse Explained* §990).

If the atmosphere be agreeable in quality, and altogether suitable for nourishment, the nose opens wide to receive as much as possible, encouraging the lungs, also, to expand their little chambers and breathe in freely the healthful odors, which it transmits to them warmed and moistened with a vapory saliva. By the combined effect to the opening of the nose and the expansion of the lungs, the air is drawn freely through the upper part of the nose where the olfactory nerves are distributed, that the pleasant refreshment may be more fully recognized and received.

But if the air be laden with pungent or putrid exhalations, the veinlets and even the nostrils contract to shut it out; a peremptory warning is sent likewise to the lungs, so that they may either refuse to admit it at all, or may expand with caution, drawing the air slowly through the lower nasal passages, and holding themselves ready to check it entirely, or to expel, by convulsive cough, any particles of unendurable foulness or acridity.

Besides these peculiar functions of the nose analogous to those of the mouth, the nose cooperates with the mouth in its discernment of the quality of food. The mouth alone, by its exquisite touch, perceives the quality of saline, sugary, and other comparatively coarse particles; but the volatile, aromatic flavors or odors are not clearly distinguished by the papillae of the tongue, but are instantly recognized by the nose. They are faintly perceived as the food is presented to the lips, and the perception has much to do with the state of reception induced upon the lips and tongue and other parts of the mouth. Within the mouth these subtle elements seem to be freely liberated—assisted, perhaps, by the warmth and moisture—so as to affect sensibly the back part of the mouth, the pharynx, and even the nose itself with a sort of compound sense which is at least as much smell as taste. It is this which Swedenborg ascribes to spirits instead of taste:

> I have discoursed with spirits concerning the sense of taste, which they said they had not, but that they had something whereby they nevertheless know what taste is; which they compared to smell, but were not able to describe. This brought to my recollection that taste and smell meet in a kind of third sense; as appears also from animals, which examine their food by the smell to discover whether it be wholesome and suitable for them. (*Arcana Coelestia* §1516)

From the frontal sinuses superfluous mucus is discharged into the upper part of the nose. The eyes also discharge their tears upon its lining membranes; and its own mucous follicles furnish it with additional moisture. These varied fluids are distributed over the undulating surface of the inner nose, where their watery vapors moisten pleasantly the entering atmosphere, and the viscid fluids hold fast to every particle of dust, and carry it wither they themselves are hastened by the cilia lining the nose, through the esophagus and stomach to the intestine.

The objects upon which the sense of the nose is exercised are the air and the various odors and spheres that mingle with it. That the amount and variety of these spheres are very great is evident from the fact that every existing thing is giving forth a sphere composed of its own particles. We are aware of a very strong sphere, pleasant or unpleasant, from certain animals, also from some plants, their flowers, fruits, leaves or wood; from a few minerals and metals, also, as from copper, iron, and sulphur. Other animals, endowed with more exquisite sense than we, because their life is confined to the body, perceive distinctly odors which to us are obscure; as the sheep the odors of the plants upon which it feeds; the dog the faint odors of footsteps upon the sand or grass, even hours after they have passed. That this immense amount of exhalation is scarcely at all detected by chemistry proves nothing; for chemistry takes cognizance of only the grossest forms of matter, and most of the aerial and etherial fluids with which we are now concerned are above its reach.

In the chapter on the lungs, we saw that the breathing corresponds to the purification of the life by thinking the truth and applying it to our affections and natural desires. Swedenborg says that the air corresponds to "all things of perception and thought" (*Apocalypse Revealed* §708). The pure air must correspond to pure, abstract wisdom of thought, and may be compared to the spirit of truth. *Spirit* also means *breath*, or wind; and the various exhalations with which the air is laden correspond to the spheres of as many states of life, which come to us as perceptions or thoughts of those states. Spheres of life are made sensible in the other world by odors which, Swedenborg teaches, "spirits perceive much more exquisitely than men" (*Arcana Coelestia* §1514); and, "what is wonderful, odors correspond to those spheres." He gives many instances of particular odors, with the spheres to which they correspond: "The spheres of charity and faith, when they are perceived as odors, are most delightful; they are pleasant odors, as of flowers, lilies, spices of various kinds, with indefinite variety" (*Arcana Coelestia* §1519).

"I perceived a winey odor, and was informed that it was from those who from friendship and lawful love speak courteously, but so that there is truth in their compliments; this odor is with much variety, and is from a sphere of beautiful manners" (*Arcana Coelestia* §1517).

"They who have cultivated eloquence for the end that all things may contribute to admiration of themselves, when their sphere is made odorous, it is like the smell of burnt bread"; because the instruction is like bread, and the zeal of self-love burns it. "They who have indulged in mere pleasures, and have been in no charity and faith, the odor of their sphere is excrementitious."

"Where men have lived in violent hatred, revenge, and cruelty, their sphere, when changed into odors, has the stench of a dead carcass. Such as have been immersed in sordid avarice give forth a stench like that of mice" (*Arcana Coelestia* §1514). But he says that spheres are not always made sensible as odors, but these are "variously tempered by the Lord, lest the quality of spirits should always appear before others" (*Arcana Coelestia* §1520).

By these odors of life the minds of spirits and angels are exhilarated and delighted; the good with the pleasant fragrances of good life, and the evil with the stenches of evil life; and they are to them manifest perceptions of the life of those whom they meet.

In the province of the nose we shall find those who excel in such perception. Not the taste, nor the touch, nor even the sight can give so true a revelation of the interior quality of substances presented to it as the nose; and they who constitute this province in the Greatest Man must enjoy unerring perception of the quality of the lives and inner thoughts of those to whom their attention is directed.

> To that province belong those who are in general perception, so that they may be called Perceptions. The smelling, and hence its organ, corresponds to them. Hence also it is that to smell [a thing out], to get scent of, to be keen-scented, and also [especially in Latin, quick] nostrils are predicated in common speech of those who divine a matter accurately, and also who perceive; for the interiors of the expressions of man's speech derive many things form correspondence with the Greatest Man, because man as to his spirit is in society with spirits, and as to his body with men. (*Arcana Coelestia* §4624)

> They who relate to the interiors of the nostrils are in a more perfect state as to perception than they who relate to their exteriors. . . . It is permitted to relate these things concerning them. There appeared to me as it were a bath with long seats or benches, and heat was exhaled from it. There appeared there a woman, who presently disappeared in a darkening cloud; and also children were heard, saying that they did not wish to be there. Afterwards some angelic choirs were apperceived, who were sent to me for the sake of averting the efforts of certain evil spirits. And then suddenly above the

forehead appeared little openings greater and less through which there shone beautifully golden light; and in that light within the openings women in snowy white were seen. And there again appeared little openings in another order, through which they who were within looked out; and again other little openings through which the light did not thus pass. At length a brightening light was seen. It was said to me that there were the homes of those who constituted the province of the inner nostrils, for they were of the female sex, and that the keenness of perception of those who are there is represented in the world of spirits by such openings; for the spiritual things in heaven are represented by natural, or rather by such things in the world of spirits as are like natural. Afterwards it was permitted to speak with them, and they said that by those representative openings they can see exactly the things which take place below; and that the openings appear turned to those societies which they are trying to observe; and because then they were turned to me, they said that they could perceive all the ideas of my thought, and also of those who were about me. They added further that they not only perceived the ideas, but also saw them variously represented to them, as the things of affection for good by appropriate little flames, and those of affection for truth by variations of light. They added that they saw certain angelic societies with me, and their thoughts [represented] by things variously colored, by purples as in embroidered tapestry, and also by rainbows in a darker plane, and that thence they perceived that

those angelic societies were from the province of
the eye. Afterwards other spirits were seen who
were cast down thence and dispersed hither and
thither of whom they said that they were such as
had insinuated themselves among them for the
sake of percceiving something, and of seeing what
went on below, but for the purpose of ensnaring.
This casting down was observed as often as angel
companies approached, with whom also I conversed. They said that those who were cast down
relate to the mucus of the nostrils, and that they
are heavy and stupid and also without conscience,
thus altogether without interior perception. The
woman who was seen, as mentioned above, signified such ensnarers; with whom also it was permitted to speak, and they wondered that any one
has conscience; they were utterly ignorant what
conscience is, and when I said that it is an interior
apperception of goodness and truth, and if anything is done contrary to that apperception that it
causes anxiety, they did not understand it. . . . The
light was then shown me in which they live who
relate to the interiors of the nostrils; it was a light
beautifully varied with veins of golden flame and
of silver light; affections for good were there represented by the veins of golden flame, and affections for truth by the veins of silver light. And it
was shown further that they have openings at the
side, through which they see as it were the heaven
with stars in the blue. And it was said that in their
rooms the light is so great that the midday light
of the world cannot be compared with it. It was
said moreover that the heat with them is like ver-

nal warmth upon the earth; and that there are also children with them, but children of some years; and that they are not willing to be there when those ensnaring women, or mucuses, approach. (*Arcana Coelestia* §4627)

Among the objects to which these keen perceptions direct their attention, are the new spirits coming from the earths, who at their entrance into the other life are received by the lips. At their first approach, while the lips still wait to receive them, their real quality is perceived in a general way by the angels of the nose; and lips and mouth and stomach, and indeed all provinces of the body, are notified, and prepared accordingly. In the further exploration of their quality, when the interiors of the memory are opened in the province of the mouth, the same angels assist; though not manifestly present, they perceive the spheres of the life, as it is opened, and add their more interior perception to the knowledge of fact and form acquired by the tongue.

From the earths themselves, where this food for the heavens is growing, ascend odors of the spiritual quality of the people upon them, which come to the manifest perception of the angels of the nose; thus we are told that from a wife who is tenderly loved, the angels perceive a sphere which is sweetly fragrant (*Conjugial Love* §171).

To the hells likewise these angels direct their attention, and to any part of the heavens or world of spirits which needs such attention; and by their perception the whole man is instructed, admonished, or encouraged, and assisted in its general efforts to remove evil and to promote the growth of all things of heavenly life.

Besides the duty of perceiving and notifying the body of the quality of odors which come to its sense, the nose has a more constant duty of receiving, tempering, and transmitting to the lungs the pure air of heaven. As odors corresponds to the spheres of life of individuals or societies, the pure air corresponds to the sphere of the Lord's life, as accommodated to the state of the heavens; it is the pure wisdom of the Divine thought, which shows what is absolutely true and wise. The purity of this truth the nose perceives and delights in; but it needs to be tempered and still further accommodated to the general life of the heavens, before it can be received without causing injurious discouragement. And this the angels of the nostrils perform by means of the abundant knowledge of the states of the body which they possess, and which is represented by the moisture of the nose. With such knowledge they temper the application of the pure truth of thought which they admit, and thus prepare it for ready acceptance by the lungs. Grosser thoughts, and spirits who embody them, who desire pure truth for selfish purposes, and not for the uses of heavenly life, also necessarily intrude, but are detected and quickly thrust down to the world of spirits, and then below.

Similar uses to these which are done for the whole heaven by angels of the nose are performed for each society by angels appointed for the purpose; for, Swedenborg says:

Each society is an image of the whole; for what is unanimous is composed of so many images of itself. The more comprehensive societies, which are images of the Greatest, have particular societies within themselves, which have like correspondence. I have sometimes conversed with those who, in the society into which I was sent, belonged to the province of the lungs, of the heart, face, tongue, ear, eye, and with those who belonged to the province of the nostrils, from whom also it was given to know their quality, namely, that they are Perceptions; for they perceived whatever happened in the society in general, but not so particularly as they who are in the province of the eye; for these latter distinguish and consider the things which are of perception. It was also given to observe that their faculty of perceiving varies according to the general changes of state of the society in which they are. (*Arcana Coelestia* §4625)

Every angel, spirit, and man possesses, in some degree, the same faculty, which is the faculty of perceiving what is abstractly true and wise, and also of perceiving truly the spheres of human life which are presented; and it does not deny the use for which the faculty was intended, that it may be employed to search out the spheres of foul life, and thoughts of unwisdom.

The things which have been said of the nose relate especially to the sensitive lining of it. Besides this, the great body of the nose is composed of cartilages and bones which protect the nerves and expand and support the membranes in the forms and positions which are necessary to their uses. The angels who are in these parts of the nose of the Greatest Man hold strongly and firmly to the right and duty to examine all the spheres of life that come to it, and to admit to the Heavenly Man the sphere of the Lord's genuine truth.

The same parts in an individual correspond to his hold of the right to think for himself as to the agreeableness or disagreeableness to him of states or spheres of life and thought. Hence a prominent nose indicates a certain degree of independence of thought and opinion.

In animals, the same faculty appears as the faculty of examining and exploring, chiefly for the sake of finding appropriate food. It is a more prominent faculty in them than in man, and is embodied in long noses, snouts, or probosces. The elephant, in which the development of the nose is most remarkable, corresponds to a love of justice. His ivory tusks, from which the throne of Solomon was made, correspond to the truth by which appearances are stripped off, and the real life is exposed; and the wonderful trunk represents a perception of real quality, of genuineness or of sham.

The Organs of Speech

We have studied the nose and the lungs in their relation to breathing, and the mouth in its use of eating. Let us now attend to their common use of speaking, in which the larynx and trachea are added to them, and indeed with a leading part.

The larynx lies behind and below the prominence in the throat called the "Adam's apple." This prominence consists of a large cartilage, closed in front but open behind. Just within the open edges behind, and extending below, lies another large cartilage; and across the space between the Adam's apple in front and the top of the second cartilage in the rear are stretched two membranous cords called the vocal cords. These are attached in front to the middle of the Adam's apple, just where we feel a depression; but behind they are attached not immediately to the other large cartilage, but to the edges of two little cartilages which are hinged upon the great cartilage. Resting upon this great cartilage, these little cartilages, as they open and shut, open and shut also the vocal cords, to regulate the amount of air that passes to the lungs; and the two great cartilages play upon each other in such a way as to tighten or loosen the cords, and so to vary the pitch of the voice.

There are several little muscles by which these motions are effected; and some muscular fibers are said to be attached to the vocal cords themselves, to regulate their length of vibration, like fingers upon a violin string.

The tension alone of these cords produces no sound; but when they are made tense, and the lungs also arouse themselves and forcibly puff upon the cords, they instantly respond with a sonorous tremble, like the reed of an organ pipe, or the strings of an aeolian harp. Then, the horseshoe-like cartilages of which the trachea or windpipe is composed, and the scarcely less sonorous elastic membrane by which they are connected together and their circle is completed, all join in the audible vibration, like the pipe of an organ when its reed is blown upon. The tense lungs, also, elastic and made to delight in every kind of aerial motion and vibration, resound like the body of a viol, with a tremble in which the lining membranes of the chest, and even the ribs and the very skin, are compelled to join, and which is communicated by elastic fluids and tissues to the extremities of the body. From the larynx the vibration extends upward, affecting all the parts contiguous to the breathing passages—namely, the pharynx, the palate, tongue, teeth, and lips, the nose, and the sinuses of the forehead; indeed, the whole skull and the brain partake of the contagious thrill, and join in the song or speech. Nor is their part merely that of passive spectators carried away by enthusiasm; they all contribute to the quality of the tone, each one modifying it in its own way, as we see plainly in regard to the nose, teeth, tongue, and lips, and as would appear from the other organs observed attentively.

There are two kinds of modifications to which vocal utterances are subject, one affecting the quality, of the tone as to force, pitch, harshness, or tenderness, and the other producing the articulations of speech. The lungs, trachea, larynx, nose, and bones of the head, are concerned especially with the first class, producing and modifying the tone of the voice; the lips and teeth, the palate, and especially the tongue, are principally instrumental in forming words. In singing, tone predominates; in speaking, articulation; yet the words of speech are imperfect unless filled with sonorous sound from the lungs and larynx; and the tones of singing are incomplete until shaped by the mouth.

The lungs, in their office of breathing, correspond to the love of perceiving and thinking truth in its application to the affections; or, in the Greatest Man, to the states of life of the heavens. In other words, they correspond to the faculty of exploring our own affections and ends, and purifying and correcting them according to the pure truth from the Lord. And it is meet that the organ which corresponds to the faculty of knowledge of the affections and ends, should express that knowledge by means of the very air which corresponds to the truth by which the exploration is made. As vocal organs, therefore, the lungs correspond to the love of confessing the thoughts of the heart. In the heavens it is the love of confessing to the Lord, or from the Lord to men and angels, the thought and the affection of the heavens.

Swedenborg relates:

> There were angelic choirs which praised the Lord together, and this from gladness of heart. Their praise was heard sometimes as very sweet singing; for spirits and angels have sonorous voices, and hear one another as men do; but human singing, as to the sweetness and harmony, which were heavenly, is not comparable to that. From the variety of the sound I perceived that there were many choirs. I was instructed by the angels who were with me that they belonged to the province and uses of the lungs; for they have song, because this office

belongs to the lungs; this also it was given to know by experience. It was permitted them to rule my respiration, which was done so gently and sweetly, and also interiorly, that I felt my respiration scarcely at all. I was further instructed that they who are assigned to the involuntary respiration are distinct from those assigned to the voluntary. It was said that they who are assigned to the involuntary respiration are present while man sleeps; for as soon as a man goes to sleep, the voluntary control of his respiration ceases, and the involuntary takes it up. (*Arcana Coelestia* §3893)

On another occasion, to correct the unfavorable opinion which spirits from the planet Jupiter had formed of the spirits from our earth, choirs of the angels from this earth came to them, one after another. "Choirs," he explains, "are when many think, speak, and act one thing together, in a continuous series; the celebration of the Lord in the heavens is for the most part by choirs. . . . Those choirs so greatly delighted the spirits of Jupiter who were with me, that they seemed to themselves to be caught up into heaven. That glorification lasted about an hour. It was given me to feel their delights which they derived from it, which were communicated to me. They said that they would tell it to their friends who were elsewhere" (*Arcana Coelestia* §8115).[1]

To the larynx are related those members of the community in heaven and on earth whose love it is to catch the shades of affection which come to them, and express them by modulations of tone. The larynx is the only

1. For an account of a general glorification in the heavens, see *Conjugial Love* §81, and for further details about choirs, *Arcana Coelestia* §3350–3351.

musical instrument in the body; and the things that relate to the musician's art, which is strictly the art of expressing affection by sound, are there concentrated. A true musician is not led by his ears but by his affection; the tones that agree with this he seizes, whether they are sweetest to the ears or not. He will be true to his feeling in his playing and in composing. As he writes, his throat sings silently; and his ears, possessed by the same affection, hear the silent music, and help to guide the throat. If orchestras and choirs are added they are only developments of the larynx, carrying out its efforts; in which case the original musician is like the sensitive and moving fibers of the larynx, and the rest are like the masses of muscle, cartilage, and ligament which compose its principal substance.

The part which the lungs have in this expression in the individual and the Greatest Man, is to furnish the breath, that is the thought, modified by the life of the man, and full of its heartthrobs. They represent the inspiration of exalted thought and feeling, springing from the life of the community, which they of the larynx put into form.

Other organs that are interested in the reception of the breath, as the nose and the membranes and passages connected with it, partake of the resonance of the expired air; and no doubt the angels of the corresponding provinces in heaven join sympathetically and joyfully in the sonorous thought of the lungs of the heavens.

They themselves sought and examined the truth which furnishes the means of thinking; and they share in the delight of expressing the truth.

To this the lips, teeth, palate, and especially the tongue, contribute definiteness of articulation, which corresponds to distinctness and definiteness in the expression of thought, especially from the love of instructing.

"They who correspond to the mouth," Swedenborg says "continually wish to speak; for in speaking they find the greatest pleasure. When they are perfected, they are brought to this, that they do not speak anything but what is of use to their companions, to the community, heaven, and the Lord. The delight of speaking thus is increased with them as the lust of regarding themselves in their speech, and of seeking wisdom of their own, perishes" (*Arcana Coelestia* §4803).

No argument is needed to show that if the whole heaven ever speaks as one man, it is through those who are in the province of the mouth; and that if either of the heavens, or any society in heaven, should so speak, it would be by those related to it in this manner.

Now, the whole heaven does speak to man, or the Lord through the heavens; for He speaks His Word to man, and He speaks it not immediately, but through the heavens; thus by degrees accommodating it to man, and forming in it the various heavenly senses. On this subject very much might be quoted from Swedenborg; but one passage will suffice:

The Lord spoke through heaven with John, and He also spoke through heaven with the prophets, and through heaven He speaks with everyone with whom He speaks. The cause is that the angelic heaven in the general is as one man, whose soul and life is the Lord; wherefore all that the Lord speaks, He speaks through heaven, as the soul and mind of man through his body. . . . But I will declare this mystery: the Lord speaks through heaven; but still the angels there do not speak, and do not even know what the Lord speaks, unless there be some of them with the man, through whom the Lord speaks openly from heaven, as with John and some of the prophets. For the influx of the Lord through heaven is like the influx of the soul through the body; the body indeed speaks and acts, and also feels something of the influx; but still the body does not do anything from itself as of itself, but is acted upon. That the speech and all the influx of the Lord through heaven with man is of such a kind, it has been given me to know by much experience. (*Apocalypse Revealed* §943. See also *Arcana Coelestia* §6982, 6996, 8443, 4677 end, 10033 end, 8899, 5121)

Usually the Word of the Lord seems to have been spoken by "an angel of the Lord"; but sometimes by "a great voice out of heaven" without the presence of an individual. In either case, it is from the Spirit of the Lord filling the heavens, and expressing His thought and affection through those who are in the organs of speech. During the scenes of the Last Judgment, no doubt Swedenborg had a great deal of experience of the ways in which the Lord speaks in the world of spirits.

Returning now to the use of the mouth in receiving food, we remember that it corresponds to the use of receiving new spirits into the heavenly kingdom, and, more generally and abstractly, to the love of gathering in their experiences of the providence and goodness of the Lord; for it is only that which men receive and live of the goodness and wisdom of the Lord, that is food to the heavens. The two uses of the mouth, therefore, are as closely related as sowing and reaping; for the Sower soweth the Word, and the harvest is the ripened lives of men. "Twin offices," Swedenborg calls them—"the office of serving speech, and that of serving nutrition"; and he adds: "as far as the tongue serves nutrition, it corresponds to the affection of knowing, understanding, and being wise in truths; wherefore, also, *sapientia*, wisdom, and *sapere*, to be wise, are from *sapor*, taste; and, as far as it serves speech, it corresponds to the affection of thinking and producing truths" (*Arcana Coelestia* §4795; see also §4791).

Even the silent angels whose special office it is to prepare the spirit to be raised from the body, and thus to receive additions to the heavens, as they sit quietly by his head look into his face with the effort to communicate their own thought, which relates to eternal life in heaven; and this is the means of doing their use.

The influence of the angels of the mouth into our minds produces therefore not only the love of obtaining useful knowledge, which corresponds to the love of receiving food, but also the love of bringing the thought into good form for expression; or, more simply, to the love of speaking, of communicating knowledge, and of teaching (see *Arcana Coelestia* §6987).

In any company or society of persons associated for some use, there are many who have some perception of what should be done; but it is usually the case that a few speak for the rest, and express their thoughts for them. The feelings and perceptions of the many correspond to the action of the heart and the lungs, and perhaps other interior organs; and the expression of these feelings and perceptions in form, to the action of the mouth. Hence, we not infrequently call one who speaks a mouthpiece for others. And if there are any who only wait for the conclusion, that they may know what is to be done, they are like hands and feet to the company.

In ancient days, before men learned to speak by words, they expressed their feelings and thoughts by changes of the face, and especially by delicate motions of the lips, which in innocent persons are still so expressive. They were taught by angels by similar changes of the face; and their teachers also were from the province of the mouth, and particularly from that of the lips (see *Arcana Coelestia* §4799).

THE PLEURA

WHAT THE PERITONEUM IS TO THE ABDOMINAL CAVITY, the pleura is to the thorax. It is the common bond of all the organs and vessels which the thorax contains; and its office is to hold each in its place with the utmost freedom of motion, and at the same time to impart to each the motions and wants of the whole; so that each may accommodate itself to the necessities of the others, and all may be combined in due proportion in the common use.

The heart and the lungs are not made independent of support through the nobleness of their office. The other parts of the body depend upon them; but there is no organ upon which these do not depend for the means of doing their use. Especially do they need the immediate and constant support of the pleura.

The heart lies between the great lobes of the lungs; but its action is not synchronous with that of the lungs; it expands and contracts three or four times during one respiration; and, without some means of accommodation, in dilating it would press upon air cells when they too were in the effort to expand, and the action of both would be impeded. Again, the heart to contract freely and uniformly, must be maintained in the same relative position during all the changes and motions of the body; and still it must not be attached and bound except at the base, where it gives forth the arteries and veins. And, further, the lungs must be maintained in their proper position, and not allowed in state of collapse to fall upon the heart or to suffer displacement; and in their place they must be protected from the ribs, and provided with the means of working without frictions, freely and smoothly.

Other needed uses will be mentioned hereafter; but these are plainly required, and to perform them is the duty assigned to the pleura.

One can hardly avoid a feeling of affection for the friendly ministry of one part of the body to another; and for none is the feeling stronger than for the modest service of the pleura, which does not pretend to be of the least importance itself, but just helps others to be important, and does for them essential service, perfectly, constantly, and without the slightest intrusion.

In itself it is composed of two membranes, one thick and fibrous, the other smooth, glossy, and moist. By its fibrous coat it applies itself closely to the lungs, covering every convolution perfectly, yet elastically, and entering between the little lobes even to the minutest air cells, as if to be in sympathy with and give protection to its inmost thoughts. Its strong outer coat at the same time invests the lungs with an almost metallic smoothness, which is rendered more perfect by constant lubrication with delicate oils.

From the base of the lungs the pleura is reflected upon itself, and forms two membranous bags loosely enclosing again the already encased lungs. The fibrous membrane of these bags, next the walls of the thorax, attaches itself closely to the ribs, and extends its little fibers among the intercostal muscles, even to the fatty tissues of the chest, while the harder, smooth coat presents inwards a polished surface for the investing coat of the lungs to play upon. Thus their easy motion is secured.

On the lower wall of the thorax the pleura unites with the diaphragm, by the flexibility of which it is enabled to apply its well-oiled coat even to the hollow inner walls of the lobes of the lungs, giving them the support they need to keep them always in position, but not imposing the slightest restraint upon their free motion.

Between the great lobes the membranous walls of these bags unite, forming a partition in the chest, extending from the breastbone to the backbone; but in this partition the two walls part, and leave space between them for a roomy closet for the heart, which is thus suspended in its place between the folds of the pleura. And in order to protect the heart and the lungs still further from mutual annoyance, still another fold of pleura, or, as some hold, a little pleura by itself, forms an inner bag of smoothest surface, and loosely encloses the heart; which is thus separated from the lungs by two spaces and four thicknesses of membrane.

Besides achieving this apparently impossible duty of giving to these active organs the closest and most intimate support without in the least affecting their freedom, and holding them closely related in their common work but preventing any chance of mutual irritation, the pleura through smaller chambers between its folds, behind that of the heart, furnishes safe conduct to the esophagus on its way to the stomach, to the great aorta as it descends to distribute the life blood to the lower viscera and members, to the great ascending vein also and the chyle duct; and it imparts to them all—and by means of the diaphragm, to the lower viscera also—the alternate motions of the lungs—motions of alternate reception and action, which are essential to their life and usefulness.

Many subordinate duties the pleura performs; but these are its chief and governing uses.

As the province of the peritoneum is held by angels of simple quality (*Arcana Coelestia* §5378), not active of themselves but readily acting from others, and above all things loving harmony, so the angels of the pleura are modest angels delighting in the harmony of the uses of the heart and the lungs. To the angels of these provinces they attach themselves closely, rendering them every support and assistance. With ready sympathy and affection for both, they interpose to receive and accommodate their strong but not coincident activities; for the impulses of affection and the thoughts of wisdom are not synchronous; they need to be accommodated to each other by intermediates who respect and love them both. They interpose also between these and the rougher, less sensitive angels, who, holding merely to the facts of the use and necessity of these vital organs, are like stony walls of protection to them, and constitute the ribs of the Greatest Man; but who would grate harshly and injuriously in immediate contact with the angels who are so full of the love of doing the Lord's will that they are unwilling to think of themselves, and those who are intent upon applying the Lord's wisdom to the life of the heavens, and cannot bear to be reminded of their own importance. The support and protection of the facts they bring them, without disturbing their unselfish activity; and from full sympathy with their life, they impress it upon all comers, new and old, who pass within their domain.

Our admiration for the pleura is admiration for these modest, unselfishly useful angels; or, for the generous, devoted love for ministering to others which these receive from the Lord. Other organs of the body partake, even in a greater degree, of the spirit of mutual service; and in that service they all are images of angels' love, and of the Lord's multiform love of serving, which creates heaven and earth, and is the life of every part of them.

THE DIAPHRAGM

THE DIAPHRAGM FORMS A PARTITION BETWEEN THE THO-
rax and the abdomen. Its upper side consists of the lower
part of the pleura, its lower side of the upper part of the
peritoneum. These two membranes come into immediate contact and close union in the central part of the
diaphragm, in three spots which are likened to the lobes
of a clover leaf; but from this center there radiate bundles
of muscular fibers between the membranes, to the line of
attachment at the extremities of the ribs; two large bundles of fibers reach well down the lumbar vertebrae.

When the muscular fibers are relaxed, the diaphragm
extends up like a dome into the thorax, lying close to the
compressed lungs; and then the liver, and some other
organs of the abdomen, lie partly above the line of the ribs
in the thorax, and are then in a state of expansion. But
when the muscles of the diaphragm contract, they bring
down the dome, expand the cavity of the chest, and press
the abdominal organs out from it, inducing upon them
their turn of contraction.

When the chest is in its state of expansion, it draws in
the air from without, and also the fluids of the body from
within, sucking upon every vein and lymphatic; and, as
the viscera of the abdomen are at the same time compressed, they freely yield up their fluids to the demand of
the thorax. And when the thorax contracts, it presses

upon arteries, lymphatics, and veins, hastening the departure of the streams ready for the nourishment of the body, and retarding the return currents; and as the abdomen is at that time in a state of expansion, its vessels gladly seize the opportunity to fill themselves full. Liver, spleen, pancreas, kidneys, and even the stomach and intestines depend upon this alternate motion for their power of usefulness; and their common container, the peritoneum, secures this motion to them by uniting itself with the pleura in the diaphragm.

We have, then, on the one side the pleura, loving its trust of serving the heart and the lungs, enjoying the free motion of the lungs, and desiring to extend its delightful animations; and on the other hand the peritoneum, caring for the common wants of the digestive organs, and here desiring for them the active life of the lungs, and the preparation which that activity ensures to receive the fresh streams of blood from the heart. And these two make a compact to help each other in this common use; and they unite almost as one membrane in the center of the diaphragm, availing themselves of the assistance of many urgent fibers to bring their purpose into effect.

Swedenborg's common statement is that the middle heaven includes the body from the neck to the knees; but the image seen by Nebuchadnezzar was as to the breast and arms, of silver, as to the belly and thighs of brass, and the legs and feet were of iron. This was a representative of the successive churches, and consequently of the heavens formed from them (*Arcana Coelestia* §10030), and it marks strongly the division between the chest and the abdomen.

Also in *True Christian Religion* §119, he says that the highest heaven is the head, the second is the breast, the lowest is the gastric region, and the church on earth is the loins and feet. Perhaps this last statement refers to the heaven before the Lord's coming, when there was no Christian heaven, and the ancient was imperfectly formed.

Swedenborg says nothing about the angels of this province of the Greatest Man; but their quality is mirrored in the uses of the organ. They are intermediates between the spiritual and the natural heavens—between the angels whose delight it is to perceive and appropriate spiritual wisdom from the Lord, and to cherish and exercise the love of heavenly uses to the neighbor, and the angels whose duty it is to receive new spirits whose spiritual minds are not yet open, to separate the evil from the good, and to train the good to habits of right thought and action.

These intermediates on the one hand delight in the activity of spiritual thought and affection, and on the other in the use of preparing new angels to receive that thought and affection. Each class loves first its own use, and then that of the other; for the use of each is indispensable to the other. There is no purpose in the action of heart and lungs, unless their influence be received beyond their own province; and there is no satisfaction in preparing spirits to receive the life of heaven, unless heavenly wisdom and love which constitute that life be abundantly provided. And in order that any use may be accomplished in either domain, there must be submission to the universal law of all created beings, alternate reception and communication, expansion, and contraction; which the lungs, as is becoming to the province of wisdom, perceive most clearly, and by means of the diaphragm impress upon all their associates.

Into this alternation, and thus into the respiration of the heavens, all good spirits are introduced in the province of the lungs (*Arcana Coelestia* §3894); they are continued in it by the animations of the lungs extended to the remotest parts of the body, and the degree of their vitality and usefulness depends upon the degree in which they partake of this animation.

MUSCLES IN GENERAL

THE POWER OF THE BODY IS EXERTED BY THE MUSCLES, which represent the love of work in the mind, and, in the heavens, societies of those who love the active uses corresponding to those of the muscles respectively. Thus, the diaphragm is not a passive means of communication between the thorax and the abdomen; its active force is essential both to the motions of the lungs and to the communication of those motions to the rest of the body. And the muscles of the diaphragm correspond to the angels who have active pleasure in the animations of wisdom and in the communication of them through the heavens. They combine and exert an animating pressure upon the provinces of digestion, inviting the expansion of the lungs; which, without this powerful cooperation, would be greatly confined in their action, as in cases of rheumatism of the diaphragm.

The heart itself is almost wholly muscular, and they who constitute it are in the active love of communicating love from the Lord to all whom they can influence, and sending them forth to do the uses of love. So all the active force exerted by the hands and feet, by the mouth in receiving food and in speaking, and by all parts of the body in their several uses, is exerted by muscles; which, accordingly, represent the active zeal of the provinces for those uses.

In these activities many angels combine, and exert their influence as a one. "How many spirits," Swedenborg says, "concur in one action, was shown me by those who are in the muscles of the face, from the forehead even to the neck. . . . It was observed that they were only the subjects of very many, so that in every muscular fiber very many concur. . . . In heaven, or the Greatest Man, there are innumerable societies thus unanimous, to which the muscles correspond" (*Index to Spiritual Diary*, "Musculus").

But the muscles exert their force mostly through tendons, or tendinous sheaths, by which they are attached to bones or to other parts of the body, and direct their action. And these tendons or ligaments correspond to passive subjects, who love indeed to receive the influence and to communicate it, but do not themselves modify it.

Bones

THE LEAST LIVING PARTS OF THE BODY ARE THE BONES, which are composed largely of earthy material, and seem to have a use like that of the rocks in nature; that is, they serve as a basis and fulcrum for the softer parts, keeping them extended and in their right places, and serving also for protection to the organs that specially need protection.

The rocks, and likewise the bones, correspond to the fixed facts upon which all other elements of mental life depend; and, in the Greatest Man, the provinces of the bones are occupied by those who have little other life than that of holding firmly to certain facts of experience which serve for support and protection to those who live more active lives. They serve to preserve the proportions and relations of the parts of the man—not exerting any force themselves except that of stolid resistance when their facts are in question.

The societies of spirits to which the cartilages and bones correspond are very many; but they are such as have very little spiritual life in them, as there is very little life in the bones relatively to the soft parts which they enclose; as, for example, there is in the skull and the bones of the head compared with either brain and the medulla oblongata, and the sensitive substances there; and also as there is in the vertebrae and ribs in comparison with the heart and lungs; and so on. It was shown how little spiritual life they have who have relation to the bones; other spirits speak by them, and they themselves know little of what they say; but still they speak, having delight in this alone. Into such a state are they reduced who have led an evil life, and still had some remains of good; these remains make that little spiritual life, after the vastations of many ages. . . . They who come out of vastations, and serve the uses of bones, have not any determinate thought, but general, almost indeterminate; they are like those who are called distraught, as if not in the body; they are slow, heavy, stupid, sluggish about everything. Yet sometimes they are not untranquil, because cares do not penetrate, but are dissipated in their general obscurity. (*Arcana Coelestia* §5560–5562)

He explains that the lack of spiritual life is lack of spiritual intelligence and charity, not necessarily lack of natural intelligence. Therefore, in the *Diary*, he says:

They correspond to bones, in the other life, who have studied various sciences and have made no use of them, as they who have studied mathematics only to find the rules, and have not regarded any use; or physics and chemistry only for the sake of experiment, and for no other use; also philosophy to find its rules and terms, only for the sake of the terms and for no other use; and likewise other things. They who become bones also, when they reason, hardly discuss anything else than whether it is or is not. Hence it is evident that the greatest part of the learned within the church become bones. They are those who are finally sensual; the church also is in this state today; hence is its end. (*Spiritual Diary* §5141)

CARTILAGES

CARTILAGES ARE REALLY THE RECEPTACLES OF THE EARTHY materials of which bones are made. All bones begin as cartilages, and gradually become hardened by receiving earthy deposits. Their use, therefore, would be performed in the heavens by spirits who are more simple and pliable in their stupidity than those who represent the bones— by those who know a few general truths, while the bones are those who hold their own particular experiences. Such would much more readily enter into easy relations with others than those who must intrude their small experiences. Hence the bones are capped with cartilage at the joints.

The breastbone also terminates in a cartilage, for the sake of greater flexibility in accommodation to the motions of the chest. The angels who belong to this province in the Greatest Man, Swedenborg says, are from our moon; and he describes their dwarfish appearance, but says nothing about their character (*Earths in the Universe* §111).

In speaking of the various qualities in the Greatest Man, he says:

> It has been provided by the Lord that those whom the Gospel has not been able to reach, but a religion only, should also be able to have a place in that Divine Man, that is, in heaven, by constituting the

parts that are called skins, membranes, cartilages, and bones; and that they like others should be in heavenly joy; for it is not a matter of concern whether they are in such joy as the angels of the highest heaven have, or in such as the angels of the lowest heaven have; for everyone who comes into heaven comes into the highest joy of his heart; he does not bear a higher joy, for he would be suffocated in it. (*Divine Providence* §254)

The Skin

WE ARE IN THE HABIT OF THINKING OF THE SKIN AS A covering for the body of a sort of delicate untanned leather, with no great vitality of its own, but serving to protect the more sensitive and important organs within. There is some truth in this—the skin does protect much nobler organs than itself; and the outer skin is not sensitive; yet no other part of the body is more sensitive than the inner skin; which possesses also a delicacy and complexity of structure which will excite our admiration. There exist in nature multitudes of little animals too minute for the unaided eye to perceive, endowed each with organs of sense, of digestion, of circulation, and of action, all contained within a compass too small for us to notice. From Swedenborg's marvelous description it would appear that there is not a point in the inner skin less exquisitely organized than these.

The outer layer of the skin, which is the part with which we are best acquainted, is composed of little horny scales laid one upon another like armor of mail to a greater or less thickness according to the exposure. This is perforated by the hairs and by innumerable little pores, which we shall consider hereafter. This outer skin is detached by blisters and chafings, and then we discover a most tender, sensitive surface under it, which we are glad to protect by a plaster till its proper coat of scales is repaired. Yet even these scales do not rest immediately upon the sensitive skin, though they are thrown into little ridges and spirals in accommodation to its papillae. They rest upon a soft, jelly-like vascular membrane (*rete mucosum*), which encases the papillae of the inner skin, protecting them and combining their sensations.

The surface of the inner skin, thus protected and encased by two outer layers, is composed of little papillae, finer than needle points, each of which under a powerful glass is seen to be a bundle of still more minute papillary fibers. In these papillae are seen looped nervous fibers, and also what are called "tactile corpuscles," both of which serve as organs of touch, and many more nerve fibers are seen splitting into almost invisible filaments. Besides these exquisitely sensitive papillae in which the touch resides, the skin contains the roots of the hairs, with their anointing glands, innumerable sweat glands, each one looking like a little convoluted intestine—which unraveled, it is estimated, would amount to two and a half miles in length in a single person—also arteries, which in states of inflammation are seen in a network over the papillary surface, and veins and lymphatics without number.

So much is commonly known of the skin, and not much more. Microscopic investigation shows some of the nerve fibers ending in the papillae in loops or "tactile corpuscles" but many more divide into little brushes; and what they do there, or what becomes of them, modern science does not know. And here Swedenborg's more than microscopic insight takes up the subject. "Not know," he would say, "what the fibers do in those most delicate of fleshy forms, when you know that the vessels are woven from the fibers, and that the intermediates are formed by the extremes! The nervous fibers are weaving there the beginnings of the blood vessels, or the fleshy fibers. They coil themselves into minute invisible tubes, called corporeal fibers, and these again into larger tubes which are the finest fleshy fibers of the papillae, and are the last subdivisions of the arteries, too fine in their ordinary state to carry red blood, and these combining extend their delicately woven walls to the lining of the arteries; and thus through the arteries, the heart, and again the carotid arteries, the nervous fibers return to the brain."

The idea that the beginning of the arterial system is in the skin, not the heart, at first may seem surprising; but it is illustrated by the similar and well-known fact that the beginnings of the woody fibers of trees are in the leaves, not in the stem or the roots. Through the pith and the delicate fibers of the bark, nourishment ascends to expand the first tender leaves, and from these descend the first woody fibers between this bark and the pith, as well as new fibers of bark, and extend themselves to the extremities of the roots. Through these woody and cortical fibers sap afterwards ascends to the leaves, and by their means new buds and leaves are formed, which in turn send down other fibers, and thus the trunk of the tree grows in concentric layers of wood, every fiber of which has descended from the leaves.

In Swedenborg's view a similar process goes on from the membranes which are the ultimates of the body, and especially from the skin. Before the heart exists in the embryo, ramifications of blood vessels are seen, which indeed soon unite in the heart and afterwards act from it; and these undoubtedly assist in the formation of other vessels and tissues, which are, however, everywhere woven from the nervous fibers, the blood vessels cooperating and afterwards sustaining them.

It is a familiar fact that through the skin there are continual exhalation and absorption. There is exhalation of watery vapor, of fatty vapor—as we see by touching the

fingers for a moment to clean glass—of more subtle effluvia which affect the sense of smell, sometimes pleasantly
as from an infant's skin, and of most delicate, perhaps
magnetic influence to which some persons are very sensitive, and which is often used in relieving nervous pains;
these exhalations are all of materials no longer needed in
the body, but partaking of the life of the body, and capable of doing more or less use in the extremes or beyond
the surface of the body.

There are also inhalations correlative to these exhalations. It is said that the thirst of exhausted men may be satisfied by immersion in the sea or by wetting their clothes.
Nutritious vapors and steam are also absorbed, no doubt
in quantities which go far to satisfy hunger.

The volatile oils of poisonous ivy and of dogwood, inap-
preciable by any conscious sense, are absorbed by the skin
to its great discomfort. And more subtle still, the "animal
magnetism," as it is called, the most active but delicate of
the exhalations of a living body, is absorbed by the minutest pores of another body, and is a powerful agent in restoring disordered or tired nerves. These are things of common experience which show that the skin is a most active
agent both in absorbing and in exhaling materials related
to animal life of many kinds. Thus the skin has already,
upon the surface of the body, some of the properties
which are further developed in its continuations which
line the stomach and the lungs.

Throughout the viscera, as well as upon the surface of
the body, the mouths of the little pores are in the extremities of the little papillae of touch, which by their exquisite sense perceive the quality of the materials offered for
their acceptance or rejection, and rule over the action of
the ducts according to their perception and to the wants
of the body. The knowledge they acquire they report in

part to the cerebrum, in which dwells the conscious, thinking mind, but in greater part, especially from the viscera, to those nerve centers which preside over the vital functions of the body without reference to our perverted sense or ignorant reason.

The sense of touch gives substance and reality to all our sensations. Sight and hearing and smell, without touch, would be almost like affections of the imagination; their objects would seem forever unreal, unsubstantial, unless they could be touched. By touch they are brought into substantial, satisfactory relations to us; by it we perceive their substance, their texture, their size, and hardness or softness, their general relation to ourselves. To the sense of touch we apply the term "feeling," which is also the name of the inner sensation produced in our mental organs by contact with thought and affection.

Sight is necessary to correct the very limited impressions of touch, and the inner feelings are modified by the understanding; but in both cases the sense of relation to us comes through the touch. Therefore it is that touch signifies in spiritual language communication of affection; for by touch the sensitive papillae are modified in form to agree with the object of contact, and they either extend themselves with pleasure and open their little pores to receive the influence presented to them, or they shrink with aversion and close their doors. Spheres of life, and of effluvia partaking of the quality and activity of the life, are both communicated and received through the skin; and the touch, including the delicate sense of the quality of spheres, guards all the doors.

At the approach of danger, real or imaginary, it orders the doors to be shut, the armor of the skin to be more firmly held, and even the little hairs to be erected and put forth as feelers. But when agreeable influences are felt, the armor is loosened, the advanced capillary guards withdrawn and laid down, and the doors thrown open wide for sweet interchange of congenial life. Hence the highest use of this sense is with two whose lives are one, and Swedenborg says that it is dedicated to marriage.

Swedenborg says that the coverings of the tabernacle of the Israelites, composed successively of fine linen, of goats' hair, of rams' skins, and of a coarser skin outside, represent the four layers of skin which cover the body (*Arcana Coelestia* §9632). Here he treats as two the papillary layer of the corium and the fibrous layer beneath. Upon the inner curtains of fine linen were embroidered cherubs, which Swedenborg says represented the guard of the Lord lest the Holy Divine should be approached except by the good of love (*Arcana Coelestia* §9509). Applied to the heavens this would mean the sensitiveness of the heavens from the Lord lest they should be approached or entered except by those who are in love to the Lord and the neighbor. And this sensitiveness resides with those who constitute the inner skin.

I have been speaking of the spheres of the body and of the mind as if they always acted together as one and were received as one. This may be so and may not. In any case the sense of touch properly has to do only with the body and the spheres of the body; and spiritual substances and influences are perceived by the corresponding sense of the mind, which, indeed, is commonly called, in its nice discriminations of mutual relation, "tact" or touch. In the spiritual world, mind and body are in agreement; and those who have delicate tact, or perception of spiritual relations, have also delicate skins. Swedenborg says:

> The conformation of the interweavings of the skin
> has been shown me representatively. The for-

mation with those in whom those most external things correspond to the interiors, or the material things there are obedient to spiritual, was a beautiful weaving of spirals wonderfully intertwined in a kind of lacework which cannot at all be described. They were of blue color. Afterwards were represented forms still more elaborate, more delicate, and more beautifully connected. Of such a structure appear the cuticles of a regenerate man. But with those who have been deceitful, these extremes appear conglutinations of mere serpents; and with those who have used magical arts, like filthy intestines. (*Arcana Coelestia* §5559)

Of the scarf-skin of the body, he says:

That skin is less sensitive than any other of the coverings, for it is covered with scales which are almost like delicate cartilage. The societies which constitute it are they who reason concerning all things whether it be so or not so, nor do they go any further. [This is like the obtuseness of the cuticle which has no life or perception of its own, but merely collects impressions of all sorts, not discriminating among them itself.] When I talked with them, it was given to perceive that they did not at all apprehend what is true or not true, and they who have reasoned most apprehend the least. Still, they seem to themselves wiser than others, for they place wisdom in the faculty of arguing. They are utterly ignorant that the essential thing in wisdom is to perceive without arguing that it is so or is not so. Many such are from those who in the world were made so by a confusion of good and truth through philosophicals; who have hence the less common sense. (*Arcana Coelestia* §5556)

This appears to be said of the horny scarf-skin proper. But in *Arcana Coelestia* §5553, it is said that "the societies to whom the cuticles correspond are in the entrance to heaven, and there is given to them perception of the quality of the spirits who approach the first threshold, whom they either reject or admit; so that they may be called entrances or doorways to heaven." Apparently in "the cuticles" he here includes the whole skin in general, and also the linings of the stomach and intestines, and what is said may, in part, refer to these last (compare *Arcana Coelestia* §8980). But it also true that the orifices of the minute ducts, as to their function of absorbing ethereal aliment for the body, are like portals to heaven, through which they who die in earliest infancy and before the embryonic state is completed, are caught up by the quickest and shortest ways into their appropriate province in heaven.[1]

There are very many societies who constitute the external integuments of the body, with differences from the face to the soles of feet; for there are differences everywhere. I have talked much with them. As regards spiritual life they are such that they allow themselves to be persuaded by others that a thing is so; and when they heard it confirmed from the literal sense of the Word, they altogether believed it, and remained in the opinion, and resolved upon a life, not bad, according to it. Intercourse with them cannot easily be had by others who are not of

1. *Spiritual Diary* §1022 and 1035, and *Index to Spiritual Diary*, under "Infans."

a similar disposition, for they adhere tenaciously to the opinions they have formed, nor do they suffer themselves to be led away by reasons. There are a great many such from this earth, because our planet is in externals, and also reacts against internals, like the skin. (*Arcana Coelestia* §5554)

The people of our earth are like the skin in this, that their whole natures are turned outwards to receive impressions from the world. Therefore the impressions of sense are here organized into sciences which do not exist upon any other earth. Therefore also the Word, by which the whole heaven is made, received its literal sense upon this earth; and this literal sense can be turned hither and thither, and is composed of facts of little or no spiritual life, which understood literally by us convey impressions of far different character to the angels, and serve to ultimate, generalize, contain, and suggest the wisdom and spiritual life of the heavens.

The order of development of the body, from the purest fibers by means of the extremities of the vessels in the skin, and then the interiors, must also be the order of development of the Greatest Man, consisting of the heavens and the church, and also of the Word itself. Swedenborg says, "The Lord flows in from firsts through lasts, thus from Himself into the natural sense of the Word, and calls out or evolves thence its spiritual and celestial senses, and thus illustrating, teaches and leads the angels" (*Posthumous Theological Works*, "Concerning the Sacred Scripture or the Word of the Lord from Experience," §18).

"The Word in ultimates is the sense of the letter; the Word in firsts is the Lord, and the Word in interiors is its internal sense which is perceived in the heavens.... Man in ultimates is the church on the earths, man in firsts is the Lord, man in interiors is heaven, for the church and heaven before the Lord are as one man" (*Arcana Coelestia* §10044).

Before there were angels, men were created upon the earths by the Lord, and by their interior development the heavens were filled with angels. And before the Divine truth could be taught to the heavens, it must have been taught in a very pure, simple, literal sense of the Word, given immediately from God to men. From this literal sense were evolved the spiritual truths which make the heavens; and these were received in the minds of men who became angels; and these angels were the mediums of making still further revelations of the Lord to men, which again were the beginnings of new heavenly forms; and thus the man grew, every new growth springing from life from God through the internal, first received, lived, and fixed in the external.

It is a knowledge of the mere letter of the Word which is like the insensible cuticle; a perception of the natural goodness of God in dealing with men, of His providence, and of His wisdom, belongs to the sensitive papillae beneath the cuticle. Of the varieties of these Swedenborg says nothing, and very little of their uses of absorption and perspiration; but I cannot doubt that they have relation to the loves of receiving the spirit which breathes through the letter of the Word, and which is genuine truth for the deepest thought; and of separating from the thought that which has done its use, and should no longer circulate in the thought.

Of the mode of action of those in the Greatest Man whose duty it is to accept the true and to separate the useless thought, Swedenborg says, "There are spirits who when they wish to know anything say that it is so, thus one after another in society; and thus, when they say it, they observe whether it flows freely, without any spiritual resistance; for when it is not so, they generally perceive a resistance from within; if they do not perceive resistance, they think that it is so, and do not know it in any other way. Such are they who constitute the glands of the skin" (*Arcana Coelestia* §5558).

Swedenborg often speaks of the skin as corresponding to those who are in truths of faith only, and not in goods of charity, and who act therefore not from a love of good in themselves but by direction from without: "They who are such even to the end of life, after death remain in that state, nor can they be led out to a state in which they will act from affection of charity, thus from good, but from obedience. These in the Greatest Man, which is heaven, constitute the things which serve the interiors, like the membranes and skins" (*Arcana Coelestia* §8990).[2] For, after all, the skin is a passive sort of agent, which loves to absorb, to test, and to excrete, but not to do or to produce; and it must correspond to those who are of like character. As a covering, also, it goes where it is carried, touches what it is made to touch, and has no power of seeking or shunning, but merely of warning others.

Life is covered with forms and usages which are neither good nor bad in themselves. To do away with these neutral things, and make everything a matter of conscience, is like removing the cuticle and exposing the cutis to pain from every touch.

If we are very sensitive about things which are of little importance in themselves, we are what is called thin-

2. See also *Arcana Coelestia* §8588, 8870, 8980, 9959.

skinned, and in associating with others we are continually getting hurt. It is the wise way in such cases to withdraw our life from such really unimportant things, let them become dead and like callosities, which can bear friction without pain. But to become indifferent and callous about things of real importance to spiritual life is to become stupid.

The Hair

HAIRS GROW FROM THE SKIN, AND IN A SENSE CONSTITUTE a part of the skin. In themselves they have very little life or sensitiveness, though they may be strongly and sensitively held by the skin. They play a great part in the adornment of the person, and they have an important use in the protection of the more living surfaces, especially of the head, beneath them.

They correspond to the formalities and courtesies of thought and of life, which are of small account in themselves, and yet add greatly to the beauty of life, and certainly present a most useful shield to the more sensitive feelings beneath. They may indeed be presented with perfect sincerity, and may rightly interpret the feelings; but it is easier to meet in pleasant formalities about which we are not very sensitive, than to be always exposing our feelings, and receiving personal affronts and injuries.

As is the correspondence of the bones and cuticles so is that of the hairs, for these put forth from roots in the cuticles. Whatever has correspondence with the Greatest Man, this the spirits and angels have; for each one represents as an image the Greatest Man; therefore the angels have hair, arranged becomingly and in order. Their hair represents their natural life and its correspondence with their spiritual life.... There are many, especially women, who have placed everything in elegancies, nor have they thought higher, and scarcely anything concerning eternal life. This is pardoned to women until the age of womanhood, when the ardor which is wont to precede marriage ceases; but if they persist in such things in adult age, when they can know better, then they contract a nature which remains after death. Such appear in the other life with long hair spread over their face, which also they comb, placing elegance in it; for to comb the hair signifies to accommodate natural things so that they appear becoming. From this they are known by others; for spirits can tell from the color, length, and arrangement of the hair, what the persons were as to natural life in the world.

They who have believed nature to be everything, and have confirmed themselves in this, and therefore have lived a careless life, not acknowledging any life after death, nor any hell or heaven; such, because they are merely natural, when they appear in the light of heaven, do not seem to have any face, but instead something bearded, hairy, unshorn; for, as was said above, the face represents the spiritual and celestial things interiorly in man, but hairiness the natural things. (*Arcana Coelestia* §5569–5571)

That the hairs of the head and of the beard correspond to the Word in its ultimates, may seem wonderful, when it is first seen and heard; but that correspondence derives its cause from this, that all things of the Word correspond with all things of heaven, and heaven with all things of man; for heaven in its complex is before the Lord as one man.... That all things of the Word correspond to all things of heaven, has been given me to perceive from this, that the chapters of the Word correspond respectively to the societies of heaven; for when I ran through the propheticals of the Word, from Isaiah to Malachi, it was given me to see that the societies of heaven were aroused in their order and perceived the spiritual sense corresponding to themselves. From these and from other proofs it was evident to me that there is a correspondence of the whole heaven with the Word in a series. Now, because there is such a correspondence of the Word with heaven, and heaven as a whole and in detail corresponds to man, therefore the ultimate of the Word corresponds to the ultimate of man; the ultimate of the Word is the sense of the letter, and the ultimates of man are the hairs of the head and of the beard. Hence it is that men who have loved the Word even in its ultimates, after death, when they become spirits, appear in becoming hair as the angels do; the same also, when they become angels, let their beards grow. But, on the other hand, they who have despised the sense of the letter of the Word, after death, when they become spirits, appear bald, which also is a sign that they are without truths; wherefore also lest it should seem to others disgraceful, they cover their heads with turbans. (*Posthumous Theological Works*, "Concerning the Sacred Scripture or the Word of the Lord from Experience," §10)

Swedenborg describes a certain council called in the world of spirits, in which "on the right stood those who in the world were called Apostolic Fathers, and who lived in the ages preceding the Nicene Council; and on the left stood men renowned in succeeding ages for their books, printed or written out by scholars. Many of the latter had their faces shaved, and their heads covered with curled wigs made of women's hair ... but the former had long beards, and wore their natural hair " (*True Christian Religion* §137). And it appeared that the shaven men had no regard for truth; but the bearded men were angels from heaven.

The beard seems to represent the clothing in which one expresses his rational thought—the generalities which one advances as it were tentatively, indicating his thought but not making it a matter of personal feeling.

Women have no beards, for when they speak they usually express their feelings; but they have beautiful hair, for they love to make this expression decorous and agreeable.

Such uses as these are evidently performed for the Word by its literal sense. Expressions of affection are there, in graceful, poetic language, which both adorns and protects them; and the wisdom by which the heavens were made, and are daily led in goodness, is there also; but it is clothed in neutral expressions which may be rejected without much harm, but which if understood rightly, reveal the Divine thought of the Lord.

THE HANDS

THROUGH THE HANDS IS EXPRESSED THE LOVE OF DOING, of forming for use, and of communicating. The working strength of the body is exerted by them; also its skill or wisdom of work.

"To speak well," Shakespeare says, "is a kind of good deed"; and it is a kind that is performed by the tongue. But the words of the tongue have for their purpose to affect the works of others' hands, by filling them with wiser thought and better feeling, if not by changing their form or direction; and even words are expressed more perfectly and permanently by the hand, in writing, than by the tongue; and, moreover, they who speak express their personal life and love more fully by what they do with their hands than by their words (*Divine Love and Wisdom* §361).

The use of the arms is almost exclusively to make the hands effective. The upper arm, to the elbow, including the muscles of the shoulder, raises, extends, and gives broad, sweeping motions to the lower arm and hand. The lower arm adds to the variety of motions of the hand that of rotation, and also contains in itself the strong muscles which extend and those which contract the fingers. The compact upper part of the hand, with its bones strongly and almost immovably bound together, gives firmness and solidity to all the deeds which require the action of the whole hand. The skin of it, especially upon the palm, though firm and thick, is exquisitely sensitive and very porous, and thus is peculiarly fitted as an instrument to receive and to communicate such influences as can be communicated through the skin. Here, also, snugly packed between the bones, lie the little muscles which give quick, light motions to the fingers; and, of course, through this part of the band pass the tendons which convey the power of the forearm to the fingers; and all are bound down and protected by smooth, strong, sinewy, sheaths, which no one can see without admiration.

Each hand terminates in four fingers and a thumb. The fingers, from their flexibility and quickness, perform most of the light, skillful motions of the hand, guiding its smaller tools, or striking the keys of its instruments by their separate motions, or combining to grasp the implements which require their united strength; and the thumb takes upon itself the task of holding within the grasp of the fingers and subject to their operations the objects upon which, or the instruments by which, they are to do their work. For this purpose the thumb has the power of opposing itself to each finger separately, and pressing a small object, as a pencil, a needle, a bit of paper or cloth, upon its point; and also of opposing them all, and retaining a larger object, as a cane or an axe or the hand of a friend, within their grasp. And both fingers and thumbs share, perhaps in even larger measure, the sensitive openness of skin of the palm. The papillae arrange themselves at the tips in beautiful spiral sweeps, which were Swedenborg's delight, expressing to him the perfection of their structure, and the infinite variety of their possible adaptations.

This beautiful apparatus for expressing the love of doing and communicating is itself very much modified by its work. By some kinds of work in which great strength is exerted, the cuticle is thickened and made hard and firm to protect the tender parts; at the same time, the muscles and even the bones are enlarged, and the shape of the hand is broadened and thickened. By other kinds of work the cuticle is made thin and flexible, and the hands themselves slight and delicate. By long continued exercise of the fingers in separate motions, as in playing upon an instrument, the little muscles of the fingers are separated from one another, and acquire great freedom of motion; and even, in some cases, new little accessory muscles may be formed; while in work which exercises all the fingers jointly, there is a tendency to combine the muscles for mutual support; at least, they often do grow together to such a degree that the power of separate motion is very much diminished.

Every employment has its own peculiar motions to which the hands and fingers must be trained; and by training they acquire skill and deftness. No doubt it is true, also, that the kind of love which is put into the work, whether gentle and considerate or selfish, affects the motions and even the organic forms of the hands. We are not skilled to judge of interior things from the hands; but Swedenborg says that an angel can read from the hand the whole of a man's life, what it has been exteriorly and interiorly; which means that all the affection and thought from which a man has *lived* are actually worked into the forms of his hands.

Possibly it is true, also, that the delicate forms of the fibers and papillae of the hands are affected by the outflow and the reception of the effluvia which constitute the spheres of human lives. Certain it is that the love of *doing* throws all its power into the hands, and expresses itself there not only in works, but by a helpful and strengthening communication of itself, and thus of the life of the man.

We read that when John in the vision saw the Lord in the midst of the seven golden candlesticks, he fell at His feet as dead; by which is signified a sense of his own lifelessness in the presence of the Lord; and then the Lord laid His right hand upon him, and communicated His life to him. Of this, Swedenborg says:

> That the Lord laid His right hand upon him is because communication is effected by the touch of the hands; the reason is that the life of the mind and thence of the body puts itself forth into the arms and through them into the hands; therefore it is that the Lord touched with His hand those whom He raised from the dead and those whom He healed; and that He also touched His disciples when they saw Him transfigured, and fell upon their faces. (*Apocalypse Revealed* §55)

In all these cases, the Lord's Divine love of doing good and giving life was actually put forth through His hand, and was received according to the state of the recipient. For a like reason, when we desire to express sympathy, and to help one who needs it, we naturally stretch out our hand.

On this subject, Swedenborg further writes:

> That to touch is communication, translation, and reception, is because the interiors of man put themselves forth through the exteriors, especially through the touch, and thus communicate themselves to

another, and transfer themselves into another, and as far as the will of the other agrees and makes one, so far they are received. This is especially manifest in the other life; for there all act from the heart, that is, from the will or love, and it is not allowed to express by actions separate from these, nor to speak with simulating lips, that is, separately from the thought of the heart. It is manifest there how the interiors communicate themselves to another, and transfer themselves into another by the touch; and how the other receives them according to his love. The will or the love of everyone constitutes the whole man there, and the sphere of his life flows thence from him like a breathing or vapor, and surrounds him, and makes as it were himself around him, hardly otherwise than like the exhalation about plants in the world, which also is perceived at a distance by odors; also about beasts, which is exquisitely perceived by a sagacious dog. Such exhalation also pours out from every person, as also is known by much experience. But when man lays aside his body, and becomes a spirit or angel, then that effluvium or exhalation is not material as in the world, but it is the spiritual flowing from his love; this then forms a sphere about him, which causes his quality to be perceived at a distance by others.... This sphere is communicated to another, and transferred into him, and is received by the other according to his love. (*Arcana Coelestia* §10130)

This sphere of life comes forth with special strength from the hands, because it comes from the love which is the life, and which concentrates its active power in them.

Upon this is founded our custom of shaking or pressing hands when we meet as friends, by which a mutual interchange of spheres of life is not only represented but effected. Sensitive persons perceive in the touch of the hands a sense of pleasure when the states of life are in harmony, and a peculiar feeling of contraction of the fibers and closing of the pores when they disagree, even though they do not know the state of the person they meet, nor the cause of their feeling. As all the power of one's life throws itself into the hands and expresses itself through them, so the life of the heavens and their power to do good operates through the angels who are in the province of the hands. Swedenborg says:

> In the Greatest Man, they who correspond to the hands and arms, and also to the shoulders, are they who are in power by the truth of faith from good [which is the same as saying that they are in the Lord's wisdom of life from good love]; for they who are in the truth of faith from good, are in the Lord's power; for they attribute all power to Him, and none to themselves, and the more they attribute all power to Him and none to themselves, the greater power they are in; hence the angels are called Powers and Abilities. That the hands, arms, and shoulders in the Greatest Man correspond to power is because the forces and powers of the whole body and of all its viscera concentrate themselves there; for the body exerts its forces and powers by the arms and the hands.
>
> A naked arm bent forward has been seen by me, which had in it so great force and at the same time such terror that not only was I terrified, but it

seemed as if I might be crushed to atoms, and even as to inmosts; it was irresistible. Twice this arm has appeared to me; and hence it has been given me to know that arms signify strength, and hands power. There was also felt a warmth exhaling from that arm. That naked arm is presented to view in various positions, and according to them strikes terror; and in the position just mentioned incredible terror; for it appears able to break to pieces in an instant the bones and the marrows. They who have not been timid in the life of the body, are nevertheless in the other life driven into the greatest terror by that arm. (*Arcana Coelestia* §4932–4935)

This arm, we are told in *Heaven and Hell* §231, is presented from those who are in the province of the arm, and is an embodiment of their power; but their power is not theirs separate from the rest of the heavens; they are in the practical truths of the uses of the heavens, and "into their truths good flows in from the whole heaven," and hence is their power. They exert their power in doing the work of the heavens, especially for those who are out of the heavens. "In general," Swedenborg says, "angels of every society are sent to men, to keep them, to withdraw them from evil affections and thoughts, and to inspire good affections as far as they receive them freely, by which also they rule the deeds or works of men, removing as far as possible evil intentions" (*Heaven and Hell* §391). Again he says:

The will and understanding of man are ruled by the Lord, by angels, and spirits; and because the will and understanding, also all things of the body are

so ruled, since these are thence. And if you will
believe it, man cannot even move a step without the
influx of heaven. That it is so has been shown me by
much experience; it has been given to angels to
move my steps, my actions, my tongue and speech
as they would, and this by influx into my will and
thought; and I found that I could do nothing of
myself. They said afterwards that every man is so
ruled, and that he might know this from the doctrine of the Church and from the Word, for he prays
that God will send His angels who may lead him,
guide his steps, teach him, and inspire what he
should think and what he should speak, and other
such things; although when he thinks in himself
apart from doctrine, he says and believes otherwise. These things are related that it may be known
how great power angels have with man.

But the power of angels in the spiritual world is
so great, that if I were to publish all that I have seen
about it, it would exceed belief. If anything there
resists, which must be removed because it is contrary to Divine order, they throw it down and overturn it merely by an effort of the will and a look. I
have seen mountains which were occupied by the
evil thus cast down and overthrown, sometimes
shaken to pieces from one end to the other, as is the
case in earthquakes, rocks also rent in the middle
even to the deep, and the evil who were upon them
swallowed up. I have also seen some hundreds of
thousands of evil spirits scattered and cast into
hell. Multitude avails nothing against them, neither arts nor cunning nor combinations; they see
all and in a moment dispel it. . . . Such power they

have in the spiritual world. That angels have similar power in the natural world also, when it is granted, is manifest from the Word; as that they gave whole armies to slaughter, that they caused a pestilence of which seventy thousand men died; of which angel it is thus written, "The angel stretched out his hand against Jerusalem to destroy it, but Jehovah repented Him of the evil, and said to the angel that destroyed the people, It is enough; stay now thy hand. And David saw the angel who smote the people.". . . Because the angels have such power, they are called Powers; and it is said in David, "Bless Jehovah ye His angels, most powerful in strength." (*Heaven and Hell* §228–229)

We could hardly ask for a plainer account of the work of the hands of the heavens. They bring forth, and are the instruments of the angelic love of doing good to men. They rule the spirits that are with men, removing the evil and strengthening the good. They are about us, as the organs of the Lord's Providence to protect, guide, and care for us; and through them the whole heavens reach forth to share with men their love and power to do good. We see their work in the protection from danger which we experience daily and hourly; in the leadings which we so often follow away from unseen danger, or to unknown good; in the sense of strong support which comes in trouble; and especially in the lifting of the mind above the pains of the body and the cares of the world even to the gates of heaven, as the time of death gradually approaches.

They inspire the strength of a just cause, giving both protection and power to individuals and to armies. They are an irresistible power present with us, which can do anything that it is wise to do for the benefit of mankind.

"All the powers of the life of the Greatest Man, or heaven, terminate in the two hands and two feet; and the hands, as also the feet, terminate in ten fingers or toes" (*Apocalypse Explained* §675 end).

The power of the Lord through heaven is exerted through the angels of these provinces; and it is of them in a special sense, as the means of the Lord's protection and providence about men, that the Scriptures say, "The eternal God is thy dwelling place, and underneath are the everlasting arms" (Deuteronomy 33:27).

The general functions of this kind are exercised by the hands as a whole; particulars of the function are performed by individual fingers. The angels of the thumb, like the thumb itself, can have no leading part, but are effective in cooperating with all those in the fingers.

The nails are of hairlike structure, protecting and stiffening the ends of the fingers. They have a correspondence with literal truths or precepts concerning the uses to be done, held not intelligently, but resolutely and inflexibly—thus for the support of those who are sensitive and yielding.

THE FEET

THE FEET HAVE MANY POINTS OF RESEMBLANCE TO THE
hands; their general structure is similar, with some modifications, so that in cases of necessity they are taught to
do in some degree the work of hands, and the hands are
degraded to the work of the feet. But they are not formed
for so great a variety of motions; their solid part is larger
and firmer, and the movable divisions are shorter and
with much less capacity for varied and quick movements.
Their thumbs, also, or great toes, are not intended to meet
and assist the individual motions of the other toes, but
step squarely with them, bearing a great part of the bur-
den, and merely balancing the others. As to touch, again,
though the feet are perhaps more sensitive than the hands
to impressions from without, they have far less power of
examining and individualizing the sources of those
impressions. It is enough for them to know quickly that
they are there, and, if injurious, must be avoided or
removed. They leave it to the hands to examine into the
nature of them and do the work of removing. Their work
is to support the body, and carry it firmly from place to
place. They are not intended to express and communicate
what is in us, nor to operate upon objects outside of ourselves. They are simply to carry ourselves forward, feeling
the ground as they go, and stepping firmly.

Swedenborg makes a curious statement in regard to the sensitiveness of the feet, which ought to be presented here. He says:

> I wish also to add that those papillae or glands which provide the sole of the foot with an acute sense of touch, appear to be woven of fibers from the cerebrum itself, which flow down the length of the spinal cord, even to its extremity, and afterwards go off in the nerves; so that the sense of touch of the sole itself communicates more immediately with the cerebrum than the touch of other parts of the body, whence there is a more acute sense in the papillae, and their changes of state are instantly presented to the cerebrum; thus also the lasts are connected with the firsts in the corporeal system. (*Animal Kingdom* part 7, p. 27)

In treating of the correspondence of the hands and the feet, Swedenborg says that "the hands signify the interiors of the natural, and the feet the exteriors of it " (*Arcana Coelestia* §7442); also, "To lift the hand signifies power in spiritual things; and to lift the foot signifies power in natural things," and he explains, "By spiritual is meant that in the natural which is of the light of heaven, and by natural that which is of the light of the world" (*Arcana Coelestia* §5328).

In describing the position of the heavens in the Greatest Man, he states that "the highest heaven forms the head even to the neck, the second or middle heaven forms the breast to the loins and the knees, and the lowest or first heaven forms the feet even to the soles, and also the arms to the fingers " (*Heaven and Hell* §65). To this he adds, "The church on earth corresponds to the soles of the feet" (*Apocalypse Explained* §606). And again, "The church not conjoined to the church in the heavens is meant by 'under the feet'; but when it is conjoined it is meant by the feet" (*Apocalypse Revealed* §533).

In explaining the words concerning the Two Witnesses, that the Spirit of Life from God entered into them, and they stood upon their feet, he says:

By the Spirit of Life from God is signified spiritual life, and by standing upon the feet is signified natural life agreeing with spiritual, and thus vivified by the Lord. That this is signified is because by the Spirit of Life is meant the internal of man, which is called the internal man, which regarded in itself is spiritual; for the spirit of man thinks and wills, and to think and to will in itself is spiritual. By standing upon the feet is signified the external of man, which also is called the external man, which in itself is natural; for the body speaks and does what its spirit thinks and wills, and to speak and do is natural. . . . Every man who is reformed is first reformed as to his internal man, and afterwards as to the external; the internal man is not reformed by merely knowing and understanding the truths and goods by which man is saved, but by willing them and loving them; but the external man by speaking and doing the things which the internal man wills and loves; and as far as it does this, so far the man is regenerated. That he is not regenerated before is because his internal is not before in effect, but only in cause, and the cause unless it be in the effect is dissipated. It is like a house built upon the ice, which falls to the bottom when the ice is melted by the sun; in a word, it is like a man without feet upon which he can stand and walk; such is the internal or spiritual man unless it is founded in the external or natural. (*Apocalypse Revealed* §510)

The two witnesses were the acknowledgment of the Divine Human of the Lord, and a life according to the Commandments; and they stood upon their feet full of the spirit of life from God when these two essentials of the New Church were fully received by Swedenborg and the angels associated with him, and were brought down into the world in his life (see *Apocalypse Explained* §665).

In general, to walk is to live; and, in a good sense, it is to live in the Lord's ways, and to carry the spirit into the new states to which His ways lead. As the hands, therefore, are the love of communicating and doing good, the feet are the love of obeying and of doing right.

The provinces from the knees to the feet are in this love of obedience; and men on earth are in conjunction with them and live with their power when they love above all things to live the Commandments from the Lord. Through this love the Lord leads the race into new states and conditions of life. In the heavens the experiences acquired here are better understood, and attain fuller development; but here the advance is made into the new conditions and applications of truth, which is appropriately done by those in the province of the feet.

If we may trust Swedenborg's statement about the connection between the sensitive soles of the feet and the cerebrum, we should infer that not only are they who love the commandments living in unity with the lowest heaven, but they receive also the immediate attention and care of the angels with whom the Lord is most sensibly present, the wisest of the angels, who thus are enabled to care for their state with all the resources of the heavens, especially by commanding for their service the provinces of the hands and arms and legs and feet.

I will add only a word in regard to the difference between the right and the left sides. "The things which are on the right side," Swedenborg tells us, "correspond to good from which are truths, and the things of the left side correspond to truths by which is good" (*Arcana Coelestia* §10061).

The right hand, therefore, responds to the call of the will, and expresses the power of the will; but the motions of the left are made with thought and comparative difficulty, and are also weaker.

But in walking, the left foot is by common usage made the leading foot, and Swedenborg declares that evil spirits turn their bodies about from right to left, but good spirits from left to right (*Divine Love and Wisdom* §270). The cause of this he ascribes to the direction of the heavenly gyres in the good, and the contrary direction in the evil. But the cause of this may be that it is good and heavenly for the will to be guided by the understanding and to learn to love what is true and right; but it is infernal for the will to compel the understanding to think from and to confirm the natural desires and impulses.

THE EAR

THE EXTERNAL EAR IS AN ORGAN FOR RECEIVING AND COL-
lecting the vibrations which we recognize as sound. This
outer ear is composed of elastic, vibratory cartilage, covered closely with a protecting skin, and thrown into sweeping folds, no doubt conforming to the natural sweeps of
aerial undulations and designed to catch them all, coming from every direction, and conduct them to the inner
ear. This is a conduction of vibrations, not of air; and it
is accomplished partly by the reception of the vibrations
by the cartilage itself, and partly by the reflection and con-
centration of these vibrations into the column of air leading into the auditory tube. No doubt the vibrations of the
cartilage and those of the adjacent air make one; and, as
the cartilage reflects and turns the little waves towards the
inner ear, it accompanies them with sympathetic tremblings to the bony passage, and, on the under side, even
halfway through the passage; nor does it leave them till it
has had time to impart its tremulous sympathy to the
bone itself, with which it is strongly and closely connected.

Across this bony tube, at a distance of a little less than
an inch from the surface of the skull, is stretched a membrane commonly called the drum of the ear. It is really a
triple membrane, composed of a fibrous layer in the middle stretched from bone to bone, covered outside by a delicate continuation of the skin which lines the tube, and

inside by another delicate membrane continuous with the lining of the middle cavity of the ear.

Upon this drum, or tympanum, are concentrated all the motions which have been gathered from the atmosphere, which are now imparted to the drum by the air itself, which is in contact with it; by the lining membrane of the tube, which forms the outer skin of the drum; and by the tremblings of the bone in which the circumference of its middle layer is inserted.

The sounds that thus come to the drum of the ear are a confused mass, in immense variety as to force, pitch, and quality, mingled together apparently in hopeless perplexity. It is like the stream of fluids brought to a gland—as, for instance, by the portal vein to the liver—there to be strained and sorted; the worthless to be cast out, the better sort to be put to a low use, and the pure, refined stream to be sent into the circulation for the benefit of the life of the body.

In the ear the stream to be examined is not a stream of fluid, but of motion; and we must look not for open passages, but for conductors of vibrations.

In the drum of the ear, with its adjacent bony wall, the expectant mass of vibrations is collected, searching for avenues of entrance. Conspicuous among these avenues is a chain of three small bones, one end of which is attached to the middle of the drum, at the point of greatest motion, and the other, in shape like the flat plate of a stirrup, is continuous as to its periosteum with another little membranous window on the opposite side of the chamber across which the chain is extended. That inner membranous window is the entrance to another chamber, properly called the inner ear, whose wonderful structure we will consider presently. The chamber crossed by the chain of bones is called the middle ear. The bones are arranged as a series of levers in such a manner that whatever motion is imparted to them by the drum is carried to the inner window with a somewhat diminished range of motion, but proportionately increased force. They seem capable of receiving and transmitting every variety and form of atmospheric tremble; but, however rapidly the tremblings may succeed one another, only one pulsation can be conveyed at a time, and thus the pulsations to be examined are in a degree strained of their conflicting elements, arranged in a sequence, and transmitted distinctly to the inner ear. Other vibrations not thus conveyed successively and distinctly by the bones, are transmitted more obscurely by the air which fills the middle ear, and also by its lining membrane and bony walls, and are received obscurely by the free rim of the membranous window to which the chain is applied, by another membranous window, called the round window, and by the bony wall of the inner ear. The most violent vibrations, which, if allowed to act with unmodified force would injure the inner ear, are as it were rejected by the way of the Eustachian tube, which leads from the middle ear to the pharynx; and perhaps are neutralized in part by the air of the large air cells in the mastoid process, which opens into the middle ear opposite to the Eustachian tube.

The particular stream of pulsations which shall be received by the little bones is in a considerable degree determined by small muscles, which, by pulling upon the bones, regulate the tension of the membranes, and thus tune them to receive most distinctly the sounds selected. In this, too, the ear resembles the glands, every one of which draws to itself a stream of such materials as it desires.

It is in part because the ear has this power of selection that the Lord commands us, "Take heed what ye hear."

It is by the action of these muscles that we are enabled to attend to the sounds of a single instrument in an orchestra, one part in a choir, one voice in a company, an individual bird or cricket in the chorus of a summer's day; which sound thus chosen is carried to the inner ear distinctly by the chain of bones, and is accompanied obscurely by the other sounds.

Arrived at the oval window of the inner ear, the current of pulsations finds ready admittance, and permeates with its successive thrills a delicate fluid which fills all the chambers of the inner ear, containing freely suspended in itself minute stony particles. And, first, it is received in a somewhat spacious anteroom, or vestibule, whose wall is loosely lined with an inner wall of membrane plentifully supplied with fibers of the auditory nerve.

As the pulsations advance successively to the inner chambers, their more subtle elements will be disclosed and set free; but here at the entrance their general quality is first perceived, as to its loudness or softness, continuity or interruptions; to which general perception the simple form of the anteroom is well adapted.

From the part of the vestibule sometimes called the "utriculus," open three semicircular canals. These, like the vestibule, enclose loose membranous linings which repeat their own forms, and which, in a bulb-like swelling at one end of each canal, contain a large supply of nervous fibers.

At present the scientific view of these canals is that their use is not as organs of hearing, but as means of preserving the equilibrium. No doubt they have this use; but it is not so easy to believe that they have no part in the function of hearing. The eyes, also, in some persons, are an important means of equilibration; but no one can doubt that this is secondary to their function of sight. In the eyes, however, the assistance in preserving the equilibrium is dependent on the sight; but this service from the canals does not at all depend upon the hearing, but upon the motion of the fluid contents.

The membranous canals exist in fishes, and their bony walls also in reptiles, which have scarcely a trace of the inmost part of the ear, the cochlea, which receives its full development only in warm-blooded animals, and especially in mammals.

If the canals do have any part in the hearing, probably it is to distinguish articulations; for the first process in analysis should be to measure the last modification given to the tones, which, in speaking, is by the mouth in forming words. It seems as if the canals lying on three sides of a cube could measure any form that could be given by the mouth.

Having received from the stream of sound the impression of force and quantity in the vestibule, and possibly of the forms of its articulations in the canals, there remain to be distinctly perceived its pitch and musical quality, and those more delicate thrills within the tones, which express the interior affection of the speakers or singers, and which are commonly attributed wholly to the "overtones," but may in part have another origin. For this analysis, we have left an instrument of exquisite adaptation to the purpose called "the cochlea."

Into the hollow center of a spiral staircase, resembling in its outer covering two and a half turns of a snail shell, enters a large nerve, which extends its fibers plentifully over the elastic, bony stairs. These delicate plates of bone are attached at their inner ends to the core of the shell. At the lower part, where the diameter is large, they are long; but they diminish with the spiral to the top, like the diminishing teeth of the comb of a musical box. At their outer end they are free, but there the membranes which cover them above and below separate, and leave a triangular space between them as they run divergently to the outer wall of the shell. In this little spiral chamber, coiled at the outer edge of the stairs, is a most delicate apparatus of nervous fibers and cells and hairs, almost too minute for the microscope, called the "organ of Corti."

We must not forget to notice that the shell is filled above and below the staircase with conducting fluid, which passes freely from one side to the other through an opening over the stairs; that the space over the staircase opens immediately into the vestibule; and that under the staircase is the membrane of the round window, communicating with the middle ear.

The elastic, bony fibers of the staircase are sufficient in number and variety to harmonize in vibration with musical tones of any shades of pitch which we have the power to appreciate; and at their extremities lies an apparatus distinctly more minute and exquisite, capable of appreciating an inner music within the music, if such there may be.

The organ of Corti does not exist in birds; though they undoubtedly can distinguish variations of pitch quickly and accurately.

It is still a question among physiologists, whether the vibrations which are perceived as sound affect the bones and fluids of the ear as to their masses or as to their particles—whether, for example, the little chain of the middle ear is shaken as a chain, or communicates the thrills of sound by the vibrations of the particles of bone and membrane of which the chain is composed.

Swedenborg believed that both motions existed—that the larger forms of motion and of sound were communicated by the general motions of the bones and fluids, and that a more subtle tremor permeated the very substance of the bones, membranes, and fluids.

The things extracted or secreted from the stream of sound by the laboratory of the ear are not fluids or solids, but motions; they are not even forms of fluids or solids, as are the impressions received by the organs of touch, taste, and smell; but they are forms of living activity. And these varieties of living motion are distinctly communicated to the fibers of the auditory nerve, and by them imparted to the brain. The portion of the brain which is the seat of the conscious reception of sounds through the ear, lies quite near, in what is called the superior temperosphenoidal convolution. But an important part of the auditory nerve goes directly to the cerebellum, which is the seat of the affections of the life, and of involuntary motion, and there has a tendency to produce immediate impulsive action in response to its impulses.

The optic nerves are cerebral nerves, having no direct communication with the cerebellum. They minister, therefore, primarily to the intelligence; but the auditory nerves minister directly to the affections as well as to the intelligence. Probably the conscious hearing, with intelligent reception of the ideas conveyed by the sounds, is in the convolution of the cerebrum especially devoted to this sense. Other effects of warning or guidance or direction are produced through the cerebellum, and by indirect communication with other parts of the cerebrum.

The things which enter by the sense of sight, enter into man's understanding and enlighten him . . . but the things which enters by the sense of hearing, enter into the understanding and at the same time into the will; wherefore by the hearing is signified perception and obedience. Hence it is that in human language it is a received form of expression to speak of hearing anyone, and also of giving ear to anyone;

likewise of being a hearer, and of hearkening; and by hearing anyone is understood to perceive, and by giving ear to anyone is meant to obey; as also by being a hearer; and both are signified by hearkening. This form of expression has flowed down from the spiritual world, in which the spirit of man is; but whence this is in the spiritual world shall also be explained. They who, in the spiritual world, are in the province of the ear, are forms of obedience from perception... and the province of the ear is in the axis of heaven, and therefore into it, or into those who are there, the whole spiritual world flows, with the perception that it must so be done; for this is the reigning perception in heaven; hence it is that they who are in that province are forms of obedience from perception.

That the things which enter by hearing, enter immediately by the understanding into the will, may be further illustrated by the instruction of the angels of the celestial kingdom, who are the wisest. Those angels receive all their wisdom by hearing, and not by sight; for whatever they hear of Divine things, from veneration and love, they receive in the will and make of their life.... From these things it is manifest that hearing is given to man chiefly for receiving wisdom, but sight for receiving intelligence; wisdom is to perceive, will, and do; intelligence is to learn and perceive. (*Apocalypse Explained* §14; also *Heaven and Hell* §270–271)

The spirits who correspond to the hearing, or who constitute the province of the ear, are they who are in simple obedience, that is, who do not reason whether a thing be so, but because it is so said by others, they believe that it is so. .... There are many varieties of the spirits who correspond to the ear, that is, to its functions and offices; there are those who relate to each little organ in it, to the external ear, to the membrane which is called the drum of the ear, to the interior membranes which are called windows (*fenestrae*), to the malleus, the stapes, the incus, the canals, the cochlea, and to parts still deeper, even to those substances which are nearer to the spirit, and which at length are in the spirit, and lastly are intimately conjoined with those who belong to the internal sight, from whom they are distinguished by this, that they have not so much discernment, but assent to them as if passive. (*Arcana Coelestia* §4653)

There was a spirit who spoke with me at the left auricle, at its hinder part, where are the elevating, muscles of the auricle; he told me that he was sent to say that he does not at all reflect upon the things which others say, provided he takes them in with his ears. .... It was said that such as attend little to the sense of a thing, are they who belong to the cartilaginous and bony part of the external ear. (*Arcana Coelestia* §4656)

To the interiors of the ear belong those who have the sight of the inner hearing, and obey what its spirit there dictates, and express its dictates fitly. (*Arcana Coelestia* §4658)

After describing some who seem to have been perversions of the faculty, he says that one came to him who was said to have been "a person of the highest reputation in the learned world, and it was given me to believe that it was Aristotle."

Swedenborg perceived that the things which he had written were from interior thought, and that the philosophical terms which he invented were not mere terms with him, as they were with many of his followers, but were descriptive of interior things; "and that he was excited to such things by the delight of affection and the desire of knowing the things which were of thought, and that he followed obediently the things which his spirit had dictated; wherefore he applied himself to the right ear."

After relating some intelligent conversation with him concerning analytical knowledge, and about the Lord, Swedenborg continues:

> A woman appeared to me, who stretched out her hand, wishing to stroke his cheek; when I wondered at this, he said that when he was in the world such a woman often appeared to him, who as it were stroked his cheek, and that her hand was beautiful. The angelic spirits said that such women sometimes appeared to the ancients, and were called by them Pallades, and that she appeared to him from spirits who when they lived as men in ancient times, were delighted with ideas and indulged in thoughts, but without philosophy, and because such spirits were with him, and were delighted with him because he thought interiorly, they presented representatively such a woman. (*Arcana Coelestia* §4658)

These things are said to illustrate the quality of men who relate to the inner ear, namely, that they have an interior perception of truth as if it were told to them; and that they speak and write it obediently, delighting in it, and perceiving that it is true because it agrees with their interior life.

In the Greatest Man they are in the outer ear who love to receive by hearing and impart what they receive without discrimination of quality, though as they are a part of heaven, they must have greater general delight in receiving and faithfully repeating good things. The drum of the ear loves to collect in a summary, in which all particulars are fairly and fully presented, all that comes from the outer reporters. The bones love to draw from that summary whatever coheres in a sequence, and with an inflexible stiffness to prevent anything from passing which will not make part of a receivable sequence. The vestibule loves to perceive and to transmit to the brain and to the whole heaven its impressions of the power and quantity of the truth received. As organs of equilibration, the correspondence of the semicircular canals is perhaps indicated by the common expression "to keep a level head," that is, to keep a clear sense of our position and relation to circumstances, and of what is to be done. If they have any part in the hearing, as suggested, it is likely to be a part relating definitely to what is to be done, and this, perhaps, is the discernment of articulation. And the cochlea loves to know the inner wisdom and purpose of the instruction, in its effect upon the harmony of the heavens and their openness to receive interior life from the Lord, which effects conjunction with Him.

All the desire of the heavens for these things is concentrated in the ears; and the ears, in turn, transmit to the desiring angels the instruction they receive, with their own love for it, and desire to obey it.

As to whence come the sounds to the angels of the ears, we have no instruction. But they may come in part from spirits and men outside of the heavens; for we read that the thoughts of these from affection are heard in heaven:

> The supplication, although tacit, of those who supplicate from the heart, is heard as a cry in heaven. This is the case when men only think, and more when they bemoan themselves, from a sincere heart. . . . It is the same with those who mourn; (*dolent* for *docent*) they are heard in heaven as crying. Not only the thoughts, but more especially the affections, which are of good and truth, speak in heaven. . . . Affections for evil and falsity are not at all heard in heaven, even if the man who supplicates from them cries aloud with his hands tightly closed, and raises them and his eyes to heaven. These are heard in hell, and there also as cries if they are ardent. (*Arcana Coelestia* §9202, see also *Spiritual Diary* §4821)

Affections and prayers that are only individual, we should suppose would be heard only by individuals or small societies; but those that express general states of the community might be heard by larger bodies.

Also those in the province of the ears may be affected by the speech of those in the provinces of the lungs and the mouth, who utter the Word of the Lord and thoughts of Divine wisdom from it.

To the inner ear, besides the interior wisdom received from this source, may there not come also interior perceptions of wisdom from the Lord Himself, as we now receive them from spirits and angels?

THE EYE

"The light of the body is the eye." Through the eye the light affects the body, informs the brain, and through the brain all other organs of the body. And in the brain it meets the mind, which there delights in the forms of life which the eye presents to it, and flashes forth through the eye a responsive, spiritual light, expressive of intelligence and love of knowing.

With a peculiar tenderness, the body guards and protects its delicate organ of light, enclosing it in a strong, bony socket, just beneath the brain, which socket it softly wads, and then lines with smooth and carefully lubricated membranes. It shades it and protects it from blows by projecting the roof over it like eaves, and turns away the descending moisture of the forehead by the capillary eaves-trough of the eyebrows.

It closes and rests the eyes with smoothly-fitting, elastic shutters, which are provided each with a reservoir of tears, and are ever on the watch to remove with moistened touch every particle of dust, and to keep the surface of the eye bright, clear, and moist.

As to these protecting parts, there is slight analogy between the eye and the ear; for the ear deals with the undulations of the air and needs protection only from the insects and coarser particles which fly in the air; its protective organs are therefore limited to a few hairs and the adhesive cerumen which guard and moisten the auditory passage. But the eye is concerned with the undulations of the ether, and needs protection from the drying, chilling, and chafing of the air itself as well as from all the foreign particles contained in it.

Internally the structure of the eye is more closely analogous to that of the ear, and we may obtain valuable aid from the grosser organ in tracing the sequence of uses in the more delicate.

First, in the ear, we observe the visible auricle with its convolutions turned every way to catch and concentrate the vibrations of the air. In the eye the correlative function is performed by the cornea—a totally different organ in appearance, but perfectly qualified to receive and concentrate upon the inner parts of the eye the undulatory rays in the ether.

In the ear next we find the tympanum, which receives in a confused mass all the sounds gathered by the outer ear, and begins the work of assorting them; first by neutralizing the most violent shocks, with the help of the inner air chamber, the mastoid process, and the Eustachian tube, and then by transmitting its central undulations in a successive stream to the little chain of bones.

The multitude of rays of light gathered by the cornea from various directions are received similarly upon the iris, which immediately absorbs and neutralizes by its own pigment cells and dark lining membrane the rays that are too divergent and scattering for service, also cutting off by the closing of its pupil those that are too intense, and transmits through its center—the pupil of the eye—the rays that are most fit to form distinct images.

Over the bones of the ear are communicated successively, one by one, the vibrations of the air, to the window of the inner ear, where the first branches of the auditory nerve are expanded, and the sense of hearing properly begins. And through the pupil and the lenses of the eye—aqueous, crystalline, and vitreous—are brought together upon the surface of the retina, or the first general expansion of the optic nerve, the rays that proceed successively from the same objects, and are capable of leaving a distinct impression of their form and colors. The ear has the power of selecting the series of sounds to which it will attend, as the notes of a single instrument in an orchestra, by attuning in agreement with them the tympanum and the window of the inner ear, by means of the little muscles attached to the chain of bones; and those sounds to which it is attuned are transmitted distinctly, but others obscurely. And so the eye has the power of adjusting its sequence of lenses to receive and concentrate distinctly the rays that come from a particular object, at the same time that they transmit obscurely those that come from other objects. This power it has partly from the muscles which turn the head, and the smaller muscles which direct the eyeball in a particular direction; but especially from the ciliary muscle which encircles the crystalline lens, and by increasing or diminishing the convexity of its face, attuning it, as it were, to the rays that come from different distances, according to the desire of observing.

Within the inner ear we traced in order the apparatus for distinguishing quantity or intensity of sound, articulation, pitch (including harmony and melody), and pathos. And the greater part of this apparatus is on a comparatively large scale, because the undulatory forms which it measures are those of the lowest atmosphere, which is the air.

The correlative qualities of light, which the eye measures, are those of light and shade, or intensity—which seem to correspond to the qualities perceived in the vestibule of the ear, and which first strike a child's eye, or our own half-closed—then the particulars of form, corresponding to those of articulation; and then the varieties of color, to which we apply the term harmony.

The instruments by which these qualities are appropriately received, and their properties of varied motion are conveyed to the brain, must be as delicate as the vibratory forms of the ether. It is no wonder that, except as to their most general structure, they have so long escaped observation. The closely-woven, nervous network, from which the retina has its name, has, until recently, been the only sensitive part of the apparatus described; but now, behind the retina, and extending from its fibers outward to the layer of pigment cells of the choroid coat of the eye, is described a minute and highly complicated nervous structure of granules and fibers and interlacing, terminating in a closely set apparatus of minutest rods alternating with cones. It is like an exquisitely organized velvet nap standing upon the expanded tissue of the optic nerve.

The precise functions of the several parts of this structure are not known; but it is plain that we have here presented forms sufficiently varied and delicate for the wonderful work required of them.

The nerves of sight seem to be connected especially with the convolution of the brain which is called the "angular gyrus," and also to have connection with the whole of the occipital lobes. If any part of these is in good order, and the connection undisturbed, the sense of sight is possible. No doubt there is indirect communication with other parts of the brain; but not such as to give the sense of sight. The auditory nerve, as has been said, as to one important branch, communicates directly with the cerebellum, and is the means of affecting the feelings directly as well as the intelligence. The nerve of sight affects the intelligence, and the feelings only through the intelligence.

There is a further difference between the animations of sound and those of light, as between generals and particulars. For the ether by its compositions produces the air, as materials of the air again are consolidated into water. The activities of the ether, therefore, affect the minute forms of the brain of which the generals are composed, or the single glands by the combination of which are formed composite glands.

As, therefore, through the air and by the ears, general animations are communicated, through the ether and by the eye are given particulars which fill those generals, and which never can be described to the hearing. We know this to true, practically, in regards to scenery and to every work of nature; and Swedenborg says that in heaven the angels express to the eye by the curves and points of their writing, ideas which cannot be communicated by sound.

The hearing corresponds to the love of being instructed, guided, and affected obediently; and the correspondence of the sight is with the love of obtaining clear, distinct ideas, of being intelligent in spiritual things and wise in heavenly things.

Swedenborg says:

> That the sense of sight corresponds to the affection of understanding and being wise, is because the sight of the body altogether corresponds to the sight of its spirit, thus to the understanding. For there are two lights, one which is of the world from the sun, and another which is of heaven from the Lord; in the light of the world there is no intelligence, but in the light of heaven there is intelli-

gence. Hence as far as the things in man which are of the light of the world are illuminated by those which are of the light of heaven, so far man is intelligent and wise; that is, as far as they correspond. (*Arcana Coelestia* §4405)

The eye is the most noble organ of the face, and communicates with the understanding more immediately than the other sensory organs of man. It is also modified by a more subtle atmosphere than the ear. (*Arcana Coelestia* §4407)

It has been made plain to me by much experience that the sight of the left eye corresponds to truths which are of the understanding, and the right eye to affections of truth which also are of the understanding; hence that the left eye corresponds to truths of faith, and the right eye to good things of faith. (*Arcana Coelestia* §4410)

Perhaps we might interpret these words as meaning that the left eye corresponds to the understanding of things that we clearly perceive to be so; and the right eye to the understanding of things that we love; or that the left eye corresponds to the understanding of what is true, and the right eye to the understanding of what is good.

All things in the eye have their correspondences in the heavens; as the three humors, aqueous, vitreous, and crystalline; and not only the humors but the coats also—yea, every part. The more interior things of the eye have the more beautiful and pleasant correspondences, but differently in each heaven. The light which proceeds from the Lord, when it flows into the inmost or third heaven, is received there as good which is called charity; and when it flows into the middle or second heaven, mediately and immediately, it is received as truth which is from charity; but when this truth flows into the lowest or first heaven, mediately and immediately, it is received substantially, and appears there as a paradise, and elsewhere as a city in which are palaces. Thus the correspondences succeed one another even to the external sight of the angels. Likewise in man, in the ultimate of sight, which is the eye, it is presented materially through the sight, whose objects are the things of the visible world. Man who is in love and charity, and thence in faith, has his interiors such; for they correspond to the three heavens, and he is in form a very little heaven.

There was a certain person who was known to me in the life of the body, but not as to his disposition and interior affections; he has occasionally conversed with me in the other life, but a little at a distance. He usually manifested himself by pleasant representatives; for he could present such things as were delightful, as colors of every kind, and beautiful colored forms; he could introduce infants beautifully decorated, and very many like things which are pleasant and enjoyable. He acted by a gentle and soft influx, and this into the coat of the left eye. By such means he insinuated himself into the affections of others, with the end of making their life pleasant and delightful. It was said to me by the angels that such are they who belong to

the coats of the eye, and that they communicate
with the paradisal heavens where truths and goods
are represented in substantial form. (*Arcana Coelestia* §4411–4412)

These paradisal heavens, or societies, I infer are in the
eyes of the lowest heaven, and communicate by correspondence with the same provinces of the interior heavens.

The eyes of the inner heavens are delighted with the
perception of interior goodness and truth, presented in
simplest forms; but the eyes of the lower heavens love to
see and to cause others to see the same things in full representatives. Of these Swedenborg further teaches:

The eye, or rather its sight, corresponds especially
with those societies in the other life, which are in
paradisal things, which appear above, a little to the
right, where are presented to the life gardens with
so many genera and species of trees and flowers
that those in the whole world are respectively few.
In every object there, there is something of intelligence and wisdom which shines forth, so that you
may say that they are at the same time in paradises
of intelligence and wisdom. These are the things
which affect those who are there from the inmosts,
and thus gladden not only their sight, but also at
the same time their understanding. Those paradisal things are in the first heaven, and in the very
entrance to the interiors of that heaven, and are representatives which descend from the higher heaven
when the angels of the higher heaven converse
together intellectually concerning the truths of
faith. The speech of the angels there is by spiritual

and celestial ideas, which to them are forms of expression, and continually by series of representations of such beauty and pleasantness as cannot at all be described. These beauties and pleasantnesses of their discourse are what are represented as paradisal things in the lower heaven. This heaven is distinguished into several heavens, to which correspond the particulars which are in the chambers of the eye. There is the heaven where are the paradisal gardens which have been spoken of; there is a heaven where are variously colored atmospheres, where the whole air glitters as if from gold, silver, pearls, precious stones, flowers, in minute forms, and innumerable other things; there is a rainbow heaven, where are most beautiful rainbows, great and small, variegated with most splendid colors. Every one of these things exists by the light which is from the Lord, in which are intelligence and wisdom; hence there is in every object there, something of intelligence of truth and of wisdom of good, which is thus presented representatively. (*Arcana Coelestia* §4528)

Swedenborg also describes "beautiful shrubberies and most pleasant flower gardens of immense extent," in which everything shines with the changeful light of intelligence and wisdom. And he adds:

They who are in the intelligence itself and the wisdom, from which those things originate, are in such a state of happiness that the things which have been mentioned are esteemed by them of but little importance. Some also who had said when in the paradisal things that they exceeded every decree of happiness, were therefore taken more toward the right into a heaven which shone with still greater splendor, where was likewise the blessedness of the intelligence and wisdom which was in such things; and then when they were there, speaking with me again, they said that the things which they had seen before were respectively nothing. And at length they were taken to that heaven where from the satisfaction of interior affection they could scarcely subsist; for the satisfaction penetrated to the marrows, which being as it were dissolved by the satisfaction, they began to fall into a holy swoon. (*Arcana Coelestia* §4529)

Here are described, apparently, those who constitute the successively interior parts of the eye. Possibly they who are in the first sensitive coat and the adjacent humor love the paradisal representatives; those in a more interior province delight in the intelligence and wisdom represented; and those in an inmost department are satisfied with the interior affection from which that wisdom exists.

These provinces, as here described, appear to have been near together and closely related—not in widely separated heavens. Probably they were all in the inmost Christian heaven, the situation of which agrees with what is said of these paradisal heavens.

Here, also, in the eyes of the Christian heaven, are the homes of those who now die as infants (*Apocalypse Revealed* §876). They are in the province of the eyes (*Heaven and Hell* §333); those of a celestial disposition in the right eye, and those of a spiritual nature in the left, "directly in the line or radius in which angels look to the Lord" (*Heaven and Hell* §332). "They are surrounded by atmospheres according to the state of their perfection . . . especially there are presented to them atmospheres as of playing infants in least inconspicuous forms, but perceptible only by an inmost idea; from these they receive the heavenly idea that all the things about them are alive, and that they are in the life of the Lord, which affects them with inmost happiness" (*Arcana Coelestia* §2297). "They are instructed by representatives . . . and these are so beautiful, and at the same time so full of wisdom from within as to surpass belief" (*Heaven and Hell* §335). Indeed, by simplest representatives they are instructed in the holiest things of the Lord's mercy and providence, which they perceive very clearly, though in a simple and infantile manner. And in their delightful gardens, the flowers of which flash gladness through their glowing colors (*Heaven and Hell* §337), they enjoy delightful perceptions of innocence and charity.

It is impossible not to see the likeness of infants in the transparent humors of the eye, full of the forming images of light. And among these humors that most delicate fluid immediately under the cornea, receiving all light, but without distinctions, is unmistakably like the first state of infancy, open to all impressions, yet seizing none but the most general—even in regard to sight, being content with the light, and scarcely discriminating even the brightest colors. The next medium is the crystalline lens, which is strongly characterized by the effort to receive distinctly the light from particular things, and seems plainly to correspond to infants in their effort to fix their attention, to discriminate, and to recognize particular objects. The vitreous humor continues the effort to concentrate the light in distinct images, and lies all around in contact with the retina, upon which such images are formed. Is not this the heaven in which children are taught by elaborate representatives, carefully and fully presented? Here also must be the paradises in which are so many perfect forms of human intelligence and affection.

It is in the different heavens corresponding to the chambers of the eye that the beautiful atmospheres appear. It is in one of these, possibly the outer chamber, that "the universal aura glitters as if from gold, silver, pearls, precious stones, flowers in their least forms, and innumerable things" (*Arcana Coelestia* §1621). In an inner heaven, which seems beautifully like the crystalline chamber surrounded by the iris, "the whole atmosphere appears to consist of very small, continued rainbows. . . . Around is the form of a very large rainbow, encompassing the whole heaven, most beautiful, being composed of similar smaller rainbows, which are images of the larger. Every single color thus consists of innumerable rays constituting one general, perceptible ray, which is as it were a modification of the origins of light from the celestial and spiritual things which produce it, and which at the same time present to the sight a representative idea" (*Arcana Coelestia* §1623; see also *Arcana Coelestia* §4528).

With the children in these beautiful heavens are the mothers and maidens who care for them, themselves in sympathy with the open innocence of the children, but wise to guide them in their heavenly sports. And penetrating everywhere through the humors are said to be, and no doubt there are, delicate tubes and fibers, as transparent as the humors, keeping them constantly changing according to their needs and the requirements of the eye.

The objects of delight to the eyes, and sight and enlightenment to the heavens, are revelations of truth and goodness from the Lord Himself, with the representatives of them. These revelations have a general ultimate in our Scriptures, just as all possible human uses and relations have a general representative in the human body. Divine wisdom concerning the development of human life is contained in the Word, and shines from it as light to the eyes of angels, or can be presented as beautiful representatives of human affection and thought. There are no beautiful things in heaven or on earth that are not representatives of these.

> The Word of the Lord, when it is read by a man who loves it and who lives in charity, and even by a man who from a simple heart believes what is written, having formed no principles contrary to the truth of faith contained in the internal sense, is displayed by the Lord to the angels with such beauty and with such pleasantness, accompanied also by representatives—and this with an inexpressible variety according to the whole state of the angels at the time—that every particular is perceived as if it had life. (*Arcana Coelestia* §1767)

> The angels have a clearer and fuller understanding of the internal sense of the Word when it is read by little boys and girls than when by adults who are not in the faith of charity. The reason is, as was told me, that little children are in a state of mutual love and innocence, consequently their vessels are most tender and alm ost heavenly, so as to be pure faculties of receiving, which therefore are capable of being disposed by the Lord, although this does not

come to their perception except by a certain delight suitable to their genius. (*Arcana Coelestia* §1776)

In the literal sense, scarce anything appears but a something without order; still, when it is read by man, particularly by a little boy or girl, it becomes by degrees, as it ascends, more beautiful and delightful, and at length is presented before the Lord as the image of a man, in and by which heaven is represented in its complex, not as it is, but as the Lord wills it to be, namely, as a likeness of Himself. (*Arcana Coelestia* §1871)

From this that is said of children in this world we can have an idea of the use of the province of children in heaven; for children here are associated with children in the other world, and their uses are one.

To children in heaven comes the light which is the Word, representing before them good ways of life and lovely varieties of human affection and thought from Himself, such as the Lord desires the heavens to receive from Him. These the children perceive in their childlike way; but from their very perfect childlike ideas, angels corresponding to the optic nerves, of quickest and most interior perception, whose special delight it is to receive new desires from the Lord, perceive the Lord's desires and plans for the formation and perfection of the heavens.

This pure and beautiful wisdom they communicate to the societies of the whole inmost heaven (or brain), by whom it is adapted and sent forth to all other parts of the heavens, according to their functions.

Swedenborg's description of children in heaven is so full and sympathetic as to show a remarkably minute acquaintance with them. And there are other things which show his familiarity with the province of the eyes. His account of the visit of the ten strangers to the heavenly society where they were instructed in the nature of heavenly joy, seems like the account of an eyewitness. And in that society were seen children with their nurses. Its emblem, also, was an eagle brooding her young at the top of a tree; which seems perfect as representing those who are in clear sight, and engaged in the education of children. The nearness of Swedenborg's own state to this is evident from the remark that "a man who draws wisdom from God is like a bird flying on high, which looks about upon all things that are in the gardens, woods, and villages, and flies to those things that will be of use to it" (*True Christian Religion* §69). It will be remembered that the angels of the nose perceived that the angelic societies with Swedenborg were from the province of the eye (*Arcana Coelestia* §4627).

A few words only remain to be said with regard to the correspondence of weeping:

That weeping (or lamentation—*fletus*) is grief of heart may appear from this consideration, that it bursts forth from the heart, and breaks out into lamentations through the mouth; and that shedding of tears (*lacrymatio*) is grief of mind may appear from this consideration, that it issues forth from the thought through the eyes. In both, as well weeping as shedding tears, water goes forth, but bitter and astringent, which goes forth by influx from the spiritual world into the grief of man, where bitter water corresponds to defect of truth on account of falsities, and hence to grief. (*Apocalypse Explained* §484)

The proper function of the tears is to keep the eye moist and clear, and they correspond to thoughts from the love of clear sight. Tears of joy correspond to thoughts from delight in perceiving good things; tears of sorrow, to bitter thoughts in not perceiving what is loved; "bitter tears of disappointment" is a common expression.

Generation and Regeneration

There are heavenly societies to which correspond all and each of the members and organs allotted to generation in each sex. Those societies are distinct from others, as also that province in man is properly distinguished and separate from the rest. That those societies are heavenly is because marriage love is the fundamental love of all loves. . . . It excels the rest also in use, and consequently in delight; for marriages are the seminaries of the whole human race, and also the seminaries of the Lord's heavenly kingdom, for heaven is from the human race. They who have loved infants most tenderly, as mothers who do so, are in the province of the womb and of the organs round about, namely in the province of the neck of the womb, and of the ovaries; and they who are there, are in the sweetest and most delightful life, and in heavenly joy above others. (*Arcana Coelestia* §5053–5054)

Of these heavenly societies we read further:

They who are there are in peace beyond all others. Peace in the heavens is comparatively like the spring season in the world, which gives delight to all things; it is the heavenly itself in its origin. The angels who dwell there are the wisest of all, and from innocence appear to others as children. They also love infants much more than their fathers and mothers do. They are present with infants in the womb, and by them the Lord takes care that infants there shall be nourished and perfected. Thus they have charge over those who are with child. (*Arcana Coelestia* §5052)

It was told me that the organs of generation form a distinct kingdom by themselves, as in man also they are distinct or separate. (*Spiritual Diary* §499 ½)

This province is said to be separate from the rest of the heaven as the corresponding organs of the body are; and although in position the lowest of the abdominal provinces, the angels who compose it are said to be the wisest and best of the angels. And this is because they constitute the ultimate in which the Lord is immediately present, and through which He produces the mediates. By means of these provinces the minds of men are formed, even to their inmosts in which life from the Lord is immediately received; therefore there is a greater fullness of the Divine Life here than elsewhere. And, as we shall see presently, here in the ultimate the three heavenly degrees exist simultaneously.

Swedenborg says that "the spirits who are below heaven wonder very much when they hear and see that heaven is below as well as above; for they are in a similar faith and opinion with men in the world, that heaven is nowhere else than above; for they do not know that the situation of the heavens is as the situation of the members, organs, and viscera in man, of which some are above and some below" (*Heaven and Hell* §66).

The world of spirits, in which are the spirits who wonder thus, is in the plane of the stomach; and some provinces are above and some are below that plane. The position of the organs of generation, below that plane, seems to be referred to in Psalm 139, where it is spoken of as "the lowest parts of the earth."

> Thou hast possessed my reins: Thou hast covered me in my mother's womb.
>
> I will give thanks unto Thee; for I am fearfully and wonderfully made.
>
> Wonderful are Thy works; and that my soul knoweth right well.
>
> My frame was not hid from Thee, when I was made in secret, and curiously wrought in the lowest parts of the earth.
>
> Thine eyes did see my unperfect substance, and in Thy book were all my members written, which day by day were fashioned, when as yet there was none of them. (139:13–16)

This position of the organs is like that of the altar of burnt offerings in the court at the door of the tabernacle; and all the worship at that altar had a correspondence with processes of regeneration, and these correspond to natural generation. More will be said of this correspondence presently.

It is necessary that these provinces should be in immediate relation with men on the earth, because both generation and regeneration must be effected, or at least begun, in the natural world. Like the work of the hands and the feet, this is one of the ultimates of the work of the heavens, in which they act together with men upon the earth.

As the work of regeneration is a work of purification from evil, as well as of reception of new life from the Lord, the corresponding organs of generation are also organs of excretion; for the beginnings of new life from the Lord are received as false and evil things are repented of and rejected, and the sense of reception is in the faculty of rejection. The embryo is matured between the bladder and the rectum; and so the things of regenerate life are nourished and grow in the midst of efforts to control and put away evil and falsity.

In approaching the more particular explanation of the uses and correspondences of these things, we are met by the difficulty which Swedenborg expresses as follows:

> But who and of what quality the societies are which pertain to the particular organs of generation, it has not been given me to know; for they are more interior than can be comprehended by one who is in a lower sphere. They also relate to the uses of those organs, which are concealed, and also are withdrawn from knowledge for a reason which also is of the Divine Providence, lest such things as are in themselves most heavenly should be hurt by unclean thoughts of lasciviousness, scortation, and adultery, which thoughts are excited with very many when those organs are only mentioned. (*Arcana Coelestia* §5055)

We shall, however, I trust, be able to describe and interpret the uses in general; and I have hope that the innocent and holy thoughts that will appear to belong to them, will be permanently associated with them in our minds, and be a lasting influence for purity and protection. Natural prolification is from spiritual, and they help to illustrate each other. Swedenborg says, "The seed of man is conceived interiorly in the understanding, and is formed in the will, and thence is transferred into the testicle, where it puts on a natural covering; and so it is carried on into the womb, and enters the world" (*True Christian Religion* §584).

It is inmostly the masculine perception of truth, which is formed in the will by the intent to propagate it. In regard to spiritual propagation—truth to be propagated must first be clothed and expressed. In its purest state it is only the form of love; its purest clothing is that of ideas of thought; then follow illustrations or formulated thoughts which can be retained in the memory, and then words. When thus triply clad, it can be expressed and communicated. And upon reaching a receptive mind there is a correlative series of unclothings. First, the words or natural expressions are cast aside, and the illustrations or formulas are understood; then the pure ideas are seen interiorly, and received; and then the love, which affects the mind inmostly.

There is a corresponding series of clothing and unclothings of the seed which embodies naturally the spiritual truth.

Its first natural embodiment is in the pure animal spirit separated in the testicle; without being too sure of the exact series of clothings, it appears to be true that this receives a first clothing in the epididymes, which are a series of much convoluted tubes attached to the testicles; the second clothing is apparently imparted in the seminal vesicles, where the seed may be stored, like ideas in definite thoughts, until ready for utterance; and the last is added in the very act of ejections, by the prostate gland. But when received, this outer clothing appears to be separated, or absorbed, by the neck of the womb; the second, by the womb itself, before the entrance into the Fallopian tubes; and the third by the Fallopian tubes, setting free the pure spirit to enter the ovum. Thus, if I understand the parallel correctly, the ovum answers to the testicle, and receives only the pure spirit secreted by it; the Fallopian tubes answer to the epididymes; the womb to the seminal vesicles; and the neck of the womb to the prostate gland. It may be that in the ovum even the first natural embodiment of the spiritual substance from the mind is separated, and the mental substance is set free for an entirely new embodiment from the mother; for Swedenborg says that "all the spiritual which man has is from the father, and all the material is from the mother" (*True Christian Religion* §92).

There seems to be in this successive clothing a series of degrees answering to the degrees of the heavens; the inmost answering to the state of wisdom of the inmost heaven, which is love and the perceptions of love, rather than thought; the clothing of the epididymes answering to the intelligence of the angels of the second heaven; that of the vesicles answering to the representatives, or the formulas of knowledge in the memory, of the first heaven; and that of the prostate to the literal expressions.

Of the angels of the inmost heaven we are told many beautiful things; the following (from *Apocalypse Explained* §828) illustrate what has just been said of the inmosts of this province:

They appear before the angels of the lower heavens as infants, some as children, and all as simple. They also go naked. They appear as infants and as children because they are in innocence, and love to the Lord from the Lord is innocence; hence also by infants and children in the Word innocence and also love to the Lord is signified. They appear simple because they cannot speak about the holy things of heaven and the church; for they do not have them in the memory, whence is all thought, but in the life, and thence in the understanding— not as thought, but as affection for good in its own form, which does not come down into speech, and if it did descend it would not speak, but only sound; and they who cannot speak of such things appear to themselves and to others as simple; and also they are in humility of heart, knowing that it is wisdom to perceive that what they know is scarcely anything compared with what they do not know. They go naked because nakedness in the spiritual sense is innocence, and because garments signify truths clothing good, and the truths which clothe are in the memory and thence in the thought; but with these, truths are in the life, thus hidden, and do not manifest themselves except to the perception whilst others speak them, and their ministers preach them from the Word. (See also *Heaven and Hell* §178–179; *Spiritual Diary* §5179)

The three degrees are present simultaneously in the ultimates, in the giving of the Word, and in the prolification which corresponds to it. But the ultimate of prolification, which corresponds to the propagation of wisdom, is not a communication of words, or of distinct thoughts, but of the living soul itself—of the specific modifications of which, thoughts and words are the interpretation (*Conjugial Love* §220).

If it were a propagation of definite thoughts, children would be born thoughts; but as it is a propagation of soul they are born affections for wisdom or goodness, with an aptitude for thoughts of wisdom and enjoyments of goodness.

"Children born of parents who are in true marriage love, derive from their parents the faculty of marriage of good and truth, from which they have an inclination and faculty, if sons, to perceive the things of wisdom, and if daughters to love the things which wisdom teaches" (*Conjugial Love* §202).

And so, also, if there were a propagation of distinct thoughts, the wife would receive from her husband such definite thoughts. It is evident that she does not; but receives such affection for wisdom as keeps her in sympathy with him, and in a state to understand and enjoy such spiritual wisdom as he enjoys.

In marriages in the heavens there is no begetting of separate human beings; but there is the multiplication of spiritual affections and perceptions in the minds of the partners. On earth there is this spiritual prolification, and also a natural prolification; the spiritual prolification is from the actual reception of the soul of the husband by the wife, and her cherishing of it in herself and in him; and the natural prolification is from the reception of the propagations of his soul in the ova which are cherished and nourished, even till the time of birth, in the womb.

To speak first of the spiritual effects: In a true marriage the husband is in the love of doing good to the wife, of sharing his life with her, and increasing her life. What might have been a selfish and lustful thing is changed to this pure and beneficent thing; and he ceases to act from any mere selfish motive. The wife, also, is in the love of receiving the life of her husband, and making it delightful to him, which she does by her bosom love. And in both, in this interchange, there is a sense of openness to the Lord, and of reception of life from Him, as in no other act. This is so with those who are in marriage from religion, and with an interior acknowledgment of the Lord. In such marriage there is a full ultimate of the marriage of the Lord and the church (*Apocalypse Explained* §984), and a fuller sense of union with Him than is possible otherwise. It comes down from within, and opens all the vessels of mind and body to the reception of life from the Lord.

Interiorly this is called the marriage of good and truth; for it is a marriage between the love of receiving wisdom from the Lord and the love of the goodness of that wisdom. A true man of the church is in love for the Lord's love, and for the wisdom that reveals that love. And a true woman of the church is stirred by the nobleness of that wisdom, and by a sense of the goodness to which it will lead in life. And when they unite in loving the wisdom and the goodness of it, and doing the good works which it teaches, they are a full recipient and embodiment of the Lord's love; and He unites them to Himself, and Himself to them, filling them with the sense of life from Him. In such marriage, it is the state of the wisdom of love in the husband which arouses the love of the wife, and the love of the wife which makes it delightful to the husband, and incites to the attainment of more wisdom. Each has his enjoyment from the other, and each communicates that which is essential to the happiness of the other; and in both is the sense that all that makes them happy is from the Lord, and that the life of the Lord is in it all. Such marriage love is therefore the very spring whence comes the growth of the church and of heaven in man, and the increase of the marriage between the Lord and the church (*Conjugial Love* §65; *Apocalypse Explained* §993).

This growth and increase have an outward embodiment in the multiplication of men; but inwardly they consist in the increase of perceptions of wisdom and of joys in goodness. Perceptions of wisdom are spiritual sons, and joys in goodness are spiritual daughters.

In the begetting of sons, spiritual and natural, the masculine mind is in the perception of truth; in the begetting of daughters, it is in the perception of the goodness of that truth, which is made sensible to it by the love of the wife. The soul is from the father in both cases, and its sex depends upon the state of the father; but in the one case his state is masculine, and in the other it is relatively feminine. It is masculine when he is in the attitude of perceiving and expressing new truth; it is relatively feminine when he is in the perception of what is good. Swedenborg says, "I inquired, 'How is what is feminine produced from a male soul?' and I received for answer, that it was from intellectual good; because this in its essence is truth; for the understanding can think that this is good, thus that it is true that it is good. It is otherwise with the will; this does not think what is good and true, but loves it and does it" (*Conjugial Love* §220). A daughter born of such perception—that "it is true that a thing is good"—when she hears things that are true and wise, perceives and feels the goodness of them, and thus is wholly feminine towards them. The church as a whole is feminine toward the Lord, and in that relation every member of it is feminine. In relation to one another everyone is masculine when he is propagating new truth; and everyone is feminine when he is receiving such truth from another and perceiving the goodness of it. Sons thus begotten from the love of truth have "the faculty of perceiving the things of wisdom," and are in the love of reaching out for true things that are beyond the reach of sense, and bringing them down to the apprehension; and daughters love the good of the things of wisdom when thus brought down to affect the feelings (*Conjugial Love* §168).

The temporary clothing of the communicated soul is from the husband, and for the sake of communication only. The permanent clothing is from the wife. As to that which is received and absorbed by her, she herself is the permanent clothing. The angels say that "the prolific things imparted from the husbands are received universally by the wives, and add themselves to their life; and that thus the wives lead a life unanimous, and successively more unanimous, with their husbands; and that hence is effectively produced a union of souls and a conjunction of minds. They declared this to be because in what is prolific from the husband is his soul, and also his mind as to its interiors which are conjoined to the soul. They added that this was provided from creation, in order that the wisdom of the man, which constitutes his soul, may be appropriated to the wife, and that thus they may become, according to the Lord's words, one flesh" (*Conjugial Love* §172).

For the soul which is to make a separate human being, the mother furnishes a permanent clothing, in the ovum, which passes back through the Fallopian tube to the womb, and there is nourished to its full development by means of the placenta. The children that are brought forth may be thought of as having the father's state of wisdom as their life, clothed by the mother with her thought of the practical usefulness of it.

We have thought of the seminal vesicles as answering to the use of clothing ideas in illustrative thoughts. The womb is the feminine correlative, answering to the clothing of the wisdom received, not with illustrative thought, but with thought from the circumstances of life in regard to its applications and usefulness—thought which embodies it in a plan for usefulness, which is brought forth in useful work. It is in accordance with this that the animating fire or zeal of one's life is from the father; and the ability of practical application is from the mother. The clothing from the mother is the means by which the soul works. If wholly inadequate, it may wholly prevent its development and expression in this world, and modify it permanently; but if of great power and ability, it may make the very most of even a little spiritual energy.

In the quotation above from *Conjugial Love* §172, it is said that in what is from the father "is his soul, and also his mind as to its interiors which are conjoined to the soul." We are taught, also, that "the soul which is from the father is the man himself, and the body which is from the mother is not the man in itself but is from him. This is only his clothing, woven from such things as are in the natural world; but the soul from such things as are in the spiritual world. Every man after death lays down the natural which he has taken from the mother, and retains the spiritual which is from the father, together with a certain covering about it from the purest things of nature" (*True Christian Religion* §103).

This purest covering from nature must be added by the mother; otherwise the seed of the father would alone produce permanent offspring. That it is essential to permanence and thus to propagation is shown in "On Divine Love and Divine Wisdom" §20 (published in *Apocalypse Explained* vol. 6).

The child when born is nourished by milk from its mother's breasts; and the milk is a correspondence of the instruction from a mother's love, by which a child is nurtured. There is also a real communication with the mother's milk, not of thought, but of affection, which nourishes in the child its love of knowing, and other things of its natural disposition, so that it is common to say that a child imbibed this or that love or taste with its mother's milk.

In regard, also, to the soul of the father not separately developed, but received by the wife, and added to her soul, there is a similar affection for nourishing it through the breasts. And there is an actual nourishing of the soul of the husband by the love of the wife imparted through her breasts. Her love thus adds itself to his life as the enjoyment and delight of it. "Their intimate union," Swedenborg says, "is like that of the soul and the heart; the soul of the wife the husband, and the heart of the husband is wife; the husband communicates his soul and conjoins it to his wife by love in act; it is in his seed, and the wife receives it in her heart; hence the two become one, and thus everything in the body of one regards its mutual in the other" (*Apocalypse Explained* §1004).

This is the very process of the increase of heavenly life, by which the two become a more and more full recipient of life from the Lord. The reception of wisdom from the Lord by the husband produces a love for its goodness in the wife, and her love makes it delightful to him. In the bodily union his state of wisdom is communicated to her, and her love for it comes back through the heart to him. Thus the members of generation are means of developing receptacles of the life of the Lord in the partners, and thus are means of regeneration; and if used for this end they are holy and innocent, and full of the heavenly life for which they form receptacles.

There are other aspects of the work of regeneration, all of which have relation to natural generation, and are illustrated by it. In the *Arcana Coelestia* we read as follows:

Man knows nothing of how he is regenerated, and scarcely that he is regenerated; but if he desires to know this, let him attend only to the ends which he proposes to himself, and which he rarely discloses to any one; if the ends are good, namely, that he cares more for his neighbor and the Lord than for himself, he is then in a state of regeneration; but if the ends are to evil, namely, that he cares more for himself than for his neighbor and the Lord for himself, let him know that he is in no state of regeneration. Man by the ends of his life is in the other life; by ends of good, in heaven with angels, and by ends of evil, in hell with devils. Ends with man are nothing else than his loves; for what a man loves, that he has for an end; and inasmuch as his ends are loves, they are his inmost life. ... Ends of good with man are in his rational, and these are what is called his rational as to good, or the good of the rational. By ends of good, or by good therein, the Lord disposes all things which are in the natural; for the end is as the soul, and the natural is as the body of that soul. Such as the soul is, such is the body with which it is encompassed; thus, such as the rational is as to good, such is the natural with which it is invested. It is known that the soul of man has its beginning in the ovum of the mother [it being there first permanently clothed], and is afterwards perfected in her womb; and is there encompassed with a tender body, and this of such a nature that by it the soul may be able to act suitably in the world into which it is born. The case is similar when man is born again, that is, when he is regenerated. The new soul which he then receives is the end of good, which has its beginning in the rational, at first as in an ovum there, and afterwards it is there perfected as in a womb. The tender body with which this soul is encompassed, is the natural and the good therein, which becomes such as to act obediently according to the ends of the soul. The truths therein are like fibers in the body; for truths are formed from good. . . . Hence it is evident that an image of the reformation of man is exhibited in his formation in the womb; and, if you will believe it, celestial good and spiritual truth, which are from the Lord, are also what forms him, and thus impresses an ability to receive each of them successively, and this in quantity and quality according as he, like a man, has respect to the ends of heaven, and not like a brute animal to the ends of the world. (*Arcana Coelestia* §3570)

The angels have life from good, and have form from truths, which is the human form. (*Arcana Coelestia* §9043; see also *True Christian Religion* §583)

The end of good has a form in the definite thought of what is good. The beginning of conscious regeneration is in such definite thought with desire and determination. The clothing of this seed is by meditation upon it in regard to its application to the uses of life, and from truths which conduce to this application. And the birth is in the life.

But this end of good, which is the beginning of new life, is from the Lord's love and is communicated to man by the Word. The seed of the heavenly life is sown by the Son of Man. And this seed, or revelation of the Divine, contains the Divine love clothed successively in the several senses of the Word, and at last in the literal sense. It is received by the church, and is successively clothed by her—variously, of course—until the Divine love is perceived in it. This love becomes an end of good in those who perceive it and would live from it. The "ovum in the rational" which receives it, is from the remains implanted by the innocent angels who are most in love to the Lord in the earliest stages of infancy. "The natural and the good therein" which "afterwards encompasses it as with a body," is from the later remains laid up in childhood and youth, and even in maturer life. From these it is nourished interiorly by goodness and truth relating to the Lord and heaven and heavenly life, and exteriorly by goodness and truth relating to moral and civil life, until the man openly begins to live a good spiritual life. And afterwards he is further nourished and sustained by the affection and instructions of the church.

This circle of life is thus described by Swedenborg:

> When man is regenerated, the truths which must be of faith are insinuated by hearing and sight, and are implanted in the memory of his natural man; from that memory they are brought into the thought

which is of the understanding, and those which are loved become of the will; and so far as they become of the will, they become of the life, for the will of man is his very life; and so far as they become of his life they become of his affection, thus of charity in the will and of faith in the understanding. Afterwards from that life, which is a life of charity and faith, he speaks and acts—from charity which is of the will goes forth the speech of the mouth, and also the acts of the body, both by an intellectual way, thus by the way of faith. From these things it is plain that the circle of the regeneration of man is like the circle of his life in general; and that it is similarly established in the will by influx from heaven from the Lord. Hence also it is evident that there are two states in man who is regenerated, the first when the truths of faith are being implanted, and conjoined to the good of charity, and the second when from the good of charity he speaks by means of the truths of faith, and acts according to them; so that the first state is from the world through the natural man into the spiritual man, thus into heaven, and the second from heaven through the spiritual man into the natural, thus into the world.... This circle is the circle of man's regeneration, and hence is the circle of his spiritual life. (*Arcana Coelestia* §10057)

The subject is further illustrated by the representation of the altar of burnt offerings with its offerings and sacrifices; which in all particulars has relation to purification from evils and falsities, the reception of good and truth, and the conjunction of good from the Lord with truth, thus to the processes of regeneration.

Swedenborg says:

The place where the door of the tent of meeting was, represented the marriage of Divine good with Divine truth; for by the altar, which also was placed at the door of the tent, was represented the Lord as to Divine good, and by the tent of meeting was represented the Lord as to Divine truth. Hence by the place at the door of the tent was represented the conjunction of good and truth, which conjunction is called the heavenly marriage. (*Arcana Coelestia* §10001; see also *Arcana Coelestia* §10143, 10053, 10124)

By burnt offerings and sacrifices in general was represented purification from evils and falsities; and since purification was represented, the implantation of good and truth from the Lord, and likewise their conjunction, was also represented; for when man is purified from evils and falsities, which is effected by their removal, then good and truth from the Lord flow in, and so far as good and truth in that state flow in, so far they are implanted, and so far conjoined; for the Lord is continually present with good and truth in every man, but he is not received except so far as evils and falsities are removed, thus so far as man is purified from them; the conjunction of good and truth is regeneration. (*Arcana Coelestia* §10022)

By the altar is also signified heaven and the church as to the reception of Divine good from the Lord there; for it is the Divine of the Lord that makes heaven and the church, inasmuch as the Lord dwells there in His own, and not in the *proprium* of man. Hence also it is that by the altar is likewise signified the man himself in whom is heaven, or in whom is the church, thus in whom is the Lord; and abstractly from person the altar denotes the good itself which is from the Lord with the angels of heaven and with the men of the church. (*Arcana Coelestia* §10124)

It is on account of this representation by the altar of the conjunction of the Lord and the church, that the altar is called the Holy of Holies,

which signifies the celestial kingdom, where the Lord is present in the good of love.... That celestial good is the Holy of Holies, and spiritual good Holy, is because celestial good is the inmost good, thus also that good is the good of the inmost heaven; but spiritual good is the good proceeding from it, and therefore is the good of the middle heaven; and this good is so far good, and therefore so far holy, as it has in it celestial good; for this flows into the other, and conceives it and produces it as a father a son. By celestial good is meant the good of love from the Lord to the Lord, and by spiritual good is meant the good of charity towards the neighbor from the Lord. The good itself of love to the Lord from the Lord is the Holy of Holies, because the Lord by it conjoins Himself immediately; but the good of charity towards the neighbor is Holy, because the Lord by it conjoins Himself immediately; and He so far conjoins Himself as it has in it the good of love to the Lord. (*Arcana Coelestia* §10129)

Thus the altar of burnt offerings, and the worship there, though situated in the court of the tabernacle and at the door of entrance, was the most holy thing of the representative worship because it represented the reception of life from the Lord in the ultimates of life, and the multiplication of good and true things in the church by that life. The coals from the altar were carried into the tabernacle, and laid in the censer upon the altar of incense, and the smoke of fragrant spices ascended from it, as the love of a faithful wife goes forth from her heart, and also the prayers and praises of a faithful church.

To return again to the correspondence of these things with the heavens, we read:

> All the members dedicated to generation, in both sexes, especially the womb, correspond to societies in the inmost or third heaven. The reason is that true marriage love is derived from the Lord's love for the church, and from the love of good and truth which love is the love of angels of the third heaven. Wherefore marriage love, which descends thence, like the love of that heaven, is innocence, which is the very *esse* of all good in the heavens. Hence embryos in the womb are in a state of peace, and infants after they are born are in a state of innocence, as also their mother in relation to them. Since there is such correspondence of the genital members of both sexes, it is evident that they are holy from creation, and therefore dedicated solely to chaste and pure marriage love, and that they ought not to be profaned by unchaste and impure love of adultery; by this man turns the heaven in himself into hell; for as marriage love corresponds

to the love of the highest heaven, which is love to the Lord from the Lord, so the love of adultery corresponds to the love of the lowest hell. The love of marriage is so holy and heavenly because it begins from the Lord Himself in the inmosts of man, and according to order descends to the ultimates of the body, and thus fills the whole man with heavenly love, and induces upon him the form of the Divine love, which form is the form of heaven, and is the image of the Lord. (*Apocalypse Explained* §985)

The angels of the inmost heaven are innocences. In the next[1] and the interior heavens there are also innocences, but not the same; those innocences constitute as it were their inmost, or as it may be called their center, like an axis or nucleus. Nor can any heaven subsist unless its center, or inmost as it were, is innocence, and other things are like circumferences into which comes innocence from the center; for no one can be in heaven unless he has something of innocence. So also the inmost heaven communicates with the next by means of its center, namely innocences, and so the inmost[2] through the next with the interior. From this may be understood the quality of the communication from the inmosts and from the Lord according to the order instituted by the Lord.

It is the inmost heaven through which the Lord insinuates marriage love; the beginning or origin

---

1. "*In caelo intimiori et interiori.*" "*Intimius*" seems to mean "comparatively inmost," but not the positively inmost.

2. "*Intimum per intimius cum interiori.*"

of this is from the inmost heaven, also through the center of the lower heavens. From this also is parental love; for the celestial angels of the inmost heaven so love infants, much more than fathers or mothers. Indeed they are present with infants and take care of them; and, as has been told me, they are present in their mother's womb, and take care of them that they may be nourished; thus they have charge over those who are with child. (*Spiritual Diary* §1200–1201)

They who most tenderly love infants, so that they be only fetuses or infants, are as most tender mothers, so that they can scarcely live unless they are in a state where the tender love of infants reigns. These constitute the province in the situation of the testicles and organs thence depending; and, in woman, the neck of the womb, and the womb, with the ovaries and the things annexed. They who are in this province live in the sweetest, most delightful, and happy life, such as cannot be described; only its state is gentleness and sweetness. Their province is between the loins (*inter lumbos*). (*Spiritual Diary* §3152)

They are innocent because innocence consists in the acknowledgment from the heart that we are nothing, and that the Lord is all; and these provinces are more than others in the perception that all of life is from the Lord; and in the love of receiving life sensitively from Him, and communicating it to others. From them comes the sense of new life from the Lord to all the heavens, and thus also the sense of conjunction with Him. And, as will be seen presently, they also are the means of multiplying recipients of His life.

It would seem that those who are in the province of the testicles are primarily in the love of receiving sensitively and imparting the Lord's life in forms of wisdom, and they who are in the province of the ovaries and the womb are primarily in love for protecting and defending the things of wisdom, and showing the goodness of them (*Conjugial Love* §127).

That the organs of both sexes have their correspondence with societies in heaven, and yet the heaven is one man, may perhaps be illustrated by the following teaching:

> There are married partners there who are in such marriage love that the two can be one flesh, and also are one when they will, and thus they appear as one man. I have seen them and talked with them, and they said that they have one life, and that they are like the life of good in truth, and the life of truth in good, and that they are like the pairs in man, namely, like the two hemispheres of the brain covered with one membrane, the two chambers of the heart within a common covering, and likewise the two lobes of the lungs; which, although they are two, still are one as to life, and the exercises of life, which are uses. (*Apocalypse Explained* §1004)

As this is the most perfect form of man, and the whole heaven is more full and perfect than any individual in it, we may conclude that the heavens are such a one, and that the intercommunication is constant (compare *Apocalypse Explained* §992); and we may think of the uses and joys of marriage love as affecting the whole heaven through these provinces, as in such a married pair.

In them is chiefly the innocence of the heavens (*Apocalypse Explained* §996), or the sense that all of life even to ultimates is from the Lord alone. There is also the sense of the reception of life from the Lord in states of wisdom, and of joy in the goodness which wisdom teaches, and in the delight of the union of wisdom and goodness, in which is the fullest reception of the Lord.

The male provinces are in the actual reception of wisdom from the Lord to increase the life of the heavens; and the female, in love for the goodness of this wisdom, and in the desire to bring to full fruition.[3]

There are in these provinces the three degrees of communication, as in individuals, answering to the several planes of life in the heavens. In the inmosts are those who have the inmost sense of the reception of wisdom and love from the Lord, and of the oneness of them; in the outer parts are those who are in intelligence concerning these things of wisdom and love, and the marriage of them in the Lord and in men. And in the outmost are those who are in natural fondness for infants and for professions and forms of marriage love (*Spiritual Diary* §3704); and some there are with very little spiritual life, who yet serve as guards and for protection. (*Spiritual Diary* §3390; see also on circumcision, *Arcana Coelestia* §4462)

Through these provinces the whole heaven, and every individual in the heavens, are affected with the delight of the union of love and wisdom from the Lord; and this delight extends through all the forms of marriage love. But everywhere the chief influence received is that of innocence, of the sense that life is from the Lord alone, and also every living form of love and wisdom; and from this comes the delight in new births of love and wisdom from the Lord for the increase of the life of the heavens.

---

3. Spiritual prolification is described in *Apocalypse Explained* §991, *Heaven and Hell* §382, and *Conjugial Love* §52.

To the earths also the influence of these provinces descends for the uses of generation and of regeneration; for without them there would be upon the earth neither love nor power for propagating either the race or the truth. The life of the heavens and of every angel in it, also of every man that is born, is the Lord's love for man. From this love, through the Divine wisdom, all things are created. The Divine wisdom from the Divine love has in view an Infinite heaven, and provides means for creating it. In the continual increase of the heavens, it operates through the heavens that already exist, expanding and developing them forever towards the Infinite ideal. The angels that are in these provinces of the heavens receive the Lord's love and wisdom for the increase of the heavens most fully. They also perceive in the states of all the heavens their need and desire for increase and development, and not only inspire into them the love and wisdom that they are capable of receiving, but inspire the same into the souls of men on earth, to form new recipients. And the inspiration from the Lord through these provinces is the very desire and the ability to propagate the soul, and the wisdom which is the substance of the soul. In a discussion in the spiritual world concerning the origin of marriage love and its ability, a wise African said:

> You Christians deduce marriage power or ability from various causes rational and natural; but we Africans deduce it from the state of man's conjunction with the God of the universe. This state we call the state of religion, but you call it the state of the church; for when the love is derived from that state, and is stable and permanent, it must needs produce its own power, which resembles it, and thus also is stable and permanent. True marriage love is known

235

only by those few who live near to God; consequently the ability of that love is known to no others. This ability is described by the angels of heaven as the delight of a perpetual spring. (*Conjugial Love* §113)

Through them descends the desire and ability of propagation to man, and is received by him according to the state of his life, purely or perversely. But inmostly in it there is ever the life of the Lord, and the love and wisdom of the inmost heaven. It is not possible for a soul to live and be born but from this love and wisdom for the development of the heavens; and thus it is not possible for one to be born without capacity for doing a use in the heavens, and making them a more perfect man.

"It is provided by the Lord," Swedenborg says in *Earths in the Universe* §9, "that whensoever there is a deficiency in any place as to the quality or quantity of correspondence, a supply be instantly made from another earth, to fill up the deficiency, so that the proportion may be preserved, and thus heaven be kept in due consistence." This may refer only to the transfer of men from the natural world to the spiritual; but I think it refers also to the production of such as are needed. The sense of need would affect the heaven. In every society there must be a sense of delightful uses to be done, which yet they are not able to do, and a desire that they should be done, and to love and support those who can do them. And this is itself a love of propagating, which can only be effective through those who are in the function of prolification and are operating upon man; and it is like the supply of pure fluids furnished to those provinces from the brains and the general circulation for the sake of their use.

The perverseness of the externals through which these heavenly things of the soul come down increases the difficulty of developing and expressing them, but does not destroy them. Even an evil man has in him the inmost of the soul in which the Lord dwells immediately, also the celestial and spiritual planes of the mind, all of which are beyond his reach, and therefore unperverted. If it were not for these, there would be no propagation of his soul. The angels of these provinces arouse to activity both the internals and the externals, though the man is wholly unconscious of the heavenly possibilities of the internals, and perceives only the perverse possibilities of the externals. They also operate upon the concealed processes of the interiors of the body, of which the man knows nothing, that they may act according to the order of right development. "Many nerves of the cerebellum," Swedenborg says, "come together in the regions of the loins, for the sake of propagation.... For propagation is exempt in almost all respects from the voluntary things of man" (*Spiritual Diary* §3862).

And during and after conception, they are present with the new soul in the ovum and through all its life in the womb, to remove from it evil influences, as far as possible, and to nurture in it all the possibilities of good; that there may never be lacking in the new being the power to see and to love and to do the uses for the sake of which he is created, and the love of which is his inmost life from the Lord.

As in a man the soul acts upon the body, and the body reacts of itself, with a degree of independence—and this because the body lives from the general influx of the heavens—so in the womb the body must be *formed* by this general influx of the heavens, reacting to the life which is in the soul from the Lord. The angels of the male organs of the heavens are with the father cooperating in the propagation of the interior receptacles of life of which he knows nothing, and in the clothing of these spiritual forms so that they may be communicated to the wife. The angels of the female organs are with the mother, cooperating with her in receiving these spiritual forms, and in giving them a permanent clothing. And through the angels of the womb the whole heaven is present, forming the body of the child in response to and accord with the life from the Lord in the soul; and this in such a manner that the influence of every province of the heavens forms the corresponding organ of the body; and thus, being formed in response to the impulses of life from the soul, it continues to react to them afterwards.

When the time of regeneration arrives, and "the end of good," which Swedenborg says is the life is the spiritual man, comes to the rational perception, the capacity for perceiving it is from the very love of use which from the Lord through the angels formed from the beginning those faculties which he now first exercises consciously. And the angels who have attended him in the womb have had perception of this, and labored to provide for the right development of his organs of thought and sense and action so that he might have all the means of receiving the truth and bringing it forth in good life.

Swedenborg says:

> I have spoken with angels concerning the progression of truth to good, thus of faith to charity: that there is joy with the angels when a child or a boy on earth from affection learns and receives truths, thus when truths become knowledge, and that there is still greater joy, when from knowledge they become of the understanding—then there is joy with the angels of the Lord's spiritual kingdom;

and still greater joy when from the understanding they become of the will—then there is joy with the angels of the Lord's celestial kingdom; and when from the will they become of the act, then there is joy with the angels of the three heavens. How great are the joy and the enjoyments in that progression, cannot be described, because it is ineffable; for thus a man enters more and more into heaven, and becomes a heaven in the least form. I have perceived this, in speaking with the angels, from the progression of the enjoyments of marriage love even to the ultimate effect by which man is propagated; such is the progression of the conjunction with heaven, that is, with the Lord; and such is the new creation of man, and the formation of heaven, or of angel, in him; for heaven is the form of the Divine truth thus progressing; from this a man becomes love, and in no other way is the marriage of good and truth formed in him. (*Spiritual Diary* §6011)

In regeneration the good seed is from the wisdom of the Divine love, successively clothed in the several senses of the Word, even to its ultimate precepts (*Apocalypse Explained* §1066, 1072). The reception and successive unclothing is by the natural and the rational thought of man, even until the love within is perceived. The development is through the gathering and arrangement of truths which are the means of bringing the good end to pass, and the new birth is the bringing forth of the end in words and works. In every step of this work the influence of the angels of these provinces, and their love for the reception of the Lord's love and wisdom, is the nurturing influence which makes the work possible. And in the completed work of regeneration their innocence finds its delight in the state of the man who has learned the truth which is the very receptacle of innocence, that man has nothing of goodness and truth of his own, but all is from the Lord.[4]

In thinking of the Word as the successive clothing of the Divine wisdom by which regeneration is effected, and the heavens are multiplied, it appears to be true that the states of the church in which this clothing was effected were masculine as to their function, and the states of the church in which the unclothing is or will be successively effected, are relatively feminine; or, in other words, that the ages down to the time of the coming of the Lord were relatively masculine, and those since His coming are feminine.

We may even go further than this, and say that the giving of the Word in its successive clothing from inmost to outmost was from the masculine in the Divine, and the opening of the inner meanings of the Word and manifesting the goodness of them was from the feminine in the Divine; for, as will be seen presently, the Divine Human is feminine relatively to the inmost Divine.

It was by the unfolding of the real meaning of the Word, and bringing forth the good of it in His human life, that

4. In *Arcana Coelestia* §5056, *Spiritual Experiences* §875, and *Earths in the Universe* §79, we read of one who was intensely eager to enter heaven, and when prepared was in the province of the seminal vesicles. He was of the chastising spirits from the planet of Jupiter, was in the love of truth, acknowledged himself to be vile in himself, and was eager to be admitted into a better state and better uses. Apparently he was in such a stage of regeneration that he was ready to receive with benefit and delight the influence of those who are in the love of the good things which wisdom teaches, and to mature under their influence a fuller heavenly life.

the Divine marriage was accomplished in the Lord. For "the union of the Divine Essence with the Human, and of the Human with the Divine," we are taught, "is the Divine marriage of good with truth, and of truth with good, from which is the heavenly marriage" (*Arcana Coelestia* §2803).

"The Divine marriage of the Lord is not between Divine good and Divine truth in His Divine Human, but between the good of the Divine Human and the Divine Itself, that is, between the Father and the Son; for the Divine good of the Lord's Divine Human is what is called in the Word the Son of God, and the Divine Itself the Father" (*Arcana Coelestia* §3952).

"From the Divine marriage, which is the union of the Father and the Son, or of the Divine Itself of the Lord with the Divine Human, comes the heavenly marriage. The heavenly marriage is what is called the kingdom of the Lord, and also heaven, and this because it exists from the Divine marriage, which is the Lord" (*Arcana Coelestia* §3960).

The church which would enter into this heavenly marriage must learn from Him the truth of heavenly life, which is the truth of His own human life, and herself live it, and become a form of the good of it; and so far as she does this, the Lord unites Himself wish her, and her with Himself; for He says: "As the Father hath loved me, so have I loved you; continue ye in my love." The fruits of this marriage of the Lord and the church will be truths rationally seen and naturally expressed; and good works, heavenly in their spirit, natural in their embodiment. The first fruits of it were in the first Christian acknowledgment of the Lord as the one God, Who fulfilled the Scriptures and established a heavenly kingdom. And the bringing forth of this doctrine the Lord compared to the pains of birth: "A woman when she is in travail hath sorrow because her hour is come; but as soon as she is delivered of the child, she remembereth no more her anguish, for joy that a man is born into the world. And ye now therefore have sorrow; but I will see you again, and your heart shall rejoice, and your joy no man taketh from you."

The birth of the doctrines of the New Church is also likened in the Apocalypse to the birth of a man-child from a woman clothed with the sun, and having the moon under her feet. These doctrines were derived from the Scriptures interiorly and truly understood, and the birth of them is a type of the continual births of wisdom and goodness with which the church will be multiplied and perfected, as she receives into herself the interior things of the Scriptures, and from them receives the Lord's life and adds it to her own life.

The Lord began the unfolding of the real meaning of the Word in His teaching; in His own thought and life there was a perfect unfolding of it; and He has given the means of a perfect unfolding now to the New Church. The very life of the New Church will come from her opening the inner meanings of the Word, even till the love and wisdom of the Lord Himself are perceived in it, and she receives these into her heart, and adds them to her life. The marriage of the Lord and the church is thus effected by means of the opening and living by her of the inner meanings of the Word. And it is possible only so far as the church is in the acknowledgment of the Divine Human of the Lord; for with no other idea of Him is conjunction possible, and no other opens the Divine Love and Wisdom in the Word, the union of which constitutes this heavenly marriage. Therefore, also, we are taught that no true marriage love is possible except with those who are in the acknowledgment of the Divine Human of the Lord; for only thus can the love and wisdom be received, the union of which is the origin and essence of marriage love (*Conjugial Love* §70; *Apocalypse Explained* §995).

Some confirmation of this view of the Word, and of the churches before and after the coming of the Lord, may be had from these considerations: The age of the Race when the Lord came, answers to the time of youth, when the desire for marriage begins (*Apocalypse Explained* §641). Swedenborg also says of the Word:

> Since the members of generation in each sex correspond to societies of the third heaven, and the love of a married pair to the love of good and truth, therefore also those members and that love correspond to the Word. The reason is that the Word is Divine Truth united to Divine Good proceeding from the Lord; hence it is that the Lord is called the Word. From this also there is in every part of the Word the marriage of good and truth, or the heavenly marriage. (*Apocalypse Explained* §985)

Besides the marriage in every part of the Word, there appears to be a marriage between the Old and the New Testaments. In the Old Testament we have the Truth from God descending and clothing itself successively even to ultimates. In the New Testament we have the beginnings of the unfolding of this truth, and the explanation of the real goodness in it, at first on the natural plane. And then in the Apocalypse we have a prediction of the future unfolding of the same Scriptures for the purification of the church and the establishment of a New Church which shall be the Bride, the Lamb's Wife.

The Lord's kingdom includes both heaven and the church; and "the Word is the medium of conjunction" between the Lord and the whole (*Conjugial Love* §128). When man reads the Word in its ultimate, the literal sense, the heavens successively evolve instantaneously their several senses, even to the inmost in which the Love and Wisdom of the Lord are most distinctly perceived (*True Christian Religion* §234–239). There is thus a conjunction of the Lord with His whole Kingdom, through the letter of the Word. And while this is a fullest reception of the Lord and conjunction with Him, in every individual who reads and looks to the Lord and lives according to His precepts there is in his degree a similar unfolding of the interiors of the Word, by his natural thought, his spiritual thought, and his reception of the Lord's love into his soul, where it becomes new ends of good life.

And so far as one is thus conjoined to the Lord, from this heavenly marriage descends the love of the marriage of good and truth, and thus a heavenly marriage love, into all the degrees of his thought and feeling and life. It is a love which none can have "but those who go to the Lord, and love the truths of the church, and practice its goods" (*Conjugial Love* §70); because no others can receive from Him the sense of His merciful saving love, and the love of the truth of heavenly life, which are united in the heavenly marriage.

Of such marriage love Swedenborg says:

> It is in its first essence love to the Lord from the Lord, and hence also it is innocence; therefore also marriage love is peace, such as the angels have in heaven; for as innocence is the very *esse* of all good, so peace is the very *esse* of all enjoyment of good, consequently it is the very *esse* of all joy between the married two. Now because all joy is of love, and

marriage love is the fundamental love of all the loves of heaven, therefore peace itself resides principally in marriage love. Peace is the blessedness of heart and soul arising from the conjunction of the Lord with heaven and the church; thus also from the conjunction of good and truth, when all strife and combat of what is evil and false with what is good and true cease.... And because marriage love descends from those conjunctions, therefore also all the enjoyment of that love descends and has its essence from heavenly peace. (*Apocalypse Explained* §997)

The Brain

The form of man at first conception was represented to Swedenborg by the angels as

a most minute image of a brain, with a delicate delineation of a face in front, without any appendage. This first form was, in the upper protuberant part, a collection of contiguous globules or spherules, and each spherule was composed of others still more minute, and each of these in like manner of the most minute of all: thus it was of three degrees. . . . The angels said that the two inner degrees, which were in the order and form of heaven, were receptacles of love and wisdom from the Lord; and that the exterior degree, which was in opposition to the order and form of heaven, was the receptacle of infernal love and insanity; because man by hereditary degeneracy is born into evils of every kind, and these evils reside in the outmosts there; and this degeneracy is not removed unless the higher degrees are opened, which, as was said, are the receptacles of love and wisdom from the Lord. And because love and wisdom are man himself, for love and wisdom in their essence are the Lord, and as this first form of man is a receptacle of them, it follows that there

246

is in this first form a continual effort towards the human form, which also it successively assumes. (*Divine Love and Wisdom* §432)

Of the development of this form we read further as follows:

> All things in man relate to the will and the understanding, and the understanding is a receptacle of the Divine Truth, and the will of the Divine Good. Therefore the human mind, which consists of those two principles, is nothing else than a form of the Divine Truth and the Divine Good spiritual and naturally organized. The human brain is that form; and because the whole man depends upon his mind, all things in his body are appendages which are actuated and live from those two principles. (*True Christian Religion* §224)

> Man's life in its beginnings is in the brain, and its derivatives in the body. (*Divine Love and Wisdom* §365)

> The will and the understanding are called receptacles because the will is not a spiritual abstraction, but it is a substantial thing, formed for the reception of love from the Lord; neither is the understanding a spiritual abstraction, but a substantial thing formed for the reception of wisdom from the Lord. They actually exist. Although they are concealed from sight, yet they are within the substances which compose the cortex of the cerebrum, and also are scattered in the medullary substance of the

cerebrum, especially in the corpora striata, also within in the medullary substance of the cerebellum, and in the spinal medulla, of which they compose the central portion. There are therefore not two receptacles, but innumerable, and every one twinned, and also in three degrees.... They are the beginnings and heads of all the fibers by which the whole body is woven. From the fibers put forth from them are formed all the organs of sense and motion, for they are their beginnings and ends.... Those receptacles in infants are small and tender; they afterwards increase and are perfected according to the knowledge and the affection for it. They are sound according to the intelligence and the love of uses; they soften according to the innocence and love to the Lord, and are solidified and hardened by the opposites. Their changes of state are affections, their variations of form are thoughts; the existence and permanence of these is the memory, and the reproduction is recollection. Both taken together are the human mind. (*Apocalypse Explained* vol. 6, "On Divine Love and Divine Wisdom" §86)

From the cortical substances proceed little fibers, the first of which are invisible, and are afterwards bundled together, of which is produced the medullary substance of the whole cerebrum, cerebellum, and medulla oblongata. From this medullary substance are put forth visible fibers, which united are called nerves, by which the cerebrum, cerebellum, and spinal medulla form the whole body and all things in it; and therefore it is that all things of the body are ruled by the brains. From this it is

evident that the will and understanding, which in
one word are called the mind, and therefore also
intelligence and wisdom, reside in the brains, and
are there in their first forms; and that the organs
which are formed to receive sensations and to perform motions are derivations from them, altogether like streams from their fountains; . . . and
that those derivations are such that the brains are
everywhere present, almost as the sun is present
by its heat and light in all parts of the earth. Hence
it follows that the whole body, and all things in it,
are forms under the observation, guidance, and
control of the mind, which is in the brain, and so
constructed in dependence upon it that the part in
which the mind is not present, or to which it does
not give its own life, is not a part of the life of the
man. (*Apocalypse Explained* §775)

The fibers gather to themselves and animate the grosser
materials contained in the blood; and in order that these
may be conveyed wherever they are wanted, and so may
be always at hand, the little blood vessels are the first things
formed in the body, and from them the heart to superin-
tend their helpful service (*Divine Love and Wisdom* §370,
400).

We have become familiar with the idea that "the Lord
does not operate from first principles through mediates
into ultimates; but from first principles through ultimates,
and so into mediates" (*Apocalypse Explained* §1086, 1087;
Apocalypse Explained vol. 6, "On Divine Love and Divine
Wisdom"§105). This is true of the creation, in that the heavens were not made first, and through them the earths; but
the earths were made by means of atmospheres from the

sun of heaven, and upon the earths the successive creations natural and spiritual were built up. At the same time it is true that when the heavens were formed, they cooperated in producing further developments upon the earths. Similar things are true also of the Word, of which we read: "The Lord flows in from first principles through ultimates; thus from Himself into the natural sense of the Word, and calls out or evolves from thence its spiritual and celestial sense; and thus illustrating, He teaches and leads the angels" (*Posthumous Theological Works*, "Concerning the Sacred Scripture or the Word of the Lord from Experience" §18). And yet it is true that when man reads the Word the angels who are associated with him understand far more of its interior meaning than he does, and that their influence tends to enlighten and expand his understanding; and thus the doctrines by which the interiors of the Word are opened, are said to have descended from God out of heaven.

And so it is in the formation of the body by the brains. They do not first form the heart and lungs and other viscera, and then extend the blood vessels to the skin; but they send their fibers directly to the skin, and there form the beginnings of arteries and veins, which presently come together to form the heart. And then the heart and the arteries and veins cooperate with the fibers in the formation of all the other viscera and members.

We have already spoken about the innumerable cells, or beginnings of the fibers, "which compose the cortex of the cerebrum, and also are scattered in the medullary substance of the cerebrum, especially in the corpora striata, also within in the medullary substance of the cerebellum, and in the spinal medulla, of which they compose the central portion." There are also small collections of these cells in nervous ganglia in other parts of the body; as in the cardiac plexus, which has immediate control of the movements of the heart and lungs; the solar plexus, which presides over the organs of digestion; the sympathetic nerve with its ganglia, connecting the functions of all the viscera. In the spinal medulla there are enlargements caused by special groups of cells having charge of particular organs and members; the lowest, or sacral ganglia, preside over the organs of generation; the lumbar, over the motions of the legs; the dorsal, over the motions of the arms. Cells are origins of fibers; and wherever there are cells, there are origins of movements or operations by means of the fibers. The acts of these ganglia are not determined by our voluntary effort, nor are they the result of conscious sensations; though the sensations that cause them may also come to consciousness, and the acts of the ganglia may to some extent be controlled by voluntary effort. For example, if our hand accidentally touches a hot iron, it is instantly twitched away; and not till afterwards do we become conscious of the pain. If the hand had to wait for this consciousness and the voluntary movement of the muscles, it would be badly burned. It has comparative safety through the nearness and the promptness of the spinal ganglia which are in immediate charge. Yet, after the sensation is felt, we may, if we will, hold the hand to the burning iron, notwithstanding the effort of the ganglia to withdraw it—the larger brain exercising its authority over its subordinates.

Of these ganglia Swedenborg says:

> There are many centers and bases in each heaven; by them there is immediate communication among the heavens, and with God the Messiah. They are in

a most tranquil state, and cannot be compared more aptly than to the ganglia of the human body, and the nodes in the brain, into which flow innumerable fibers, and are there as it were formed anew, and so the things which are around are disposed according to the ends in the beginnings, and thus all these in most perfect order and form, by God the Messiah alone. (*Spiritual Diary* §305)

From the series of fibers in the body it may be seen how it is in the lowest heaven; for there are incomprehensible fascicles, as those that are about the heart, and those in lower regions, where all conjoin themselves wonderfully. One fiber flows into another, and also weaves itself with others in a wonderful way; it flows in and out, and blends itself with others, and again into others, also into ganglia, where they enter into other combinations, and flow out thence to their functions. How these things are done no one can comprehend; they are disposed according to the heavenly form. Such are the cardiac plexus, the hepatic, and other plexuses, and special plexuses in every viscus. (*Spiritual Diary* §5780)

These that have been described are the simplest ganglia, having immediate relation to the extremes of the body. Another set, larger and more comprehensive, combine the sensations of the lower body with those of the head, especially those received through the eyes, and direct the motions of the body accordingly. These are four small bodies at the base of the brain, called the corpora quadragemina; with a fifth, closely associated with them, called the pineal gland, which exercises some control over the secretions of the brain. It is by virtue of these bodies that we can walk over a rough path, even when the mind is so occupied as to pay no attention to the way. Many operations of the hands and of other parts of the body are similarly controlled by them, without any conscious effort of the mind. Lying near these, and more important than any other subordinate ganglion, is the medulla oblongata; a body which serves as the lieutenant of the cerebellum in controlling the vital functions of the body—the beating of the heart; the circulation through arteries, capillaries, and veins; the operations of all the glands of the body; the respiration, so far as it is involuntary; and even the processes of eating, swallowing, crying, and speaking, so far as these also are involuntary. It also combines the fibers of the cerebrum, which are the instruments of conscious sensation and voluntary action, with those of the cerebellum, which keep the unconscious life informed of the state of every point in its kingdom, and distribute its commands accordingly. Both cerebrum and cerebellum may be wanting; if this medulla, with its group of cells, be sound, these vital functions will be attended to as long as its powers suffice. Its animating power is small; but it holds the reins of all the vital functions of the body, and will guide them safely as long as the life holds out.

The great variety of uses performed by the fibers from a single center has its correspondence in the arrangement of the heavens, and is thus illustrated by Swedenborg:

> There came a company of spirits who said that they were dissimilar; and because this seemed to me impossible, namely, that there should be a society of dissimilars in the other life, I therefore spoke

with them about it, saying that if a common cause moved them in one direction, they still might be consociated, because all would thus have one end. They said that they are such that all speak differently, and yet think alike. . . . It was perceived that they have relation to the isthmus in the brain, which is between the cerebrum and the cerebellum, through which the fibers pass, and are thence distributed variously, and wherever they go they act diversely in externals. Also that they have relation to the ganglia in the body, into which a nerve flows, and then is separated into many fibers, some of which go one way and some another, and act dissimilarly in ultimates, but still from one principle; so that in ultimates there is dissimilarity in appearance, although there is similarity as to end. It is also known that one force acting in the extremities may be greatly varied, according to the form there. Ends are likewise represented by the beginnings from which are the fibers, such as are in the brain. Thoughts thence are represented by the fibers from those beginnings, and actions by the nerves which are from the fibers. (*Arcana Coelestia* §5189; nearly the same is in §4051)

Two other pairs of brain masses lie under the hemispheres of the cerebrum, and are closely associated with it, called the optic thalami and the corpora striata. The nerves of sense that proceed from the cerebrum pass through the optic thalami; and the nerves of motion pass through the corpora striata. The cerebrum is the organ of the conscious efforts of the mind. It desires to see; and its desire puts forth the nerve fibers that form the eye, and in the eye receive impressions from the light, and return these impressions to the brain where the reflecting mind resides. But this conscious effort can be directed to only one thing at a time—to observe, for instance, the difference between black and white, or to distinguish the form of a letter; and, if no impression could be received except by this conscious attention, we never could learn to read; the whole power would be spent upon ever-repeated efforts to make the simplest distinctions. The mind, therefore, forms for itself a depository for the impressions already received, in the optic thalami, which, after a few repetitions, recognize the familiar impressions without the effort or even the consciousness of the cerebrum, and combine them, and communicate the result to the cerebrum. Thus letter after letter, and word after word, are added to their stores of sense-knowledge, and the conscious effort is left free to attend to the meaning of the pages.

In like manner the mind desires to do something, and stretches out nerve fibers charged with this desire, and by them weaves the muscles and the bones of the arms and the hands. And then, according to the circumstances and opportunities of doing, it teaches the fingers to move, to grasp a needle, to take a stitch, or to touch the key of a piano. And if every motion must needs proceed from the direct effort and intention of the mind, the very simplest movements are all that would ever be effected; and therefore the mind forms for itself lieutenants, who shall be associated with it and cooperate in every effort, perhaps even itself doing the work under direction, and which, after a few attempts, shall be able to direct all familiar motions without special charge from the conscious thought. The corpora striata, so called from their alternate layers of cellular and fibrous tissue, are such a lieutenant. They make the familiar stitches, strike the familiar chords and runs, write the letters, and even spell the words; and the convolutions of the cerebrum, after teaching them to look after these things, are free to attend to the use and beauty of the work, the feeling of the music, the sense of the writing.

It may be true that the fibers proceeding directly from the cerebrum do not themselves extend further than to these subordinate bodies, but content themselves with forming there the cells proper to them, from which again proceed the fibers which form the organs of sense and motion; so that the cerebrum may not receive sensations immediately from, nor act directly upon, the body, but may perform both functions mediately through the cells and the fibers of the optic thalami and the corpora striata, respectively. Yet even so the secondary fibers are only modifications and extensions of the primary, and the effect is the same for most purposes as if the fibers were immediately from the cerebrum; the only difference being that, if the hypothesis be true, the cells of these subordinate lobes serve as repeating stations for both sensations and impulses, the operators in which stations are able to do of themselves, under the general control of the cerebrum, whatever it has taught them to do.

All these lower nerve centers, important as they are, are subordinate to the great masses of the brain, called the cerebrum and the cerebellum. These chief organisms of the mind are informed of every act of their lieutenants, and the cause of the act, and have power to control and revise their action. In these great masses of the brain reside the conscious sense, the powers of attention, of reflection, of comparison or choice, of intention, and the human affection. And there are the first receptacles of life from above.

The cerebrum is much the larger of the two, and occupies the whole of the upper part of the head; the cerebellum lying under the hinder lobes of the cerebrum. The cerebrum is divided into two hemispheres, the right and the left, united by masses of fibers at the base. The cerebellum, though having a right and a left which answer to each other, is not divided. Besides these most general distinctions, the brains, especially the cerebrum, are distinguished into lobes, and the lobes into convolutions of great intricacy and beauty, of which we shall have more to say presently.

It has already been intimated that the cerebellum has charge of the vital functions of the body, of which the reflecting mind is unconscious; and that the cerebrum is the abode of the conscious sense, effort, and thought. The sense of the cerebrum Swedenborg calls "voluntary"; and that of the cerebellum, "involuntary;" and of these he says:

> The voluntary sense belongs to the cerebrum, but the involuntary to the cerebellum. These two general senses are conjoined in man, but still distinct. The fibers which go forth from the cerebrum present in general the voluntary sense, and those from the cerebellum present in general the involuntary sense. The fibers of this twofold origin conjoin themselves in the two appendices which are called the medulla oblongata and the medulla spinalis, and through them pass into the body, and fashion its members, viscera, and organs. The things which encompass the body as the muscles and the skin, and also the organs of sense, for the most part receive fibers from the cerebrum; from these man has sensations and also motions according to his will. But the things which are within that enclosure, and

are called the viscera of the body, receive fibers from the cerebellum. Therefore man has no sense of them, nor are they under the control of his will.

The cerebellum shares its control of many functions of the body with the cerebrum, during the hours of wakefulness; but when the cerebrum sleeps, the cerebellum has sole charge. Dreams, therefore, flow in through the cerebellum, and from angels and spirits who belong to that province. After describing some dreams, pleasant and instructive, Swedenborg says:

> They are angelic spirits, who are on the confines of the paradisal abodes, who insinuate such dreams; to whom also is assigned the duty of watching over certain men while they sleep, lest they should be infested by evil spirits. This duty they perform with the greatest delight, insomuch that there is an emulation among them who shall attend; and they love to affect man with sweet and delightful things which they see in his affection and disposition. These angelic spirits are of those who in the life of the body have delighted and loved to make the life of others delightful, by every means and endeavor. When the sense of hearing is so far opened, there is heard as from afar a sweet modulation of sounds as of singing. They said that they do not know whence such things come to them; and such beautiful and pleasant representatives; but it was said that it was from heaven. They belong to the province of the cerebellum; because the cerebellum, as I have been instructed, is awake during sleep, while the cerebrum is asleep. The men of the Most Ancient Church

had their dreams from thence, with a perception
what they signified; from which in great part came
the representatives and significatives of the Ancients,
under which things deeply hidden were set forth.
(*Arcana Coelestia* §1977)

As has been said, in some parts of the body the voluntary fibers prevail, as in the organs of sense; and in some
the involuntary, as in the viscera; but yet both kinds go
everywhere; for there is no part of the viscera which, in a
state of disease, may not make its condition consciously
felt by fibers of the cerebrum; and there is no part of a
muscle or a membrane which does not depend for the
regulation of its nutrition upon the presence of fibers
from the cerebellum. Swedenborg says:

The voluntary things continually lead away from
order, but the involuntary things continually lead
back to order. Hence it is that the motion of the
heart, which is involuntary, is altogether exempt
from the will of man; likewise the action of the
cerebellum; and that the motion of the heart and
the forces of the cerebellum rule the voluntary
things, lest these should break down beyond limits,
and extinguish the life of the body before the time.
Therefore the agents of both, as well the voluntary
as the involuntary things, go forth in the whole
body united. (*Arcana Coelestia* §9683; similar
things also in *Spiritual Diary* §5781)

The cerebellum is said to be the abode of the involuntary things, in the sense that its actions proceed without
the consciousness and effort of man. But this is because

they proceed from the love which is his life, of the affections of which he is unaware. The evil genii who operate upon the cerebellum are said to flow into the affections, with the effort to turn them into evil lusts, carefully avoiding the thoughts lest they should be perceived (*Divine Providence* §310). The cerebellum, therefore, like the heart, is the organ of the love or the will; and the cerebrum, like the lungs, is related to the understanding. Therefore the perverse things also of man's love have their seat in the cerebellum; and the cerebellum can be instructed, and freed from perversity, by the cerebrum, as the blood from the heart is purified by the lungs.

A very simple matter illustrates the action of the cerebrum upon the cerebellum. It has been said that the cerebellum rules in the body at night while the cerebrum sleeps. But if, before going to sleep, the cerebrum fixes the hour for waking, the cerebellum thus instructed awakes it at the time.

It is possible to see in the character of the dreams a reflection of the natural tendencies of the will; and to most people they reveal evil tendencies which certainly are not of their choice or intention, and yet they are real tendencies of the natural will, having their abode in corresponding forms of the cerebellum. And if, in the preparation for the night's sleep, besides the reading of the Word and prayer, which should bring prevailing good influences into the dreams, there should be also a distinct condemning of the evil tendencies and a warning of the soul against them, much might be done to make the dreams gentle and pure, and the sleep deeply refreshing.

We read nowadays of the experiments of French physicians in what is called "hypnotism," or involuntary sleep, which is nearly or quite the same as mesmeric sleep. Hypnotized patients are not conscious of anything that is said to them, and remember nothing of it; and yet they are deeply impressed by it, and will do in their natural state, as by a natural impulse upon which they do not reflect, whatever they have been told in their sleep to do. Instances are related in which patients of violent temper and coarsest manners have been instructed not to do the things which have been habitual to them, but to do good and gentle things instead, specifying particularly what is not to be done and what is to be done, with the result of transforming apparently the natural disposition of the subjects. Evil things also are taught and executed with equal readiness. Now, without delaying to inquire the possible effect of this in regeneration—remarking only that no one is ever condemned or saved by his hereditary character, nor by that which is impressed upon him without his own choice—we may draw this lesson: If while one's own cerebrum is quiescent, another can so instruct and impress the organ of one's will or natural disposition through the auditory nerves, one may do the same for himself—may chide himself for evil and warn himself not to do it. Foreseeing times of temptation, he may resolutely instruct himself in what he is to do; and when the time of trial comes lie will find his natural disposition changing, and if he does not himself undo his own instructions, he will very likely go by in safety; at least he will find his continued efforts much more effective in securing self-restraint.

In studying the sense of hearing, we have seen that it has relation to obedience; and it is interesting to remember that the nerves of the ears, besides their extension to their special convolutions of the cerebrum, send large branches directly to the cerebellum, having thus a tendency to produce prompt and involuntary obedience, as well as voluntary. In listening to music, the effect upon the feelings, aside from any thinking, is an effect produced upon the cerebellum; the thought about the words, or about the structure of the music, and even about its beauty of form, is in the cerebrum.

There were some spirits, professedly Christian, but of evil life, who desired to enter heaven. Swedenborg relates that they were brought to the gates of a certain heavenly society, where they were examined by those whose duty it was to receive newcomers.

> And they turned them about, and saw that the hinder parts of their heads were very hollow; and then they said, "Depart from here; for you are in the enjoyment of the love of doing evil, and therefore you are not conjoined to heaven; for in your hearts you have denied God, and despised the things of religion." . . . On the way home, we conversed about the cause that the occiputs of those who are the enjoyment of doing evil are hollow. And I said that this is the cause: that man has two brains, one in the occiput, which is called the cerebellum, and the other in the forehead, which is called the cerebrum; and that the love of the will dwells in the cerebellum, and the thought of the understanding in the cerebrum; and when the thought of a man's understanding does not lead the love of the will, the inmosts of the cerebellum, which in themselves are celestial, collapse, whence is the hollowness. (*True Christian Religion* §160)

It may be supposed that the perverse exterior forms of the cerebellum remained, and were receptive of evil influx;

but the interiors shriveled away. That the same was not true of their cerebrums was because the understanding can be separated from the will; and they could know and understand the things of religion and of heavenly life, though they did not believe and love them. How forcibly does this present the consequences of evil life in the very organism of the spirits of men! They still receive from the Lord the rationality and freedom that reside in the forehead; they can still understand the truth, and for some external motive of honor or gain can compel themselves to do it. But their ability really to love it is gone forever: they themselves have destroyed it.[1]

The texture of the cerebrum also is affected by the mode of thinking, whether truly or falsely, spiritually or sensually; and becomes orderly, soft, and pellucid, or disorderly, hairy, callous, or bony, accordingly. Swedenborg relates that in the early period of his spiritual instruction there were felt hard places in the left part of his cerebrum, like rather large, hard nuclei, which, he says,

> were affected with a dull or mute pain; and it was said to me that it was perceived from the hardened spots that there were still things which were not truths of faith. Hence it appears that hardness actually exists in the organic forms when there is not faith, and the greater the hardening the less conscience there is; so that they who have no conscience after death have the brain outmostly hard.
>
> Moreover, when I received only the literal sense of the Word, then the ways were closed to the

---

1. Similar things are said of some spirits of the Dragon (*Posthumous Theological Works*, "Last Judgment" §52).

understanding of interior things. And thus with those who only stick in the literal sense of the Word; the brains are hardened and enclosed, so that there is no way open to an inner sense, and still less to the inmost; thus a crust is formed of external corporeal or sensual things glued together. It is otherwise when the way is opened to the sense of interior things, or to the spirit; which way is opened by the Lord alone. (*Spiritual Diary* §1623–1624)

"The head of those who know and believe," we are informed, "appears as if human, and the brain orderly, white like snow, and lucid, for heavenly light is received by them." But the brains of some of the wicked, who believed they lived of themselves, and refused to open their minds to the Lord, were found "rough, hairy, and dark" (*Arcana Coelestia* §4319). Not that the natural brain would so appear, but the spiritual brain when inspected by the angels after death.

The function of the cerebellum, according to the common idea of modern physiologists, is chiefly to preserve the equilibrium of the body. And this idea is founded upon the observed fact that, in cases of injury to the cerebellum, an animal tumbles about helplessly. The same is the case with man in less degree. After a time, however, the power of preserving the equilibrium is recovered in great degree, yet at the cost of close attention and much effort. It probably is true that animals walk, and perform many other actions, naturally, without much teaching, and mostly under the control of the cerebellum. Man does the same to a much lesser extent. And when the cerebellum is destroyed, all such natural motion, except as it can be continued by the medulla oblongata, ceases; and the actions can be continued only by the effort of the cerebrum. Man loses less of the power than animals, because he always moves less by nature, and depends more upon teaching. This part of the function of the cerebellum is more easily observed than the rest; but a great want of vitality is noticeable in the performance of all the natural functions of the body.

As the brain forms the body by means of its fibers, it also animates it. For the life that flows into the body to form it continues to flow in to keep it in the power to perform the functions for which it is formed.

The life also animates the body in the same order in which it formed it. It flows into the cells of the brain immediately, and from them through the fibers into all the tissues of the body. After the body is formed, and the man assumes control of it, his thought and affection are exercised in the cells of the brain, and according to the quality of this exercise is the quality of the animation of the body through them. Swedenborg states that the animating influence of the brain is exerted by means of a highly vitalized fluid which he calls "the animal spirits." And he says that one who does not believe in the existence of such an agency, stops in the beginning, and can know nothing of the operation of the spirit in the body (*Spiritual Diary* §3459).

In the cells of the brain the spiritual and the natural substances of the mind meet (compare *True Christian Religion* §38). In thinking the truth, and willing what is good, the very substance of truth and goodness is secreted by the cells of the spiritual body, and in the cells of the natural brain is embodied in the pure fluids secreted from the capillaries, and thence is sent through the fibers, inspiring every part of the body in the performance of its functions. And this vitalization is according to the quality of the thinking and willing, noble if these be noble, and vile if they be vile. From the body there is a return of the purer fluids to the brain, for re-secretion and new combinations, through the blood vessels (*Divine Love and Wisdom* §316).

It is Swedenborg's view that not only are the tissues of the body vitalized directly by fibers from the brain, but the blood itself also receives its portion of spirit which is secreted in the ventricles of the brain, together with pure lymph with which it is combined, and impure serosities and adhesive fluids discharged from among the fibers, and from which the brain needs to free itself. These fluids, he says, are directed from the ventricles through the appropriate foramina to the infundibulum, under the pineal gland, and thence to the pituitary body, which is really a gland for compounding this vitalizing fluid for the blood and separating from it the impurities.

Of the correspondence of these functions with the heavens, Swedenborg has much to say:

> There were certain spirits above the head, a little in front, who spoke with me. They discoursed pleasantly, and their influx was tolerably gentle. They were distinguished from others by this, that they had a continual eagerness and desire to come into heaven. It was said that they who have reference to the ventricles or larger cavities of the brain, and belong that province, are of this nature. The reason was also added: that the better kind of lymph which is therein is of such a nature, namely, as to return into the brain; and hence also is in such an effort. The brain is heaven: the effort is eagerness and desire. Such are the correspondences.

There appeared to me a certain face over a blue window, which face presently betook itself within. There then appeared a little star about the region of the left eye; afterwards many red stars with a white sparkle. Next appeared to me walls, but no roof, the walls only on the left side: lastly, as it were the starry heaven. But whereas these things were seen in a place where evil spirits were, I imagined that it was something foul which was presented me to see. Presently, however, the wall and the heaven disappeared; and I saw a well, out of which came forth, as it were, a bright mist or vapor; it seemed also as if something were pumped out of the well. I inquired what these things signified or represented. It was said that it was a representation of the infundibulum in the brain, over which was the cerebrum, which is signified by heaven; and what was next seen was that vessel, which is signified by a well, and is called the infundibulum; and that the mist or vapor which arose thence was the lymph which passes through, and is pumped out thence; and that this lymph is of a twofold kind, namely, what is mixed with animal spirits, which is among the useful lymph, and what is mixed with serosities, which is among the excrementitious lymphs. It was afterwards shown me of what quality those are who belong to this province; but only those who were of the viler sort. They were also seen. They run about hither and thither, apply themselves to those whom they see, attend to every particular, and tell others what they hear; prone to suspicion, impatient, restless, in imitation of that lymph which is therein, and is conveyed to and fro. Their reasonings are the fluids there which they represent. These, however, are of the middle sort; but they who have reference to the excrementitious lymphs therein, are such as draw down spiritual truths to things terrestrial, and there defile them; as, for instance, when they hear anything about marriage love, they apply it to whoredoms and adulteries, and thus drag down to these the things which belong to marriage love; and so in other cases. (*Arcana Coelestia* §4049–4050)

These descriptions seem all to be taken from the Christian heaven before the Last Judgment, thus during the process of its formation and purification from evil spirits. The Ancient heavens would be described very differently, and likewise the Christian heaven now that it is in order.

In the *Diary* we read of those mentioned above as being in the ventricles of the brain, and desiring to enter heaven:

They knew not that they had been in heaven, and had been removed from it that they might be the better perfected, and so return into heaven when hetrogeneous things had been cast out from them; altogether as it is with that serosity in the ventricles, a part of which is absorbed by the choroid plexus, as a part also is cast out from it, a part is exhaled from elsewhere, a part passes through the third ventricle under the pineal gland, and so through the infundibulum towards the pituitary body, where it is separated by three ways, and is carried thence by various passages, canals, and sinuses towards the jugular vein, that it may meet the chyle coming up through the thoracic duct, and they may there be consociated, and borne towards the heart, and thence into the lungs, and back to the left ventricle, and then onwards, a part towards the head through the carotids, a part downwards through all the viscera of the body; and all for the end that a purer blood or animal spirit may be formed, and thus the red blood, in order that material things may be united with spiritual and live one life. (*Spiritual Diary* §831; see also §914)

Certain spirits are described—deformed, cruel and beastly—who correspond to foul and poisonous humors in the brain, and also to deadly tumors. And it is said that "such are they who slew whole armies in the old times, as it is written in the Word; for they rushed into the chambers of the brain in everyone, and inspired terror, together with such insanity that they slew one another" (*Arcana Coelestia* §5717).

Others who are like the gross phlegm of the brain, and produce obstructions, dullness, and many diseases, are described as totally void of conscience, and placing "human prudence and wisdom in exciting enmities, hatreds, and intestine combats, for the sake of ruling" (*Arcana Coelestia* §5718). And still others are described who cause various disorders (see *Arcana Coelestia* §5386, 5724; *Spiritual Diary* §1783, 1793).

It seems strange to think of spirits so perverse as having access to so interior a province of the heavens. Probably it would be impossible now; but before the Last Judgment there were many evil persons penetrating even to the higher parts of the Christian heaven, and causing much disturbance. In the higher heavens, and probably in the Christian heaven now, instead of such evil spirits we might find angels who have some morbidness or sluggish-ness to get rid of, and are there subjected to some purifying processes corresponding to those by which evil spirits were separated.

A view of the brain, to one who looks upon it with the reverence which is its due, excites a feeling of awe, arising from the sense of deep mystery, and also of wonderful, if as yet unintelligible, beauty. Swedenborg says:

> When the skull and the integuments about the brain are removed, there appear wonderful circumvolutions and gyri, in which are disposed the substances that are called cortical. From these run forth the fibers which constitute the medulla of the brain. These fibers proceed thence through the nerves into the body, and there perform functions according to the command and will of the brain. All these things are altogether according to the heavenly form; for such a form is impressed upon the heavens by the Lord, and thence also upon the things which are in man, and especially upon his cerebrum and cerebellum. (*Arcana Coelestia* §4040)

The exact purpose or distribution of functions, of these wonderful convolutions, is not perfectly known; yet it is possible to obtain a general view of them which is to be trusted in the main. We have seen that the cerebellum is the organ of the love which is the life of the mind, the seat of its natural affections, and the means by which the organs performing the vital functions in the body are animated and controlled. And in general we have learned that the cerebrum is the habitation of the conscious mind, to which the sensations that come to consciousness are reported, and by which the voluntary actions are controlled.

The cerebrum is divided into two hemispheres. To the right hemisphere, we are taught, they correspond "who are in the will of good, and thence in the will of truth; but they who correspond to the left part of the brain are those who are in the understanding of good and truth, and thence in affection for them" (*Arcana Coelestia* §4052).

Besides this division into hemispheres, the whole cerebrum may be thought of in general as divided into regions of conscious sense and regions of action; the regions of sense lying in the hinder and lower part of the cerebrum, and the region of action somewhat overlying this towards the front, and occupying the whole of the lobes immediately above the temples. In front of these, both in animals and in men, are the convolutions in which resides the faculty of attention and intelligence; by which animals as well as men can be instructed to some extent, and learn to do things contrary to their natural inclinations, yet, in the case of animals, under the stimulus of other natural motives. And in the extreme front, furthest removed from the ultimates of sense and action—looking down upon all the impressions of sense, the natural desires, the acquired knowledge, with power to rule and control them all, with power also to abstract itself from these, and to appreciate not only abstract qualities, such as warmth and color, but also spiritual qualities of affection and wisdom—reside the human faculties of rationality and freedom.

In the area obliquely upward and backward from the ears, devoted to the perceptions of sensations, we have a simple arrangement of the convolutions, proceeding from below upward in the natural sequence of the senses from voluntary to intellectual. In the large convolutions in the base of the cerebrum, under the great ventricles, resides the sense of touch; and proceeding thence upward behind the line of the ears, and backward, we have successively the convolutions devoted respectively to taste, smell, hearing, and sight, the last much more extensive than the others.

No doubt, besides the direct communication of fibers from these several convolutions to their respective organs of sense, there is indirect communication with other parts of the brain, the great mass of white substance indicating that there is a multitude of fibers forming a means of intercommunication among all parts of the cerebrum, and especially between all other parts and the frontal lobes; yet the conscious perception of sensations seems limited to their special convolutions.

Above and in front of the area of sight lie the convolutions which control the movements of the legs; then over the ears and somewhat forward, those that move the arms; in the upper part of the frontal convolutions is now the control of the face; and in the lower part, just above the temples, lies the faculty of speech.

This relative position of organs of sense and organs of motion is continued in the lower nerve centers; for the corpora striata, through which pass the nerves of motion, lie below the convolutions of motion, and the optic thalami behind them, under the convolutions of sense. In the spinal medulla also, the columns of sensory fibers lie in the rear, and those of motor fibers in front; and these are attended by columns of fibers from the cerebellum accompanying them both at the sides, and running everywhere with them.

Through the fibers, as Swedenborg says,

> the mind, when it is in its thought from the understanding, and affection from the will, has extension into all things of the whole body, and there spreads

itself throughout their forms, as do the thoughts and affections of the angels into the societies of the whole heaven. The case is similar, because all things of the human body correspond to all things of heaven; wherefore the form of the whole heaven before the Lord is the human form. (*Apocalypse Explained* §775)

Many things are said of the correspondence of the brain with the heavens, and of the influx of the heavens into the brain, which will help fill out and make clear the whole subject.

The angels who correspond to the enclosing membranes of the brain, like those relating to other covering membranes of the body, are in a passive state, speaking not from themselves, but from others, and thus serving as conjoining mediums, and for protection.

They who constitute the dura mater "were such as during their life as men thought nothing of spiritual and heavenly things, nor spake about them, because they believed only in what was natural, and this because they could not penetrate further; nevertheless they did not confess this. They still, like others, worshipped the Divine, had stated times for prayer, and were good citizens."

Among those who

had reference to the outer layer of the dura mater ... were such as thought about spiritual and heavenly things only from such things as are objects of the external senses, comprehending more interior things in no other way. They were heard by me as of the female sex. They who reason from external sensuals, hence from things worldly and corporeal, concerning those which are of heaven and the spiritual things of faith and love, the more they unite and confound those things, go outward even to the external skin of the head, which they represent; but still they are within the Greatest Man, although in its extremes, if they have lived a good life; for everyone who is in good life from affection of charity is saved. (*Arcana Coelestia* §4046)

Those of the pia mater

were as they had been in the world, not trusting much to their own thought, and thereby setting themselves to think anything certain on holy things, but depending on the faith of others, and not considering whether a thing was true. That this was their quality was also shown me by an influx of their perception into the Lord's Prayer when I was reading it; for all spirits and angels, however many they may be, may be known as to their quality from the Lord's Prayer, and this by an influx of the ideas of their thought into the contents of the Prayer. From this it was perceived that such was their character, and moreover that they could serve the angels as intermediates; for there are spirits intermediate between the heavens, by whom there is communication; for their ideas were not closed, but easily opened; thus they suffered themselves to be acted upon, and readily admitted and received the influx. They were also modest and peaceful, and said they were in heaven. (*Arcana Coelestia* §4047)

The sinuses of the brain are large vessels for receiving the venous blood, and are situated in safe and quiet places, where they can relieve the brain of the surplus blood without themselves partaking in any great degree of its active motions. Swedenborg writes:

> There was a certain spirit near my head who spoke with me. I perceived from the tone of his voice that he was in a state of tranquility, as of a kind of peaceful sleep. He asked this thing and that, but with such prudence that a person awake could not have asked more prudently. It was perceived that interior angels spoke by him, and that he was in such a state as to perceive and bring forth what they spoke. I asked about that state, and told him that it was such. He replied that he spoke nothing but what was good and true; and that he perceived whether anything else flowed in, and if it did he did not admit or utter it. Of his state he said that it was peaceful; and it was given me to perceive it by communication. It was said that they are such who have reference to the sinuses or larger blood vessels of the brain; and that they who are like him have reference to the longitudinal sinus, which is between the hemispheres of the cerebrum, and are there in a state of peace, however the brain on both sides be in a state of tumult. (*Arcana Coelestia* §4048)

The cells, or glands, which constitute the cortical substance of the brain, Swedenborg says, are innumerable; and he adds:

> The multitude of these glands may ... be compared to the multitude of angelic societies in the heavens, which also are innumerable, and in the same order (as was told me) as the glands; and the multitude of

fibrillae proceeding from these glands may be compared to spiritual truths and goods, that in like manner flow from the societies like rays. (*Divine Love and Wisdom* §366)

They who are in the principles of good relate to those things in the brain which are the first beginnings there, and are called the glands, or cortical substances; but they who are in the principles of truth relate to those things which flow from those first beginnings, and are called the fibers. (*Arcana Coelestia* §4052)

The brain, like heaven, is in the sphere of ends, which are uses; for whatever flows in from the Lord is an end regarding the salvation of the human race. This end is what reigns in heaven, and also what reigns thence in the brain; for the brain, where is man's mind, regards ends in the body, namely, that the body may serve the soul, in order that the soul may be happy forever. (*Arcana Coelestia* §4054)

In regard to the influx from the heavens into the brain, we read in *Heaven and Hell*:

The influx of the Lord Himself with man is into his forehead, and thence into the whole face, since the forehead of man corresponds to love and the face corresponds to all the interiors. The influx of the spiritual angels with man is into his head everywhere, from the forehead and temples to every part under which is the cerebrum, because that region of the head corresponds to intelligence. But the

influx of the celestial angels is into that part of the
head in which is the cerebellum, and which is called
the occiput, from the ears all around even to the
neck; for that region corresponds to wisdom. (§251)

In *Apocalypse Explained* §61, we read as follows:

The Divine Influx from heaven is into man's will,
and through the will into his understanding. Influx
into the will is into the occiput, because into the
cerebellum, and from this it passes to the forward
parts into the cerebrum, where is the understanding; and when it comes by that way into the understanding, it then comes also into the sight, for man
sees from his understanding.

And again:

All good is received from behind, and all truth from
in front, since the cerebellum is formed to receive
good which is of the will, and the cerebrum to receive
truth which is of the understanding. (§316)

To understand these things we must remember that the
relation of the cerebellum to the cerebrum is like that of the
heart to the lungs; that the cerebellum causes the cerebrum
to be formed and nourished, as the heart does the lungs;
and then, as the blood of the heart is purified by means of
the lungs, so the affections of the cerebellum may be
purified by the truth perceived and willed by the cerebrum;
and that in this faculty of perceiving and willing the truth
that purifies the life's love, consists the true rationality and
freedom in which the Lord resides in man; which faculty

lies in the forehead, and is that which knows and acknowledges the Lord, and causes the whole of the man to submit to His influence: and further, as in the case of the heart and the lungs, if the love in the cerebellum is not purified by the thought of the cerebrum, it compels the cerebrum to think only the evil and false things that agree with its own perversity (compare *Divine Love and Wisdom* §413–425). In this case, the interiors of the cerebellum are destroyed, but the freedom and rationality still remain, for they are the Lord's in man, and are never destroyed or taken away (*Divine Love and Wisdom* §425). But in case the love is purified by the truth, then the Lord flows into the will's love, and through this continually incites the understanding to learn more of the ennobling truth.

> The angels of the inmost heaven correspond to those things in man which belong to the provinces of the heart and the cerebellum; but the angels of the middle heaven correspond to those things in man which belong to the provinces of the lungs and the cerebrum. . . . But to intermediate angels who are near to both heavens, and conjoin them, correspond the cardiac and pulmonary plexuses, by which the heart is conjoined with the lungs; also the medulla oblongata, where the fiber of the cerebellum is conjoined with the fiber of the cerebrum. (*Arcana Coelestia* §9670)

We are told also that the gentle, interior, and sincere spirits from the planet Mars, who are in thought from affection and in the affection of thought, relate to "that middle province which is between the cerebrum and the cerebellum."

And because they have such a relation in the Greatest Man, that middle province which is between the cerebrum and the cerebellum corresponds to them; for in them the cerebrum and cerebellum are conjoined as to spiritual operations; their face makes one with their thought, so that from the face the very affection of thought shines forth, and from the affection, with some indications also from the eyes, the general nature of the thought. Wherefore, when they were near me, I sensibly perceived a drawing back of the front part of the head towards the occiput, thus of the cerebrum towards the cerebellum. (*Arcana Coelestia* §7481)

A most interesting account is given, in *Arcana Coelestia* §4326, of the operation of the two brains upon the expression of the face, in the Most Ancient times and afterwards:

There was heard a gentle thundering, which flowed down from on high above the occiput, and continued about the whole region of it. I wondered who they were. It was told me that they were those who relate to the general involuntary feeling. And it was further said that they can perceive well a man's thoughts, but are not willing to set them forth and utter them; like the cerebellum, which perceives all that which the cerebrum perceives, but does not publish it. When their manifest operation into the whole province of the occiput ceased, it was shown how far their operation had extended. It was first determined to the whole face, then it withdrew itself towards the left part of the face, and lastly towards the ear there; by which was signified of what nature the operation of the general involuntary feeling had been from the earliest times with the men of our earth, and how it had changed. The influx from the cerebellum insinuates itself chiefly into the face, as is manifest from this, that the disposition is inscribed on the face, and that the affections appear in the face, and this for the most part without man's will—as is the case with fear, awe, shame, various kinds of joy and also of sorrow; besides other things which thus are made known to another; so that he knows from the face what affections and what changes of the feelings and of the mind there are. These are from the cerebellum by means of its fibers, when there is no simulation within. Thus it was shown that the general feeling in the earliest times, or with the Most Ancient people, occupied the whole face; and that successively after those times it occupied only the left part of it, and finally afterwards it spread itself outside of the face, so that at this day there is scarcely any general involuntary feeling remaining in the face. The right part of the face, with the right eye, corresponds to affection for good; but the left to affection for truth; and the region where the ear is, to obedience only without affection. For with the Most Ancient people—whose age was called the Golden Age, because they lived in a certain state of integrity, and in love to the Lord and mutual love, like the angels—all the involuntary feeling of the cerebellum was manifested in the face; and then they did not know how to present anything else in the face than according as heaven flowed into the involuntary efforts, and thence into the will. But with the Ancients, whose age was called the Silver Age, because they were in a state of truth, and thence in charity towards the neighbor, the involuntary feeling of the cerebellum was manifested, not in the right part of the face, but only in the left; and with their posterity—whose time was called the Iron Age, because they lived not in affection for truth, but in obedience to truth— the involuntary feeling was no longer manifested in the face, but betook itself to the region about the left ear. I have been instructed that the fibers of the cerebellum thus changed their distribution in the face, and that in their place fibers of the cerebrum were carried thither, which then rule over those from the cerebellum; and this from an effort to form the expression of the face according to one's own will, which is from the cerebrum. It does not appear to man that these things are so, but it is very manifest to the angels from the influx of heaven, and from correspondence. (*Arcana Coelestia* §4326)

We read also of another remarkable change:

The Most Ancient people, who constituted the Lord's Celestial Church, had a will in which was good, and an understanding in which was truth thence, which two made one in them. But the Ancients, who formed the Lord's Spiritual Church, had a will altogether corrupt, but a sound understanding, in which the Lord formed by regeneration a new will, and through this also a new understanding. (*Arcana Coelestia* §4328)

The change that thus took place suggests a possible explanation of the curious fact that the fibers that pass from the head to the body are crossed in the medullae, so that the fibers from the right side of the head rule in the left side of the body, and those from the left side of the head in the right side of the body. And yet Swedenborg, though he mentions the fact in the *Diary* (§1666–1667), still in his published works refers the right side of the head and of the body alike to the love of good, and the left side to the love of truth. The body is spiritual relatively to the head; and the position of the Ancient Church, relatively to that of the Most Ancient, is sometimes likened to that of the body to the head. Now, if the right side of the head may be regarded as representing the will of good and truth in the Most Ancient Church, and this will was so corrupt in the Ancient that a new will must be formed by means of the understanding, the influx of the will of good and truth from the Most Ancient into the Ancient must have been into the understanding and thence into the new will; and when this was done, then there could be influx from the understanding of good and truth into the new will. In the head the will to do good leads, the will to understand follows; but in the body the will to understand leads, and receives influx from the leading faculty of the head, and the will to do follows, and receives influx from the faculty that follows in the head. The will to do, as it descends, must become the will to understand for the sake of doing; and the will to understand, as it descends, must become the will of doing for the sake of the understanding. It may have something to do with this, that the primary principle in the Most Ancient Church was love to the Lord, and the secondary mutual love; and the primary in the Ancient Church was charity to the neighbor, and the secondary was the faith of charity. Also, that in the changes of state of the angels, in the most external state of the celestial angels, their sun passes over to the left, and adds its luster to that of the moon of the spiritual angels, which then is in its greatest brightness.

Ends of good, we have learned, prevail in the province of the brain of the heavens; that is, the Divine ends for the salvation of the human race. The angels of this heaven "have extension into the whole heaven" (*Heaven and Hell* §49); that is, they perceive the states of all in heaven— their states as to love and thought. And by the influx of affection and light—also sometimes by representatives, and through intermediate angels, and sometimes by angels sent down from their own societies—they inspire and instruct.

The influx of the angels of the cerebellum, like that of this organ in the body, is a silent influx of the love for the Lord and for doing His will, which is the life of the heavens. They perceive the states of the whole heaven as to the reception of life from the Lord, and the mutual usefulness which is the effect of that life. They control the whole process of receiving, sorting, and training the new spirits from the earths, and preparing them for heaven. They act mediately through others, and not without association with those of the cerebrum; but their sense of the need of the heavens, and of what is in harmony with its life, governs the whole process. The opening of the understandings of the angelic spirits in the province of the lungs is partly under the influence of angels of the cerebrum; but the final sending forth from the heart of the heavens, with the full inspiration to do all possible good, is from the impulse of the cerebellum.

From their sense of the state of the whole heaven as to its reception of the Lord, they not only train and assimilate new spirits—as it were for the nourishment of every part of the heavens—but they also gather into themselves the sense of need for further uses, and of preparation for new forms of reception of the Divine Wisdom and Goodness; and this they have from their sense of the Lord's love for uses not yet fully performed. And the life which they receive from the Lord, with this sense of what It would do, they impart to the angels of the province of generation, whose delight it is to assist in preparing receptacles for the Divine life. Thus these angels preside over the reception of the Divine life in the heavens, and the perfecting of the states of reception.

They flow also in man into all the functions of natural life which take place according to correspondence with the heavens, and this they do by influx into his cerebellum. They preside also over his sleep, contribute to the renovation and refreshment of sleep, and are in the effort to give sweet and helpful dreams (*Arcana Coelestia* §1977). To the Most Ancient Church, whose affections were innocent, such dreams were always given, and by them they were instructed in the general things that they needed for the perfecting of their lives (*Arcana Coelestia* §1122).

To the province of the cerebrum, which presides over the voluntary sense of the heavens, belongs the duty of attending, not to the states of life, but to the states of thought and intention of all parts of the heavens, and to their actual experiences. It is a part of their duty to attend to and interpret the representatives by which the Lord would instruct the heavens through the angels of the eyes. It is their duty to attend to the states of thought, intelligence, and intention of angels throughout the heavens, and of men on earth—for the Church also is a part of the Greatest Man—and to communicate the truth which the Lord reveals to them for the continual improvement of His kingdom, according to the states of reception in all.

Even the angels of life in the cerebellum are instructed by the cerebrum through intermediates (*Heaven and Hell* §225; *Apocalypse Explained* §831), and by such instruction their perception of life from the Lord is made more intelligent; they are helped to perceive what they had not perceived, to understand what had been obscure to them, and thus to impart a nobler life to the heavens.

Examples of the presence of angels of the brain in lower provinces, we have in the many relations which represent angels of the third heaven as presiding over the deliberations of the assembled spirits, and receiving their conclusions (see *True Christian Religion* §48, 162, 188).

Of the use of their constant presence and influence in other parts of the heavens, we have the following interesting instruction:

> All the wisdom of angels is given by means of the Word, since in its internal and inmost sense is Divine wisdom which is communicated to the angels through the Word when this is read by men, and when they think upon it. But still it is to be known that wisdom is given to them mediately by angels who were from the Most Ancient and Ancient Churches, who were in a knowledge and perception of representatives and correspondences; these were such in the world that they knew the internal arcana of the Church, and correspondences, and by means of these wisdom is communicated, and when it is communicated it appears to those who receive it as if it were their own. This is the effect of communication; and therefore angels of the Most Ancient heavens are dispersed throughout the heavens, that others may have wisdom. (*Spiritual*

Diary §5187; see also *Apocalypse Explained* §5188, 5189, 5194)

This presence is like the presence of the brain by means of the nerves in every part of the body. Besides the personal presence, there is abundant instruction by representatives and by influx.[2]

The societies of the cerebrum are, of course, arranged in correspondence with the heavenly form of the brain itself. In the hinder part are societies that correspond with the convolutions of sense. It is their duty to observe and perceive and record all things in the state of all parts of the Greatest Man that have relation or correspondence with the senses—the quality of new spirits, as perceived through the angels of the tongue and the nose; the quality of the lives of men on the earth also, as perceived through smell and sight and touch and hearing; the state of all parts of the heavens also, as manifested to the senses; the representatives given by the Lord to the transparent provinces of the eyes, with the beautiful representatives which are presented to the inmost heaven by the Lord when men upon the earth are reading the Word; also, perhaps, the spoken words of the Lord. All these impressions it is their duty and their delight to receive and treasure for the general use.

In the middle and forward part are the societies whose duty it is to direct the voluntary action of the muscles— the motions of the hands and the feet in their cooperation with the Lord's Providence in the care of men and spirits and angels; the motions of the head and the eyes; and all

2. See *Apocalypse Explained* §260, 369, 490; *Arcana Coelestia* §1971, 9125, 9139, 9166, 9457, 9577.

other voluntary motions requisite to the proper performance of the duties of the several provinces.

And in the extreme front are societies which, more than all others, perceive intelligently the relation of the heavens to the Lord—their entire dependence upon Him, yet their absolute freedom; their nothingness in themselves; their possibilities of infinite development into His image and likeness, by learning and doing His will, receiving His wisdom and His love which are Himself. To these societies it is given to interpret the impressions of sense, which the angels of the provinces of sense communicate to them by intermediates; to understand and interpret the representatives by which the Lord instructs them; to reflect upon all things relating to the state of the heavens in the light of the Lord's own teaching; to instruct the angels who control the action of the heavens as to what should be done, the angels of the provinces of sense as to what they should observe, and the angels of the love which is the life of the heavens as to the ends which the Lord sets before them, and thus as to the quality of the love which is flowing from Him to them.

Through these provinces of the forehead, therefore, the Lord unites Himself with the whole heaven, and under their guidance the whole heaven unites itself with the Lord.

Spiritual Works *by*
EMANUEL SWEDENBORG

SWEDENBORG ORIGINALLY PUBLISHED HIS BOOKS IN LATIN. Throughout the years, these books have been translated into dozens of languages, including various English editions. To find the latest translation, inquire at your favorite bookstore or visit www.swedenborg.com.

APOCALYPSE EXPLAINED
Modern Title: *Revelation Explained*
Original Title: *Apocalypsis Explicata secundum Sensum Spiritualem, Ubi Revelantur Arcana, Quae Ibi Praedicta, et Hactenus Recondita Fuerunt* [The Book of Revelation Explained as to Its Spiritual Meaning, Which Reveals Secret Wonders That Were Predicted There and Have Been Hidden until Now].
London: 1834–1840 (published posthumously).

APOCALYPSE REVEALED
Modern Title: *Revelation Unveiled*
Original Title: *Apocalypsis Revelata, in Qua Deteguntur Arcana Quae Ibi Praedicta Sunt, et Hactenus Recondita Latuerunt* [The Book of Revelation Unveiled, Uncovering the Secrets That Were Foretold There and Have Lain Hidden until Now]. Amsterdam: 1766.

ARCANA COELESTIA
Modern Title: *Secrets of Heaven*
Original Title: *Arcana Coelestia, Quae in Scriptura Sacra, seu Verbo Domini Sunt, Detecta: . . . Una cum Mirabilibus Quae Visa Sunt in Mundo Spirituum, etin Coelo Angelorum* [A Disclosure of Secrets of Heaven Contained in Sacred Scripture, or the Word of the Lord, . . . Together with Amazing Things Seen in the World of Spirits and in the Heaven of Angels]. London: 1749–1756.

BRIEF EXPOSITION
Modern Title: *Survey*
Original Title: *Summaria Expositio Doctrinae Novae Ecclesiae, Quae per Novam Hierosolymam in Apocalypsi Intelligitur* [Survey of Teachings for the New Church Meant by the New Jerusalem in the Book of Revelation]. Amsterdam: 1769.

CONJUGIAL LOVE
Modern Title: *Marriage Love*
Original Title: *Delitiae Sapientiae de Amore Conjugiali: Post Quas Sequuntur Voluptates Insaniae de Amore Scortatorio* [Wisdom's Delight in Marriage Love: Followed by Insanity's Pleasure in Promiscuous Love]. Amsterdam: 1768.

CONTINUATION CONCERNING THE LAST JUDGMENT
Modern Title: *Supplements*
Original Title: *Continuatio de Ultimo Judicio: Et de Mundo Spirituali* [Supplements on the Last Judgment and the Spiritual World]. Amsterdam: 1763.

DIVINE LOVE AND WISDOM

Modern Title: *Divine Love and Wisdom*
Original Title: *Sapientia Angelica de Divino Amore et de Divina Sapientia* [Angelic Wisdom about Divine Love and Wisdom]. Amsterdam: 1763.

DIVINE PROVIDENCE

Modern Title: *Divine Providence*
Original Title: *Sapientia Angelica de Divina Providentia* [Angelic Wisdom about Divine Providence]. Amsterdam: 1764.

DOCTRINE OF FAITH

Modern Title: *Faith*
Original Title: *Doctrina Novae Hierosolymae de Fide* [Teachings for the New Jerusalem on Faith]. Amsterdam: 1763.

DOCTRINE OF LIFE

Modern title: *Life*
Original title: *Doctrina Vitae pro Nova Hierosolyma ex Praeceptis Decalogi* [Teachings about Life for the New Jerusalem: Drawn from the Ten Commandments]. Amsterdam: 1763.

DOCTRINE OF THE LORD

Modern Title: *The Lord*
Original Title: *Doctrina Novae Hierosolymae de Domino* [Teachings for the New Jerusalem on the Lord]. Amsterdam: 1763.

DOCTRINE OF THE SACRED SCRIPTURE

Modern title: *Sacred Scripture*

Original title: *Doctrina Novae Hierosolymae de Scriptura Sacra* [Teachings for the New Jerusalem on Sacred Scripture]. Amsterdam: 1763.

EARTHS IN THE UNIVERSE
Modern Title: *Other Planets*
Original Title: *De Telluribus in Mundo Nostro Solari, Quae Vocantur Planetae, et de Telluribus in Coelo Astrifero, deque Illarum Incolis, Tum de Spiritibus et Angelis Ibi: Ex Auditis et Visis* [Planets or Worlds in Our Solar System, and Worlds in the Starry Heavens, and Their Inhabitants, As Well as the Spirits and Angels There: Drawn from Things Heard and Seen]. London: 1758.

HEAVEN AND HELL
Modern Title: *Heaven and Hell*
Original Title: *De Coelo et Ejus Mirabilibus, et de Inferno, ex Auditis et Visis* [Heaven and Its Wonders and Hell: Drawn from Things Heard and Seen]. London: 1758.

INTERCOURSE BETWEEN THE SOUL AND BODY
Modern Title: *Soul-Body Interaction*
Original Title: *De Commercio Animae et Corporis, Quod Creditur Fieri vel per Influxum Physicum, vel per Influxum Spiritualem, vel per Harmoniam Praestabilitam* [Soul-Body Interaction, Believed to Occur either by a Physical Inflow, or by a Spiritual Inflow, or by a Preestablished Harmony]. London: 1769.

The Last Judgment

Modern Title: *Last Judgment*
Original Title: *De Ultimo Judicio, et de Babylonia Destructa: Ita Quod Omnia, Quae in Apocalypsi Praedicta Sunt, Hodie Impleta Sunt: Ex Auditis et Visis* [The Last Judgment and Babylon Destroyed, Showing That at This Day All the Predictions of the Book of Revelation Have Been Fulfilled: Drawn from Things Heard and Seen]. London: 1758.

New Jerusalem and Its Heavenly Doctrine

Modern Title: *New Jerusalem*
Original Title: *De Nova Hierosolyma et Ejus Doctrina Coelesti: Ex Auditis e Coelo: Quibus Praemittitur Aliquid de Novo Coelo et Nova Terra* [The New Jerusalem and Its Heavenly Teaching: Drawn from Things Heard from Heaven: Preceded by a Discussion of the New Heaven and the New Earth]. London: 1758.

Spiritual Diary

Modern title: *Spiritual Experiences*
Original title: *Experientiae Spirituales* [Spiritual Experiences]. London: 1844 (published posthumously).

True Christian Religion

Modern Title: *True Christianity*
Original Title: *Vera Christiana Religio, Continens Universam Theologiam Novae Ecclesiae a Domino apud Danielem Cap. VII:13–14, et in Apocalypsi Cap. XXI:1, 2 Praedictae* [True Christianity: Containing a Comprehensive Theology of the New Church That Was

Predicted by the Lord in Daniel 7:13–14 and Revelation 21:1, 2]. Amsterdam: 1771.

The White Horse

Modern Title: *White Horse*

Original title: *De Equo Albo, de Quo in Apocalypsi, Cap. XIX: Et Dein de Verbo et Ejus Sensu Spirituali seu Interno, ex Arcanis Coelestibus* [The White Horse in Revelation Chapter 19, and the Word and Its Spiritual or Inner Sense (from Secrets of Heaven)]. London: 1758.

Index

Bolded page numbers refer to the main entry on that topic.

A

acids, 31, 34, 39

Adam's apple, 128

affections

  children born with, 218

  communication of, 156, 223

  corresponding to the
    brain, 109, 189, 256, 270

  corresponding to the face,
    280

  for truth, 122–123

  good, 50, 123

  knowledge of, 130

  of the Greatest Man, 26

  purification of, 74–75

  read from hands, 170

  works of, 78

air, 116, 119, 125, 130

altar

  in the tent of meeting,
    228–229

  of burnt offerings, 213,
    227, 230

angels

  becoming, 27, 64

  celestial, 6–7, 19–23,
    110–111, 190

  celestial vs. spiritual,
    238–239, 282–283

  combining, 146

  coming from men, 161

  dreams from, 258

  guards, 104

  hair of, 164–166

  innocent, 226

  new, 66–68

  of the brain, 253–254,
    273, 276–277, 283–285

  of the breastbone, 150

  of the diaphragm, 145

  of the digestive system,
    16

  of the ear, 193–194

  of the eyes, 208

  of the hands, 173, 176–177

  of the heart, 105

of the inmost heaven, 2,
216–217, 230–231, 278
of the kidneys, 95
of the mesentery, 52–54
of the mouth, 8, 10–11,
16, 135, 286
of the nose, 121, 124–126,
209, 286
of the peritoneum,
139–140
of the pleura, 140
of the reproductive
organs, 237–238, 284
of the third heaven,
25–26, 230
purification of, 74–76
silent, 133–135
societies, 104–106,
122–123, 125–126, 202,
211–212, 230, 233,
286–287
speech of, 202–203
spiritual, 111
spiritual vs. natural, 143
wisest, 212
writing of, 199
Aristotle, 57, 192
arms, 168, 173–174

B
baldness, 166
beards, 165–167
bile, 33, 38–39, 47, 68–70, 78

bladder, the, 91–93, 98–99,
214
blood, 6, 28–29, 58–60,
62–63, 72–74, 90–91,
101–103, 113–115, 266
bones, **147–149,** 150, 164
brain, the, 54, 108–109,
198–199, 208, 233,
246–287
brass, 43, 142
breathing, 112, 115, 119, 130,
132. *See also* lungs;
respiration.

C
cartilage, 147, **150–151**
cerebellum, 189, 237,
253–265, 270, 277–281,
283–285
cerebrum, 179, 189, 253–265,
267, 270–272, 276–281,
283–286
chastising, 91–93
cheeks, 8, 192
cherubs, 157
chewing, 16–17
children, 9, 14, 206–212,
217–223, 238
choirs, angelic, 121, 130–131
church, the, 240–243
ancient, 57, 282, 285
marriage with the Lord,
219–220, 228–230, 245

most ancient, 258–259,
280–282, 284–285
on earth, 143, 180
state today, 149
chyle, 29, 46, 51, 53–54, 58,
62–64
cochlea, 187, 193
colon, 29, 40, 47–48, 99
conception, 237, 246
Corti, organ of, 188
creation, the, 249–250
cuticles, 158–159, 161–162,
164, 170

D
daughters, 218, 220–221
dentists, 15
deposits, fatty, 80–81, 85
diaphragm, the, 26, 139,
141–144, 145
digestion, 5, 16, 77
Divine Man. *See* Greatest Man.
doing, love of, 112, 140,
168–170
dragonists, 76, 83
dreams, 258, 260, 263n
dura mater, 273–274

E
eardrum, 183–184, 193
ears, the, **183–194,** 196–197,
261
elephants, 127

equilibrium, 186, 264
esophagus, 25–27
esse, 230, 244
excrement, 6, 28, 40, 49, 120
excretion, organs of, 214
eyes, the, 123, 126, 186,
195–210, 254–255, 280,
286

F
face, the, 136, 146, 165, 276,
279–281
facts, 13, 140, 147
fat, 63, 77, 81, 85
fathers, 216, 220–223, 237, 241
feet, the, 142–143, 177,
178–182
beneath the soles of, 42,
45–46, 65, 77
femininity, 220–222, 240
fibers, nerve
affected by outflow, 170
connected to the brain,
248–259, 266, 272–273,
281
function of, 153–154
like truths, 225, 276
of the feet, 179
fingernails, 177
fluids
alkaline, 23–24
digestive, 31, 34–35
pancreatic, 33, 47, 74, 78

food
  corresponding to newly
    deceased, 23–24, 28–29,
    31–33, 38–39, 47–48,
    134
  for heaven, 5–6, 124
  for the mind, 37, 135
  muscle–making elements
    of, 77
  retained in the mouth, 14
  formalities, 164
  fruit, 9, 23, 39, 67–68, 78

G
gall bladder, 61, 69–70, 94
gardens, 202–203, 205
generation, organs of,
  211–245
glands
  of the brain, 275–276
  of the mesentery, 53–54,
    62
  of the skin, 162
  prostate, 216
  salivary, 19, 23
Golden Age, 280
good
  affection for, 122–123,
    217, 280
  and truth, marriage of,
    218–219, 228, 230, 239,
    241, 243–245
  celestial vs. spiritual, 229

divine, 247, 284
doing, 173, 176, 181
end of, 224–226, 238, 283
from truths, 182
love of, 48, 282
memory of, 85
natural, 81
noble, 85
perception of, 8, 117, 202,
  210, 221
received by cerebellum,
  277
spiritual, 276
understanding of, 200
goodness
  joy in, 220, 234
  love of, 63, 218–220, 223
grain, 9, 78
Greatest Man, 4, 59, 74, 130,
  146, 160–162, 164,
  179–180, 284, 286
  becoming part of, 6, 40
  bladder of, 91, 93
  bones of, 147
  brain of, 279
  breastbone of, 150
  chyle of, 54
  ears of, 193
  hands of, 173, 177
  intestines of, 39, 48
  liver of, 71
  kidneys of, 87, 91, 93, 95
  kingdoms of, 16

mouth of, 9, 13, 36
muscles of, 146
nose of, 121, 126
peritoneum of, 98
pulse of, 109
ribs of, 140
thoughts of, 26

H
hair, the, **164–167**
hands, the, 135, **168–177,**
    178–179, 181–182, 214,
    286
hearing, 156, 185, 189–190,
    193, 199, 261
heart, the, **101–115,** 277
    angels of, 6, 145
    corresponding to celestial
        things, 94
    corresponding to second
        heaven, 25–27
    movement of, 135, 143, 259
    thoughts of, 79, 130
heaven
    air of, 125
    before Last Judgment,
        268–269
    corresponding to the
        brain, 266–268, 273,
        276, 283, 286–287
    corresponding to the
        Greatest Man, 4,
        160–162, 177, 233, 273

creation of, 250
form of, 272–273
heart of, 106, 108–109
increase of, 234–235, 240
infants in, 26, 66, 204–209
influx from, 15–16, 175,
    227, 237, 273, 276–277
inmost, 204, 216,
    230–232, 236, 278
instruction about, 19–24,
    35, 52, 61, 64, 67, 76
made by the Word,
    160–161
marriages in, 218
new spirits in, 8–11, 33, 81
purification, 74–75
respiration of, 109–110,
    132, 143
three degrees, 25–26, 54,
    142–143, 179–180,
    201–203, 211–212, 216,
    246, 253–254, 278, 285
voice of, 133–134
hells, 6, 13, 40–43, 92, 95,
    124
husbands, 218–223
hypnotism, 260–261

I
incense, 230
incisors, 11–12
independence, 126
indigestion, 37

infants, 26, 66, 88, 204–209,
    211–212, 217, 232
influx, 15–16, 109, 111, 175
    body formed in the womb
        by, 134
    from the liver, 71
    into the brain, 273,
        276–277, 282–284
    like the soul through the
        body, 134
infundibulum, 266–268
innocence, 62, 111, 206–207,
    212, 217, 230–234, 244
instruction, 8, 31, 39
    by influx, 286
    concerning heaven, 18–24,
        26, 35, 52, 61, 64–67,
        76, 285
    from mothers, 223
    like bread, 120
    love of, 57, 132, 199
    places of, 33, 64–68,
        75–76
interiors
    communicated by touch,
        171–172
    conjoined to the soul,
        222
    connected to angelic
        societies, 65
    corresponding to the
        forehead, 276
    in heaven vs. hell, 41

    opening, 104, 124
    state of, 30, 32
    the Word in, 160–161, 244
intestines, 33, **38–50,** 68, 77,
    84–85, 95n
iron, 142
Iron Age, 281
ivory, 127

K, L
kidneys, the, 86–87, **90–95,**
    98–99, 109
knowledge
    of affections, 130
    of facts, 127, 161
    of goodness, 77
    of heaven, 36–37, 81
    love of, 135
larynx, 128–132
Last Judgment, 22, 76, 82–83,
    134, 268–269
left (side), 182
    brain, 108, 263, 271, 282
    eye, 200–201, 204, 267
    of a place, 49, 167
    of the face, 279–281
    of the heart, 191
life
    after death, 6–10, 19–22,
        26–27
    beginning of, 247
    circle of, 226–227
    duties of, 78

from the Lord, 4–5, 53,
    133, 171, 193, 212, 214,
    219–220, 230, 232–233,
    237–238, 256, 265, 283
heavenly, 48, 68, 105, 143,
    223, 234–235
in the womb, 237
marriage, 221, 223, 233
natural, 164–165
of man is will, 113–114
of the Lord, 242
peaceful, 85
purification of, 119
spheres of, 119, 124–126,
    156, 172–173
spiritual, 147–148,
    163–164, 180–181
states of, 37, 75, 119, 130
uses of, 71, 226
light, 20, 122–123, 179,
    195–203, 208, 283
lips, the, **3–8, 16,** 124, 129,
    136
liver, the, **58–71,** 94
Lord, the
    celestial kingdom of,
        67–68, 110–111, 239
    choirs praising, 130–131
    coming of, 143, 240, 243
    divine marriage, 228–229,
        241, 245
    goodness of, 105
    guard of, 157

guiding spirits, 35–36
healing by touch, 171
life from, 4–5, 53, 133,
    171, 193, 212, 214,
    219–220, 230, 232–233,
    237–238, 256, 265, 283
life of, 125–126, 181, 283,
    226
light from, 201, 203
love from, 108, 145, 234,
    246–247
love of, 140, 217, 231, 282
opening eyes, 37
power of, 177
presence of, 84
providence of, 176, 286
speech of, 133–134
united to heaven, 287
wisdom from, 194
Lord's Prayer, 274
love
    chaste, 88
    corresponding to the
        forehead, 276
    ends, 224, 226
    from the Lord, 105, 219,
        246–247
    is will, 172
    married with wisdom,
        108, 234, 239, 242
    nourishment of heaven, 4
    of self, 13, 48–49, 112, 120
    of the world, 13

perceptions of, 216
purification of, 77, 277–278
to the Lord, 157, 282
See also marriage love.
lower earth, 33, 40, 42–47,
  65, 82–85
lungs, the, **101–115**, 130,
  260, 277
  angels in, 194, 283
  motion of, 25, 135,
    142–144
  related to pleura, 137–139
lymph, 52–53, 76, 265–266

M
marriage, 157, 211, 218–220,
  243
  divine, 228, 241–244
  of love and wisdom, 108
marriage love, 211, 230–231,
  233–235, 242–245
masculinity, 215, 220–221
mastication, 3, 16–17
meeting, tent of, 228
memory, 85, 216
  interior, 10, 13–14, 124
mesentery, the, **51–57,** 64, 85
milk, 63, 223
modesty, 88, 98
mothers, 63, 216, 218–225,
  238
mouth, 3, 9, 11, 25, 94,
  116–118, 134–136, 194

movement, 251, 254–256,
  272, 286
muscles, **145–146**
  -making elements of food,
    31, 33, 47, 63
musicians, 132

N
nakedness, 217
nerves, 54, 254–255,
  272–273, 286
  auditory, 189, 198
  corresponding to
    sensitivity, 88
  of touch, 153–154, 179
  optical, 189, 198–199, 208
  See also fibers, nerve.
New Church, 181, 242–243
New Testament, 243
nose, the, **116–127,** 209,
  286

O
occiput, 262, 277, 279
odors
  of celestial angels, 6
  of heaven, 125
  of spirits, 49, 120
  of thoughts, 115, 124
  perceived by the nose,
    116–118
Old Testament, 243
omentum, the, **80–85**

ova, 216, 221, 225–226, 237
ovaries, 211, 232–233

P
pancreas, the, **72–79,** 94
pearl, gates of, 10
perception
  angelic, 105
  by many, 135
  corresponding to
    respiration, 113, 119
  corresponding to the
    tongue, 117–118
  cuticles, 159
  eyes, 202, 208
  hearing, 189–190, 192,
    194
  nose, 120–127
  of good and truth, 8n, 220
  of spiritual relations, 157
  of wisdom, 220
peritoneum, the, **96–100,**
  139, 142
philosophy, 57
pia mater, 274
pleura, the, **137–140,** 142
power, 145, 173–177, 182
  spiritual vs. natural, 179
prolification (reproduction),
  215, 217–218, 234n,
  236
proprium, 229
pulse, 106, 109–110

punishment, love of, 39, 48,
  68–69, 91–93
purification
  from evil, 112–113, 130,
    214, 227–228, 277–278
  in the heart, 94
  in the intestines, 33, 77
  in the liver, 58, 62–63
  in the lungs, 113, 115,
    119, 260
  in the peritoneum, 97
  in the stomach, 29
  of angels, 74–75, 270
  of heaven, 268
  of the church, 243
  stages of, 35, 65
  See also regeneration;
    vastation.

R
rainbows, 122, 203, 206
rectum, the, 6, 29, 48, 214
regeneration, 180, 213–214,
  224–228, 238–240,
  261
reins, 94, 213
reproductive organs,
  211–245
respiration, 106, 108–110,
  113, 131, 143. *See also*
  breathing; lungs.
ribs, 140
rice, 78

right (side), 182
    brain, 109, 257, 271
    ear, 192
    eye, 200, 204
    hand, 171
    of a place, 166
    of the face, 280–282
    robes, white, 82, 84

S
sacrifices, 85, 227–228
saliva, **18–24,** 36
salt, 34
seed (semen), 215–216,
    222–223, 226, 239
self-assertion, 23–24, 39, 71
self-love, 13, 48–49, 112, 120
seminal vesicles, 215–216,
    222, 240n
senses, 257–258, 271–272,
    286–287. *See also*
    hearing; sight; smell;
    taste; touch.
sensitivity, 88, 157, 162–163,
    173
service, love of, 140
shoes, wooden, 98–99
sight, 156, 189–190, 198–202,
    206–207, 210
Silver Age, 280–281
silver, 15, 142
singing, 130
sinuses, 274–275

skin, the, **152–163,** 274
slowness, 70–71, 148
smell, 8, 116–118, 121
sons, 218, 220–221
    Son, the, 241
souls, 4, 133–134, 218–225,
    229, 235–238
speech, 7
    in accord with others, 59
    induced by influx, 92–93,
    175
    of angels, 194, 202–203
    organs of, **128–136**
spirits, 6
    angelic, 15–16, 54
    animal, 265
    dreams from, 258
    evil, 76, 182, 268–269
    from Jupiter, 131, 240n
    from Mars, 278
    good, 34–35, 46, 54, 75, 182
    new to heaven, 8–11,
        18–19, 21–29, 25–27,
        36, 52, 59, 61–68, 76,
        100, 143, 283, 286
    of the bones, 147–148
    of the ears, 190–191
    of the peritoneum, 98–99
    quality known by odors,
        49, 120
    societies, 31, 121, 146
    See also angels; world of
        spirits.

spitting, 37
spleen, the, **72–79,** 94, 142
standing, 180–181
starch, 23, 30–32, 77–78, 81
states after death, 6, 9, 21–22,
    30, 35, 64, 162
stomach, the, 6–7, 26–26,
    28–37, 40, 77, 94, 213
strength, 168, 174
sugar, 23, 30, 33, 68, 78, 81
suprarenal capsules, the, 86–89

T
tabernacle, the, 157, 213, 230
tact, 12, 157
taste, 8n, 116–118, 135
tears, 209–210
teeth, **10–17,** 132
Ten Commandments, 181
testicles, 215–216, 232–233
thoughts, 119
    adopting, 16–17
    confessing, 130
    corresponding to air, 119,
        132
    corresponding to tears, 210
    divine, 125, 167
    examining, 79
    expressing, 3, 132, 134
    good, 50, 79
    heavenly, 52, 54, 62, 110
    in the cerebrum, 262, 278
    independent, 126

    intelligent, 76
    interior, 6, 30, 32, 121
    of the Greatest Man, 26
    propagation, 218
    purification of, 74–75
    rational, 167, 239
    represented by fibers, 254
    true, 161
    unclean, 40, 71, 88–89, 95,
        114–115
tongue, the, **3–17,** 106, 117,
    124
touch, 153, 156–157,
    171–173, 179
trachea, 128–129
truth, 127, 135, 200
    affection for, 68, 123
    and good, 34–35, 182,
        219, 228, 241, 244, 282
    clothing, 217
    corresponding to teeth, 14
    corresponding to water, 18
    divine, 84, 126, 161, 228,
        239, 241, 243, 247
    infants formed from, 225
    literal, 176–177
    love of, 63, 130, 221, 240,
        282
    of faith, 162, 173
    of the Lord, 37
    perception of, 8, 117, 123,
        125, 192–193, 202, 215,
        220

reception of, 23, 227
represented by reins, 94
spiritual, 276
thinking, 119
two witnesses, 180–181

U, V
understanding
affection for, 16, 135,
    199–200
and will, 174, 189–190,
    215, 226, 247–249
corresponding to motion,
    107
corresponding to the
    brain, 260, 262–263,
    271
corresponding to the
    lungs, 112–114
influx into, 277–278
ruled by the Lord, 174
sensuals of, 13
ureters, 91–93, 98–99
urine, 28, 53, 91, 95n
uses
affection for, 68
human, 4, 207
love of, 145, 237
of the heavens, 61, 64, 68
spiritual corresponding to
    the natural, 74
truths concerning, 177
vastation, 42–48, 68, 84, 148

virgins, 87–88
vocal cords, 128–130

W
walking, 181–182
water, 18, 23, 209
weeping, 209
wheat, 78
white (color), 84, 104, 122,
    264
will
and understanding, 174,
    189–190, 215, 226,
    247–249
corresponding to motion,
    107
corresponding to the
    brain, 260, 262–263,
    271, 277, 281
corresponding to the
    heart, 112–113, 172
influx into, 277–278,
    282–283
interior, 30
is man himself, 114, 172
wisdom
corresponding to
    marriage and child-
    bearing, 218–224
corresponding to the
    lungs, 143
divine, 53, 207, 234–235,
    239–240, 284–285

from the Lord, 4,
134–135, 194, 234
in the brain, 246–247
influx, 15–16
inner, 193–194
love of, 112, 115
of the ancient churches, 57
of thought, 119, 125
wives, 124, 218–223, 230
womb, the, 211, 216, 222,
225, 230, 232–233,
237–238
Word, the
corresponding to heaven,
165–166
divine wisdom in, 207,
226, 250, 285

inner meaning of,
239–244
literal sense, 160–161,
263–264
spoken, 133–134, 194
work
love of, 25, 33–34, 77, 145
good, 45, 71, 78
skill at, 168
world of spirits, 5, 7, 9n, 21,
65
correspondence with the
stomach, 28–29, 34, 37,
213
instruction on, 19
knowledge of, 36
spirits delayed in, 39